Co

Canon

Design

Media

Romanticism

Preface

The new millennium has arrived, and with it a tremendous upsurge of debate and theorizing about visual art. One event in particular seems to have set the tone: the 9/11 attack on the World Trade Center in New York City, which led to a reconsideration of the post-ideological era. The anything-goes attitude of the preceding years gave way to a renewed quest for the foundations of art. This reorientation went hand in hand with the unprecedented expansion of the art scene, expressed in part by the worldwide emergence of countless institutions, grant programmes, biennials and other forums for contemporary art. These new institutions and forums display a strong propensity for discussion, debate and theorizing. No topic whatsoever is taboo; in today's society, it seems, everything revolves around information and interpretation, even in the art world.

Now Is the Time: Art and Theory in the 21st Century is part of this development. The aim of this publication is to forge a link between contemporary art and the social issues that confront us at the start of the new millennium; it presents a provocative new context for thinking about art at this historical juncture. The book grew out of a series of lectures and debates with the same name, which took place in Amsterdam from October 2008 to January 2009. Hence its organization in terms of seven themes. Five of these themes – 9/11, Religion, Globalization, Canon and Media – offer insight into the preoccupations of contemporary society and the consequences for art and reflection on art. The other two themes, Design and Romanticism, take developments in art and culture as a point of departure for reflection on the social challenges that we face.

Each section contains two main articles on the theme in question, written by leading international scholars, critics and curators, and in one case an artist. As in the lecture series, each thematic section is concluded with a discussion among the authors and between them and the audience, in which similarities and differences in methods and interpretations are explored. In our view, it is this approach that makes *Now Is the Time: Art and Theory in the 21st Century* a proper introduction to art and art-theoretical debate in the first decade of the twenty-first century.

One recurring theme in the lecture series was the supposed resurgence of religion and the related polarization of societies. What responses does this resurgence evoke in the largely secular world of contemporary art? Opposition and disbelief, to begin with, because organized religion and the modern art world, with its history of avant-gardism, seem to be one another's opposites. Yet the many exhibitions and art events dedicated to Religion over the past few years have opened the way for a new perspective on the past and the present. Perhaps religion and spirituality were never entirely abandoned; perhaps they even form the basis of today's digital society.

The influence and aftermath of 9/11 are closely tied to this topic. Though the new millennium began with a worldwide celebration, broadcast on televisions everywhere, the tone of the new era was set on 11 September 2001, with the globally televised attacks on New York City's World Trade Center. This historic turning point is said to have had a profound influence on the visual arts. But what exactly is the nature of this 9/11 effect?

The 9/11 attacks also put the incessant process of globalization on the agenda. Globalization had already been a popular subject in the art world for many years. Yet there is now a keener sense of urgency, as international political debate is galvanized by globalization's many and paradoxical manifestations, such as the yawning gap between rich and poor, the growing commercialization and privatization of public space, and the outbreak of local and geopolitical conflicts. The ever-expanding network of biennials and grant programmes for artists is one example of globalization's direct impact on the art world. But how is the art world responding to its less agreeable effects?

The issue of canons and the way they are established perfectly illustrate the disorientation that social trends like globalization have created in many people's minds. When chaos gains the upper hand in society, it is only natural to take refuge in traditional frameworks. Against this backdrop, critical questions about the tenability of the traditional canon and the possibility of creating new canons have provoked lively discussion. That is especially true in the Netherlands, where a fierce public debate has been set off by the semi-official proclamation of a Historical Canon of the Netherlands. This example illustrates well how canons can be used to safeguard national identity in a hybrid multicultural society. But who actually takes the lead in rewriting these paradigmatic cultural standards, and what role does art play in the process? And do canons imposed from above still have any legitimacy in a democratic and interactive culture like ours, or is it time to go in search of new models?

The mediatization of society is a familiar topic of debate, but one which has gained new currency in the twenty-first century. Over the past decade various observers, including many visual artists, have produced critical analyses of the media that offer penetrating insights into their impact and significance in a rapidly changing landscape. Nevertheless, the idea of the 'new' media is often little more than a gimmick, calculated to win the hearts of the public, and should not be taken too literally. The 'oldness' of the media may prove to be a much more crucial concept as we try to understand their workings.

The other two themes, in contrast to those mentioned above, do not relate primarily to trends in society but to developments in art and culture, which serve as a jumping-off point for the exploration of broader social issues. Design is such a topic. In the 1990s, design became ubiquitous, and it seemed as if everyone had become a designer. In today's 'creative cities', design is often the most highly esteemed of all disciplines, so much so that it is even held up as an example to artists of how to become an independent economic force. Visual artists have generally responded with scepticism, and even within the design sector a critical mode of practice is developing that questions the political and economic parameters of contemporary design. This makes the issue of the trendsetting role of design in present-day social and cultural life all the more pressing.

The seventh and final theme of *Now Is the Time: Art and Theory in the 21st Century* is the current interest in Romanticism in art and culture, which can be viewed as a reaction against a number of tendencies discussed elsewhere in this book. It involves an element of opposition to the dominant discourse of neoliberalism, the politicization of art, mediatization, de-individualization, and a perceived lack of authenticity. Recent studies have made it abundantly clear that romantic thought has lost none of its relevance and can point the way to a deeper understanding of current developments.

In summary, however diverse the themes of this book may be, they show that in the new millennium, society and art are tightly intertwined. Major social and political themes are being seized on by artists, curators and critics as raw materials for their art, exhibitions and writings. Even so, individuals in society are still yearning for art as a sanctuary or critical counterbalance (Poynor), but it is also clear that art and culture only to a certain extent define a person's or a nation's foundation (Eagleton).

This book also shows that new artistic developments cannot be grasped outside of a historical context. To gain a full understanding of any of these themes, we must go back to the previous century, and much further still into the past, unearthing visual typologies that still dominate our culture today (Silverman), or have been forgotten (Marks), or form a dominant discourse in need of revision (Noack). Robert Nelson aptly recalls Marx's dictum: 'The past is remade by the present for the future.'

Yet above all, this book is concerned with the present. As W.J.T. Mitchell argues in his contribution, it is our very interest in the present day that shows that we have turned away from postmodern theory, for postmodernism tells us that everything has already happened. We are now witnessing the return of modernity. There is a widespread awareness that things are changing fast and are not the way they used to be. That truth only becomes apparent if you open your eyes to the past and have the courage to turn your gaze to the future. But you have to start with the present, believing in the power of today. *Now is the time!*

The editors

Terry Eagleton - Faith and Belief

NOW

Belief

Boris Groys - Repetition versus Progress

Art & Theory

TIME

Belief

The theme of Belief was put on the map against the background of various manifestations of religion which were until recently largely ignored by the dominant, modernist, secular world view in art theory. The attack of 9/11 and its aftermath not only confronted this world view quite intrusively with Islamic fundamentalism, but also with a conservative political response in the West, partly inspired by Christianity. As far as it concerned the art world, some major museums took up this seeming return of religion by organizing large-scale exhibitions that focused on traces of all kinds of belief systems in modern art. Elsewhere, curators and art theoreticians tried to deal in their exhibitions and especially their writings with the idea of religion in relation to contemporary art and art theory. Where exactly do the two meet nowadays?

In this contribution Boris Groys starts with discerning science from religion. The first searches for ultimate truths, the second focuses on the repetition of texts and rituals. This latter feature prompts him to analyse the special nature of the digital image with regard to fundamentalism. Digital images consist of abstract data that can be copied exactly at all times without any further interpretation. This partly explains the attractiveness of Internet distribution of photography and video to fundamentalists. Before discussing the role of the cultural in what to many people may seem a new religious upheaval, writer and literary theorist Terry Eagleton first of all goes to the very bottom of what constitutes 'faith' and 'belief'. From what begins as an etymological analysis he demonstrates that believing in the neoliberal West hardly can reach very far. He continues with noticing that instead, the idea of 'culture' in contemporary society has become a weak substitute for the place once naturally held by religion.

Terry Eagleton (UK) is a literary theorist and critic. He is professor of English literature at the University of Lancaster and holds a visiting professorship at the National University of Ireland, Galway. His recent publications show a renewed interest in theological themes. His numerous publications include: *Literary Theory: An Introduction* (1983, 1996), *Ideology: An Introduction* (1991, 2007), *The Ideology of the Aesthetic* (1990), *After Theory* (2003), *Holy Terror* (2005), *The Meaning of Life* (2007) and *Reason, Faith and Revolution: Reflections on the God Debate* (2009).

Boris Groys (GER) is a philosopher, essayist, art critic, curator, media theorist and Global Distinguished Professor of Russian and Slavic Studies at the New York University. Furthermore, Groys is an acclaimed expert on Russian avant-garde and late-Soviet postmodern art and literature. At ZKM in Karlsruhe, he co-curated the exhibitions *Iconoclash* (2002) and *Medium Religion* (2008-2009). Groys' publications include *The Art of Installation* (1996), *Under Suspicion: A Phenomenology of the Media* (1997) and *Art Power* (2008).

Faith and Belief

Terry Eagleton

Let me begin by saying something about the way the word belief behaves in our language. Would it make sense for me to say 'I believe I am the most beautiful person in this room'? Of course it would. It wouldn't be *true*, but that's another matter. Would it make sense for me to say 'I believe I'm in atrocious pain'? Of course not. Being in pain is not a matter of belief. Is this because it is a question of *knowing* that I am in pain? Not according to the philosopher Ludwig Wittgenstein. Wittgenstein claims that it does not make sense to say I *know* I'm in pain. Why not? Presumably because 'I know I am in pain' adds nothing to 'I am in pain'. The words 'I know' are completely superfluous here. They are doing no work. They have meaning but no force. Words like knowing and believing have force only where doubting is possible. And doubting is possible only against a background of accepted truths, which is why total scepticism is a fantasy. In other words, it's a mistake to imagine that we need reasons for believing, but not for doubting. You can doubt irrationally, just as you can believe irrationally. If I have a belief and no good reason to doubt it, then doubting would make no sense here. It would be a 'pretend' sort of doubt, a phantasm. I couldn't really doubt that I'm not Dick Cheney, eternally grateful though I am that I'm not.

Do I believe that I have two hands? No. Belief enters into the matter only where a proposition is up for interpretation. And generally speaking, the claim that I have two hands isn't of this kind, though one could always dream up scenarios where it might be. A postoperative situation, for example, where I peep cautiously under the bedclothes to see if my hands are still there . . .

Can I have beliefs I don't know about? Yes. It's commonly known as ideology. Much ideology consists in beliefs which are too close to the eyeball even to be objectified, beliefs which are part of the invisible colour of daily life itself. Donald Rumsfeld, President George Bush's Defence Secretary, talked famously about known knowns, known unknowns and unknown unknowns, but he forgot about unknown knowns – things we know but don't know we know, or things we believe but don't know we believe. Freud thought we could have unconscious beliefs and intentions that may be quite at odds with our conscious ones. Can one believe two contradictory things at the same time? Yes: Shakespeare's Othello does this, more or less, when he believes that his wife Desdemona is faithful to him and doesn't believe it, both at the same time.

Is *having* a belief like having a purple waistcoat or a pet tarantula, or is it more like having a pair of kidneys? Well, it depends on the belief. Not all our beliefs go all the way down. I believe that Vancouver is a pleasant sort of place, but I can quite easily imagine not believing this. I wouldn't go to the death for it. (These days, by the way, beliefs that people are prepared to die for, or kill for, are known as culture. It makes one positively nostalgic for the days of Rembrandt . . .) But could I imagine *not* believing that people are not at their finest when they're starving to death? No, not really. Some beliefs really do go all the way down. They are what we might call core or constitutive beliefs, the kind of beliefs that go to make up the self, and which we couldn't really change without transforming our identity. We couldn't really change these kinds of beliefs simply by taking thought. Too much practical stuff is bound up with them. We don't acquire these kinds of convictions as we might acquire a new iPod. Beliefs of this kind aren't a matter of the will. They aren't to do with that postmodern mantra, 'choice'. We cannot just decide to believe in the free market or the Buddha. Beliefs of this kind have us, so to speak, much more than we have them. They are what we find we can't in the end walk away from, however inconvenient that might prove to be. All our most passionate beliefs have a quality of necessity or ineluctability about them. When I believe in communism or Catholicism, I can't choose not to believe in it.

Beliefs are bound up with what we do. Imagine someone who swears blind that he adores badgers yet spends all his spare time cutting their legs off. Imagine also that he understands the meaning of the word 'adore', isn't mad and isn't a hypocrite. What would we say? We would surely have to conclude that though he thought he loved animals, he didn't. As Wittgenstein comments: It is what we do which lies at the bottom of our language games. Look at what George Bush did and then ask whether he's a Christian. Ask whether it even makes sense to talk about religious belief in such a context.

So belief is bound up with social practices and institutions. We come to believe what we do because we are brought up within a practical way of life in which beliefs are embedded. Indeed, for a materialist like myself, beliefs are not only embedded in our material forms of life, but actually generated by them. There is an interesting postmodern objection to this case, which goes like this. First, the claim that beliefs are generated by our material forms of life is itself a belief, so we have got precisely nowhere. We thought we had got outside belief, to something that caused it externally, but in fact we have not. Second, what we call our material way of life is itself a matter of interpretation, and thus involves beliefs. As far as what counts as our way of life goes, there will always be room for contention, for clashing interpretations. So the postmodern conclusion is that we never get outside belief. On this view, belief is the bottom line, the ontological foundation, the rock where our spade can dig no deeper, the horizon over which we can't peer, the a priori we can't ever peer behind. Belief – or culture (a formation of beliefs) – becomes the new transcendent reality. This is the postmodern heresy known as culturalism. However far down we dig, we find nothing but culture. Culture is wall-to-wall. As a materialist, I reject this proposition. Culture is important, but not *that* important. And it is not, I think, what is foundational about human beings.

Is belief the same as faith? No, not really. Some people think that to say you believe in God is to subscribe to the proposition that there exists somewhere a Supreme Being. But this is a theological error. It is what one might call the Yeti or Big Foot theory of faith. On this view, we cannot be sure whether there is a God or not because all the evidence isn't in, so we are left with speculation and surmise. And this is known as faith. But this is never how Judaeo-Christianity or Islam understood the word, and simply goes to demonstrate the theological illiteracy of most atheists and agnostics. Faith in God does indeed presuppose that he exists – though 'exists' isn't the right word, theologically. God doesn't exist in the sense of being an entity within the universe like a pint of Guinness. God and the universe don't make two. But what we call faith is not reducible to this claim. Faith is not primarily a matter of propositions. Abraham had faith in God, but given his cultural situation he probably could not even have conceived that God did not exist. His faith in God had little to do with accepting the claim that God existed. The devils are traditionally said to believe in God, but they don't have faith in him. You could believe in God or socialism or feminism but not have faith in it, in the sense that this belief might remain purely cerebral and make no actual difference to your life. This, I suppose, is how Donald Rumsfeld believes in God.

Faith is a question of commitment and conviction, not of believing in the existence or otherwise of some phenomenon. Faith is always faith in *something*, which is not necessarily the case with belief. (Think of believing that the weather may improve.) It is also, in its Judaeo-Christian form, a faith in redemption – and this means that you cannot understand faith unless you understand that there is some condition which needs to be transformed. You cannot grasp the idea of faith, then, unless you also grasp something of suffering, tragedy, breakdown, failure and despair. In short, what the New Testament calls crucifixion. People who believe that things are fundamentally fine with the human species – the Tony Blairs of this world – cannot have faith in transformation because they don't see that there is any real need for it.

Faith as presented by the New Testament isn't a question of signing on for certain claims about reality. It is the tenacity of a tortured political criminal at the end of his tether, the mangled victim of a brutal colonialism, floundering in darkness and agony and bewilderment, who nevertheless, despite all the evidence, despite all reasonable considerations to the contrary, continues to commit himself to what he sees as a source of transformative love. This kind of faith is more like faith in a person than it is like faith in a proposition. When I say 'I believe in you', I don't mean I accept the proposition that you are an existent entity. And that, for one thing, is because it doesn't make sense to say I *believe* that you exist, any more than it makes sense to say I believe I am in pain. How, in ordinary circumstances, could I doubt that you exist? Doubting, like any other social practice, is carried on against a background of taken-for-granted assumptions. It finds its place within a certain familiar context. And there would generally be no place or context I could assign to a doubt that you existed, not least if you were standing there before me. This is why complete scepticism is a fantasy. There is just no home we could find for such a radical doubt. It would have no force and no function.

Faith, then, is more a life-defining, identity-constituting commitment than it is a question of accepting this or that description of reality (though it involves such descriptions, to be sure). Why, let us ask, should someone today, in these dark political times, continue to be a political radical? There are many reasons. Because one can't accept that the world we see groaning in agony around us is the only way things can be; because one gazes with wondering bemusement at those who imagine that this is as good as it gets; because one simply can't shake off the primitive suspicion that this is not how things are meant to be; because there is something in this vision of change which calls to the depths of one's being and elicits a passionate assent there; because not to feel this would not to be oneself; because one is too much in love with this vision of humankind to be able to back down, walk away or take no for an answer. And so on. A believer, Kierkegaard comments, is someone in love.

The world today is divided down the middle between those who believe too much (fundamentalists, whether Texan or Taliban) and those who believe too little (liberal agnostics). And then there is a sprinkling of sane, balanced, mature people like myself in the middle. Each party helps to constitute the other, so that the more inherently secular, pragmatic and faithless advanced capitalist orders become, the more stridently others turn to absolute values of various kinds. God is suddenly back in business, just when he was looking forward to as well-deserved retirement from the public stage, and just when we seemed to be smoothly sailing into the post-metaphysical era. These sworn enemies are secretly sides of the same coin. For every sceptical cosmopolitan chief executive travelling the skies, there is a village elder somewhere beneath him who believes that evil starts just on the other side of the mountains.

Fundamentalists are men and women who have been driven into spiritual fanaticism by a shallow, two-dimensional, purely technological rationality which sweeps all the big questions scornfully to one side, thus leaving those questions open to being monopolized by the bigots. The other side of a purely instrumental rationality is a faith-based politics. There are those who are powerful and well-heeled enough not to have to ask themselves who they are, because they have enough identity to be satisfied with; and there are those in Gaza and Baghdad who carry the problem of their identity around with them like a daily burden on their back. The point is that these two narratives are interconnected. Those who have enough or too strong an identity are on the whole politically responsible for the situation of those who have too little. And those who have too little identity are likely to convert that anxiety into some form of fundamentalism. A paucity of belief and identity will be turned into a surplus of it. Those who believe too little (roughly speaking, the agnostic West) will then find themselves precisely for that reason without the spiritual or ideological resources to deal adequately with this threat, and will become deeply anxious in their turn. This is the narrative known as the war on terror.

It is important to see that for late capitalist civilizations, what you believe doesn't really matter very much. In this sense, market societies are intrinsically agnostic. As long as you roll out of bed, pay your taxes, consume a reasonable amount of goods and refrain from beating up policemen, you can believe more or less what you like. Liberal democracies do not so much hold beliefs as believe that people should be allowed to hold beliefs, as long as their beliefs, whatever they are, do not interfere with people's rights to hold beliefs. Such societies must, in other words, be illiberal about threats to tolerance. Liberal societies thus tend to be rather lukewarm about belief. Like postmodernists, liberals tend to suspect any passionate conviction of being incipiently authoritarian. But the liberal belief that one should tolerate other people's beliefs is a conviction that should itself be passionately held. In any case, if authoritarianism wreaks political damage, so can apathy. It is a serious error to mistake passionate conviction for dogmatism.

At the same time, liberal social orders like the West still feel the need for a metaphysical or theological underpinning, largely for ideological reasons. Such beliefs do not sit at all comfortably with their genuine, more secular and pragmatic articles of faith. They are like an embarrassing, rather old-fashioned superstructure added to such beliefs, always in danger of looking peculiarly hollow and hypocritical. As President Eisenhower sagely remarked: 'Our society needs a firm foundation in belief, and I don't care what it is.' The problem is that such secular societies *themselves* keep undermining their own metaphysical foundations. It is not the Richard Dawkins's of this world who are the hairy, wild-eyed, subversive atheists (indeed, Dawkins, the well-known English campaigner for a militant atheism, is an impeccable member of the British Establishment), but market capitalism itself, which simply can't help secularizing, rationalizing, pragmatizing and relativizing away its own metaphysical foundations. It is thus a culture divided against itself. The USA is both the most cynical, faithless, materialist nation on earth and the one full of the most pious, earnest, high-minded, hand-on-heart, full-blown metaphysical rhetoric about Freedom, Family and God's special regard for certain regions of south-east Texas, at which we more jaded, cynical Europeans simply shuffle our feet and wait for it to stop.

In this situation, the West gazes with both envy and alarm on cultures like radical Islam which have absolutely no problem with their metaphysical foundations (would that they did!). Islam confronts the West with the contradiction between its own will to believe and chronic incapacity to do so. So should the West try to beat them or join them? Should it seek to defend its own values by going metaphysical and foundationalist, but only at the risk of betraying those liberal values in the act of trying to save them? Or should it fall back on a familiar liberal pragmatism – but will this prove ideologically sufficient?

In this situation, liberalism is at once the West's virtue and catastrophe. Liberal society is one long, unruly, inconclusive argument, in which – astonishingly to a medieval mind, for example – we cannot even agree on fundamentals. Everyone agrees that it is not a good idea to roast innocent people slowly over fires, but we can't agree on why we agree on this. And no doubt we never shall.

Part of what has happened in our time is that God has shifted over from the side of civilization to the side of barbarism. He is no longer just the respectable, short-haired, blue-blazered God of the American suburbs, but a wrathful, dark-skinned deity who lays siege to everything civilization holds dear. One might go further, and claim that the name of this new kind of barbarism is culture. The conflict of beliefs is now one between civilization (autonomy, universality, individuality, rationality) and culture, which means all the unreflective loyalties and allegiances as built-in to people as their pancreas, in the name of which they are in extreme circumstances prepared to kill.

The idea of culture, by and large, was historically speaking a substitute for a failing religion in the industrial West. On the surface, this seemed plausible enough. Both religion and culture were concerned with absolute values, transcendent realities, felt inward experience, ritual practices, organic unities, symbolic action and so on. At first, to simplify a complex narrative, culture in the minor, aesthetic sense of the word tried to perform the task of religion, and dismally failed. The arts simply involve too few people to match a phenomenon (religion) which links the daily practices of billions of people to the most fundamental values. Then, in the West at least, politics tried to perform some of the tasks of religion – collective faith, the transformation and redemption of the earth – and that seemed to fail as well. What then happened in the West is that culture took over from politics. And this we know as postmodernism. If traditional leftist politics weren't working, perhaps cultural or identity politics would do the job instead. At the same time, this shift seemed to be happening elsewhere in the world as well. Islamic fundamentalism sprang among other things from the crushing of radical nationalist politics in the Muslim world. Fundamentalism is partly the result of a failure of politics. It represents a turn to culture, or religion, instead. Islamism, like postmodernism, is a form of culturalism, which mistakenly believes that ideas and values are what govern the world.

The shift from politics to culture, however, is deceptive. Just as the conflict in Northern Ireland was never really about religion, so the so-called war on terrorism has exceedingly little to do with religious belief. Most radical Islamists, in fact, know about as much about the Koran as Brad Pitt knows about the Bible. They are fighting largely for political reasons, not cultural ones; and so are their Western antagonists. The old political world hasn't disappeared after all. The problems which confront us today, as they did on the brink of the first millennium, are material, geopolitical ones – questions of the conflict between rich and poor, for example, not exalted questions of belief and identity. It's just that the terms in which they are being fought out have radically altered. So I suppose my attitude to belief in the modern world is that it doesn't matter all that much. More's the pity.

Repetition versus Progress

Boris Groys

I

I would like to propose shifting the terms of our discussion. Specifically, I would prefer to speak not about knowledge and belief but about science and religion. The notions of knowledge and belief both suggest one's personal relationship to truth. It seems to me that it will be more interesting to characterize the regime under which knowledge and belief function in contemporary Western society – and they function there as science and religion.

Let us start with religion. The regime under which religion, any religion, functions in contemporary secular, democratic societies of the Western type is freedom of belief. After the victory of the Enlightenment faith became a private affair. Freedom of belief means that everybody is free to believe what he or she chooses to believe, and also that everybody is free to organize their personal, private life according to their beliefs. But at the same time it means that it is forbidden to impose one's own faith on public life and state institutions. The work of the Enlightenment resulted not in the complete disappearance of religion, but in its privatization, in its withdrawal into the private sphere. Under the conditions of the contemporary secularized world, religion became a matter of private taste – it functions in a way that is analogous to the functioning of art and design. This does not mean that religion is not publicly discussed. However, the place of religion in its relationship to public discussion is the same as the place of art as it was described by Kant in his *Critique of Judgment*: religion can be publicly discussed, but such a discussion cannot result in any conclusion that would become binding for the participants of this discussion or for society as a whole. The commitment to this or that religious faith is a matter of a personal, private, sovereign decision that cannot be dictated by any public authority, including any democratically legitimized authority. And what is even more important, such a decision – as in the case of art – does not need to be publicly argued for and legitimized. Rather, it is supposed to be socially accepted without any further explanation. The legitimacy of personal faith is based not on its persuasive power, but on the sovereign right of the individual to accept or to reject this faith.

Now science is, on the contrary, a public affair. Knowledge that is obtained, formulated and presented scientifically is central for the governing of contemporary enlightened, liberal Western democracies. As Michel Foucault repeatedly stressed, under the conditions of modernity scientific knowledge equals power. Modern technology is based on sciences like physics or biology. Modern governing practice is also based on the positive sciences like law studies, political science, economics, psychology, sociology, and so on. All that means that there can be no freedom of science in the same sense as there is freedom of belief. In the context of a scientific discussion, every opinion can and must be argued for, substantiated or falsified by certain facts, proved according to certain rules. Every participant in such a discussion is certainly free – at least theoretically – to formulate his or her own positions and to argue in their favour. But one cannot insist on a certain scientific opinion without any justification, against all proofs and evidences to the contrary, without producing any arguments that would make one's position plausible and persuasive for others. Such an obstinate resistance to the obvious, such blindness toward facts, logic and common sense would be regarded as bordering on insanity. If somebody would refer to his sovereign right to insist on a certain scientific opinion without being able to legitimize this insistence by any rational argument, he would be excluded from the scientific community. And that means that he would be excluded from the public discussion altogether because today public discussion and scientific discussion are de facto identical.

So there are today two types of freedom operating in our culture. Freedom of scientific opinion is conditional. It is conditioned by one's ability to justify, to legitimize one's opinion according to certain publicly established rules. Freedom of belief is an unconditional, sovereign freedom because there is no possibility of proving that someone's faith is wrong – just as there is no possibility of proving that someone's faith is true. Or to formulate that in a different way: every religion functions as a social and political representation of individual, private non-knowledge. The ideology of the Enlightenment tends to suggest that the whole sphere of non-knowledge will eventually be replaced by all-encompassing knowledge, or, to formulate that in another way: in the future science will find appropriate answers to all possible questions. Science famously operates by the notion of progress – or rather by the notion of delay. Scientific truth is ultimately a messianic truth: the time of its full appearance and victory is always indicated as sometime later. In this sense scientific knowledge is a matter of belief, of personal trust in the promised coming of insight, of evidence that will overcome any doubt, any non-insight, any non-knowledge. Of course, one can argue that waiting for such a moment, for the revelation of the ultimate scientific truth, is actually unscientific. And, of course, it has been said again and again that doubt and non-knowledge never can be completely overcome. But progress in science is still generally seen as permanent replacement of non-knowledge by knowledge and of doubt by certainty, as a potentially unending quest for ultimate truth – and this infinite progress is at the same time infinite delay.

Religion, on the contrary, does not seek to overcome non-knowledge. Instead, it perceives non-knowledge as the ultimate, unsurpassable horizon of human existence. The religious subject does not seek truth because he knows that every quest of that kind is futile. The scientist loves truth and seeks to achieve truth. But scientific truth is *la dame sans merci*. The scientist loves truth but he is not loved by truth. The consummation of the scientific love is promised for the future – but it is always a future beyond the future, an infinite perspective of eternal delay. In the case of religious truth the situation is the opposite. The religious subject is actually passive, he does not search for the truth – like Abraham who was, as we know from the Bible, initially perfectly content and who lived a quite normal life. Rather, truth comes to him and imposes itself on him. The religious subject is sought by truth, addressed and seduced by it. Here we have a case of the active truth, of truth in love. Such a loving truth is also extremely jealous – it punishes those who do not accept it. In this case we do not have a subject who wants to possess truth but does not get it, but, rather, a subject who is chosen by truth that wants to possess him. Or to say it in other terms: the scientific subject is a producer of truth – or at least, of desire of truth – whereas the religious subject is a consumer of truth. And like every consumer, he actually does not need to know what it is that he consumes, just as we don't necessarily know how cars, planes and other things are built. It is sufficient that the consumer accepts (one can say: buys) a truth in an act of individual commitment. As Søren Kierkegaard described it, it is sufficient that the religious subject effectuates a leap of faith; an acceptance of faith on the basis of non-knowledge.

Indeed, there can be no knowledge of God and his will. God exceeds any rationality because he is sovereign – and does not need to explain or to justify his acts and decisions (as can be read in the Book of Job). This divine sovereign free will undermines all the certainties, evidences and convictions of reason. Therefore, only the religious subject is truly sceptical: he does not believe even in direct evidence, and he does not submit it to the power of a better argument. For a religious subject the face of the world is not the surface of an object that should be scientifically investigated, but an interface, a surface behind which divine subjectivity is hidden. The relationship of the religious subject to God is the same as the relationship of a spectator to an artist. One likes an artwork precisely because one does not understand it. A leap of faith functions in a same way as a decision of taste.

The difference between science and religion can therefore be described as the difference between the production of truth and the consumption of truth. That explains why the religious attitude has become so popular in our contemporary society, which is after all predominantly a society of consumption. Today we are more in the position of Abraham than in the position of Plato. And, indeed, today we are beyond the time in which an individual was offered no truth at all, or a couple of publicly recognized truths and traditions, as in the time of Plato or the early Enlightenment. The contemporary subject is addressed and even attacked from all directions by truths of every description. These truths are not simply waiting quietly somewhere to be found, to be discovered, to be engaged. Not at all. They are aggressive, they are pushy, they are busy advertising themselves – and they are often terrifying. They tell us that the earth is warming and we will all die together in the near future. And if not together, then everybody will die alone from smoking, from cholesterol, from Islamist terrorism, and so on. These and other truths are produced and distributed today by impersonal agencies and organizations.

II

The truths that demand our acceptance are mostly truths that are brought to us by the media – today by the Internet in the first place. The Internet has become the main source of our knowledge about the contemporary world and the main medium of communication with this world. At the same time, the Internet is not a medium that is controlled by any public agency. Rather, it is a public space occupied by private interests and private, sovereign commitments. The information that is brought to us by the Internet is not a result of any rational public discussion. Each individual user has a completely sovereign right to put every personal opinion and any unchecked information on the Web, without being obliged to justify this information. Today, the Internet is the main vehicle by which the private invades the public space. Moreover, the Internet does not differentiate between religious or scientific truths. The same can be said about all contemporary mass media. All truths confront us today as news: the Holy Virgin has appeared again to a group of humble believers, the mass of the dark matter was found to be bigger than the mass of the matter accessible to our senses. One can believe it or not – the opinions of the experts are always split.

Under these conditions, how can a consumer form his or her own opinion? Religion is often understood as a certain set of opinions. In that realm religion is associated with opinions about whether contraception should be permitted or women should wear head scarves. But I would argue that religion – any religion – is primarily not a set of opinions but a set of rituals, a practice of literal, ritualistic repetition. Furthermore, this religious ritual refers to a state of the absence of opinion, a state of opinionlessness – a-doxia – for it refers to the will of the God or gods, which is ultimately hidden from the minds of mortals. Religious ritual is always in one or another form a symbolic repetition and celebration of a love affair and an ultimate wedding between divine truth and human non-knowledge. Neither of the protagonists in this love affair change through time: divine truth remains unfathomable and unthinkable and human non-knowledge remains infinitely humble, and at the same time infinitely proud.

This means that ritual as such is neither true, nor false. It marks the zero level of freedom of opinion, the freedom from every kind of opinion, from the obligation to have an opinion. Religious ritual can be repeated, or abandoned, or modified, but not legitimized, criticized or refuted. Accordingly, a religious fundamentalist is somebody who insists not so much on a certain set of opinions, but rather on certain rituals not being abandoned or modified, but faithfully, correctly reproduced. Science is supposed to be progressive because knowledge grows in time, but religion is repetitive, because non-knowledge is repetitive. Non-knowledge reproduces itself in time, and every religion manifests this self-reproduction of non-knowledge by the repetitiveness of its rituals.

This is why the true religious fundamentalist cares not about fidelity to the truth, but about the correctness of a ritual, not about the theoretical, or rather, theological interpretations of faith, but about the material form of religion. The fundamentalist is somebody who believes in the primacy of the letter over the spirit. Now if we look at the religious movements that are especially active in our day we immediately see that they are mostly the fundamentalist movements. We traditionally tend to distinguish between two kinds of repetition: (1) repetition of the spirit and in spirit, for example repetition of the true, inner essence of a religious message; and (2) repetition of the external form of a religious ritual. The opposition between these two types of repetition, between living spirit and dead letter, informs the whole traditional Western discourse on religion. The first kind of repetition is almost always regarded as true repetition, as the authentic, 'inner' continuation of a religious tradition, a continuation that at the same time presupposes the possibility of a rupture with the merely external, conventional, historically accidental form of this tradition – or even requires such a rupture. According to this view an inner, spiritual fidelity to the essence of a religious message gives a believer the right to adapt the external, material form of this message to the changing historical milieus and contexts without betraying the inner truth of this message. A religious tradition that is capable of transforming and adapting itself to the changing circumstances without losing its inner, essential identity is usually praised as a living, spiritually powerful tradition that maintains its vitality and historical relevance. On the contrary, 'superficial' fidelity to the mere letter, to the external form of religion, to 'empty' ritual, is as a rule regarded as a symptom of a lack of vitality in the corresponding religious tradition – and even as a betrayal of the inner truth of this tradition through the purely mechanical reproduction of its external, dead form. Now fundamentalism is precisely that: the insistence on the letter against the spirit.

That is why religious fundamentalism always has a revolutionary dimension: it breaks with the politics of spirit, for instance with the politics of reform, flexibility, adaptation to the *zeitgeist*, and replaces it (I mean: the politics of spirit) by the violent politics of the letter. Contemporary religious fundamentalism can be seen, therefore, as the most radical product of the European Enlightenment and the materialist view of the world. Religious fundamentalism is religion after the death of the Spirit, after the loss of spirituality, because if the Spirit dies only the letter remains, the material form, the ritual as event in the material world. If meaning, sense and intention cannot be stabilized, the only possibility of authentic repetition is literal repetition, mechanical reproduction, beyond any opinion, meaning, sense and intention. In this sense fundamentalist religious movements are also religions after deconstruction.

In his book *Difference and Repetition* Gilles Deleuze speaks of literal repetition as being radically artificial and therefore as being in conflict with everything natural, living, changing and developing, including natural law and moral law. To practice literal repetition can be seen, therefore, as initiating a rupture in the continuity of life. Actually, in his remarks on the philosophy of history, Walter Benjamin also speaks about revolution as a break with the continuity of historical evolution – presenting a literal repetition of the past as a genuine revolution. (He also speaks about capitalism as a new kind of religion that is reduced to a ritual, devoid of any theology.) But literal repetition is not only a revolution, not only an act of violence against the flow of historical change, and even against life as such. Literal repetition can also be seen as a way to personal self-sacralization and immortality – immortality of the subject who is ready to submit himself to such a repetition. It is no accident that the working class that performed repetitive, alienated, one might say ritual work in the context of our modern industrial civilization was in a certain sense sacralized by the socialist movements of the nineteenth and twentieth centuries, whereas intellectuals or artists, as embodiments of the creative spirit of change, remained profane, precisely because of their incapacity to repeat, to reproduce. Nietzsche already had proclaimed literal repetition – eternal return of the same on the level of the world of appearances – to be the only chance to conceive of immortality after the death of spirit, of God. One can say that religious ritual is an Ur-form of the mechanical reproduction that dominates our contemporary world, especially our mass media – and that means that mechanical reproduction can in turn be understood as a religious ritual. That is why fundamentalist religious movements have become so successful in our time: they combine religious ritual with mechanical reproduction.

Of course, for Benjamin mechanical repetition and reproduction mean the loss of the aura, the loss of the religious experience that he understands as uniqueness. He describes religious experience as, let us say, unique spiritual experience. (In this respect it is very characteristic that he evokes an experience of being enchanted by an Italian landscape as an example of an authentic experience that gets lost through reproduction.) It is the experience of happiness, of fullness of life, of intensity of life. But one can argue that true religious experience is actually the experience of death rather than the experience of life, the experience of death in the midst of life. Thus, precisely because mechanical reproduction can be understood as the lifeless repetition of the dead image, it can also be interpreted as a source of truly religious experience. One might say that it is precisely the loss of aura that is the most radical religious experience under the conditions of modernity, because in this way a human being discovers the mechanical, machine-like, repetitive and reproductive, one might even say dead aspect of his or her own existence.

III

However, as already mentioned above, the new religious movements operate primarily through the Internet by means of digital and not mechanical reproduction. During the last decades video has become the chosen medium of contemporary religious propaganda, and is distributed through different TV channels, the Internet, commercial video stores, and so on. This is especially so in the case of the most recent, most active and even aggressive religious movements. The phenomenon of confession videos by suicide bombers and many other kinds of video production reflecting the mentality of radical Islam has meanwhile become familiar to us. On the other hand, the new evangelical movements also operate with the same medium of video. If one asks those responsible for the public relations in these movements to provide information, one is initially sent a video. This use of video as the major medium of self-presentation among different religious movements is a relatively new phenomenon. The standard traditional media rather used to be a script, a book, a painted image or sculpture. Islam is an especially good example here. It famously forbids the production of images of living persons – but it does not forbid their re-production, the use of already existing images. It (indirectly) forbids individual authorship or such images but de facto allows the practices of appropriation and the ready-made technique. It has become a banality to say that Islam is not modern – but it is obviously postmodern.

The question then arises as to what constitutes the difference between mechanical and digital reproduction and how this difference affects the fate of religion in our age. At this point, I would argue that the use of video as the principle medium by contemporary religious movements is intrinsic to the message of these movements. Neither is it external to the understanding of the religious, as such, which underlies this use. This is not to suggest, following Marshall McLuhan, that here the medium is the message; rather, I would argue, the message has become the medium – a certain religious message has become the digital code.

Digital images have the propensity to generate, to multiply and to distribute themselves almost anonymously through the open fields of the contemporary means of communication. The origin of these messages is difficult, or even impossible to locate, much like the origin of divine, religious messages. At the same time, digitalization seems to guarantee a literal reproduction of a text or an image more effectively than any other known technique. Of course, it is not so much the digital image itself as the image file, the digital data that remains identical through the process of its reproduction and distribution. However, the image file is not an image – an image file is invisible. The digital image is an effect of the visualization of the invisible image file, of the invisible digital data. Only the protagonists of the movie *Matrix* (1999) were able to see the image files, the digital code as such. The average spectator, however, does not have the magic pill that would allow him or her, like the protagonists of *Matrix*, to enter the invisible space otherwise concealed behind the digital image for the purposes of directly confronting the digital data itself. And such a spectator is not in command of the technique that would enable him to transfer the digital data directly into the brain and to experience it in the mode of pure, non-visualizable suffering as depicted by the protagonist of another movie, *Johnny Mnemonic* (1995). (Actually, pure suffering is, as we know, the most adequate experience of the invisible.) Digital data should be visualized, should become an image which can be seen. Here we have a situation whereby the perennial spirit/matter dichotomy is reinterpreted as a dichotomy between digital file and its visualization, or 'immaterial' information and 'material' image, including visible text. In more theological terms: the digital file functions as an angel, as an invisible messenger transmitting a divine command. But a human being remains external to this message, to this command, and thus condemned to contemplate only its visual effects. We are confronted here with a transposition of a dichotomy between the divine and the human, from a metaphysical to a technical level – a transposition that, as Martin Heidegger would argue, is only possible by virtue of this dichotomy being implicitly technical from the outset.

By extension, a digital image that can be seen cannot be merely exhibited or copied (as an analogous image) but always only staged or performed. Here, the image begins to function as a piece of music, whose score, as is generally known, is not identical to the music piece – the score not being audible, but silent. For the music to resound, it has to be performed. One could argue that digitalization turns visual arts into performing arts. To perform something, however, means to interpret it, to betray it, to distort it. Every performance is an interpretation and every interpretation is a misuse. The situation is especially difficult in the case of the invisible original. If the original is visible it can be compared to a copy, so the copy can be corrected and the feeling of distortion reduced. But if the original is invisible no such comparison is possible, and any visualization remains uncertain in its relationship to the original; or one could even say that every such performance itself becomes an original.

Moreover, today information technology is in a state of perpetual change: hardware, software – simply everything. For this reason alone, the image is transformed with each act of visualization that uses a different and new technology. Today's technology thinks in terms of generations; we speak of computer generations, of generations of photographic and video equipment. But where generations are involved, so too are generational conflicts, Oedipal struggles. Anyone attempting to transfer his or her old text or image files to new software experiences the power of the Oedipus complex over current technology. Many data are destroyed, evaporate in the void. The biological metaphor says it all: it is not only life that is notorious in this respect, but technology as well, which, supposedly opposing nature, has now become the medium of non-identical reproduction. Benjamin's central assumption in his famous essay 'The Work of Art in the Age of Mechanical Reproduction' (1936), namely that an advanced technology can guarantee the material identity between original and copy, was not borne out by later technological developments. The real technological development went in the opposite direction – towards a diversification of the conditions under which a copy is produced and distributed and, accordingly, the diversification of the resulting visual images. And even were technology to guarantee the visual identity between the different visualizations of the same data, they would still remain non-identical due to the changing social contexts of their appearances.

The act of visualizing invisible digital data is thus analogous to the appearance of the invisible inside the topography of the visible world (biblically speaking, signs and wonders) that generates the religious rituals. In this respect, the digital image functions like a Byzantine icon, as a visible representation of invisible digital data. The digital code seems to guarantee the identity of different images that function as visualizations of this code. The identity is established here not at the level of spirit, essence or meaning but on the material and technical level. Thus, it is in this way that the promise of literal repetition seems to acquire a solid foundation. The digital file is, after all, supposed to be something more material and tangible than an invisible God. However, the digital file does remain invisible, hidden. What this signifies is that its self-identity remains a matter of faith. Indeed, we are compelled to believe that each act of visualization of certain digital data amounts to a revelation of the same data, much as we are obliged to believe that every performance of a certain religious ritual refers to the same invisible God. And this means that opinion about what is identical and what is different, or what is original and what is a copy is an act of belief, an effect of a sovereign decision that cannot be fully justified empirically or logically.

Digital video replaces the spiritual guarantees of immortality allegedly waiting for us beyond this world with the technical guarantees of potentially eternal repetition inside this world, a repetition that becomes a form of immortality because of its ability to interrupt the flow of historical time. It is this new prospect of materialist, technically guaranteed immortality that the new religious movements de facto offer their adepts, beyond the metaphysical uncertainties of their theological past. Placing human actions in loop, both practices – ritual and video – realize the Nietzschean promise of a new immortality: the eternal return of the same. However, this new technical guarantee remains a matter of belief and sovereign decision. To recognize two different images as copies of the same image or as visualizations of the same digital file means to value immortality over originality. To recognize them as different means to prefer originality in time to the prospect of immortality. Both decisions are necessarily sovereign – and both acts of faith.

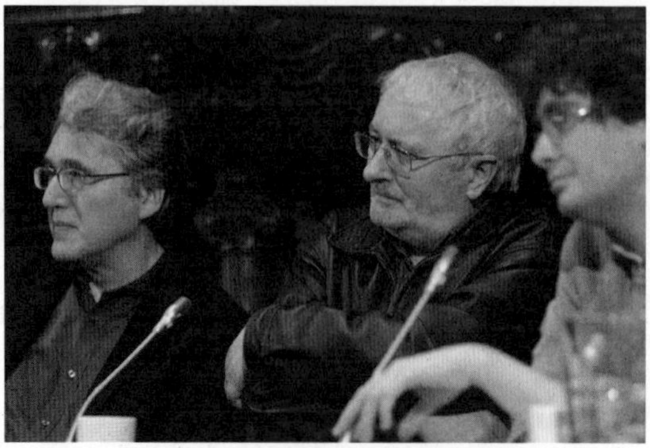

Boris Groys, Terry Eagleton and Sven Lütticken.

Discussion

The discussion was moderated by Sven Lütticken, who is lecturer in the history of modern art at the Vrije Universiteit Amsterdam and curator of the exhibition The Art of Iconoclasm *at BAK, Basis voor Actuele Kunst, Utrecht (2008-2009).*

Moderator: It struck me that Boris Groys now seems to consider the religious movements that he discussed as fully compatible with their respective monotheistic traditions. We heard him say that the digital image is comparable to the Byzantine icon, whereas a few years ago he presented Islamic fundamentalism, specifically terrorism, as a break with monotheistic iconoclasm, as a surrender to the image, so to speak. Has your opinion changed?

Boris Groys: Since I have students from Arab countries and Iran, I had a possibility to read, in translation, some of the Iranian *fatwa's*, especially with regard to the use of image. And these fatwa's are extremely subtle and in some cases unexpected. For example, one ayatollah wrote that it is forbidden to photograph somebody without a flash. But with a flash it is allowed, because at the moment a person is struck by the flash he is dead, his soul disappears for an instant. And a dead corpse may be photographed. But my general impression and my general conclusion is that in the case of contemporary, and, especially, radical Islamic movements we have to do with strategies that are comparable with postmodern curatorial or artistic strategies that actually inscribe these movements in the general context of contemporary visual culture. In Islam the individual production of images is forbidden, but the use of already produced, ready-made images is allowed. Islam may be not modern but it is postmodern.

Moderator: So these movements still function as religious movements and are not absorbed by this contemporary notion of culture?

Boris Groys: I think they are completely trans-cultural, meaning that their operative mode does not presuppose any specific education at all, any cultural knowledge. If you say that the Bible or the Koran should be understood literally, what does that mean? Literal understanding means that the text is reproduced in your mind literally. In that case you would create a complete democratization of religion, which erases every kind of upbringing and tradition and hierarchy of interpretation. So you create a direct contact between certain texts and the audience. Of course, this does fit into the contemporary political landscape, or perhaps into market practice, but there's one thing here that is missing in other political or commercial projects: the idea of immortality. At a certain point in time people don't talk about politics anymore, they start to speak about death and how to deal with it. In our society it is problematic that our secular culture does not give us any intellectual, emotional, psychological, sociological or technical means to deal with death as a public and a social experience. On this level religion and the religious movements do something that no other secular or political movement could.

Terry Eagleton: What does it say about the discussion of religion that you don't start with Thomas of Aquinas, the Eucharist or Augustine but that you start with ayatollahs? The only thing I know about imagery and religion is that Judaism is of course iconoclastic and so is Islam. That's for one very simple reason: the only image of the god of freedom, love, justice and emancipation is men and women. Human beings, who according to the Bible are created in the image and likeness of God. If you want an image of freedom, or of justice or loving, you go to people. That's why those religions are iconoclastic. They have no truck with all this fashionable stuff about the image, because they see that the image substitutes for something a lot more important . . .

Boris argued a very fine nineteenth-century positivist case about faith and science, roughly saying: science is fine, faith is not. But Aquinas believed that any faith that couldn't adduce reason, argument, discourse and evidence was bankrupt. He believed, as the Church has always believed, that there is a heresy called fideism, the belief that faith is independent of reason. A heresy! Equally I think the belief that science can do no wrong is quite heretic. Because for one thing, science requires a faith in rationality as one of its enabling conditions. A faith in rationality is not itself reducible to reason, it's axiomatic. So it's not the case that blind faith is completely on the side of religion, without reason, and pure reason is all on the side of science. We got beyond that polarity a long time ago.

Boris Groys: Yes, but we came back to it, because if we erase this polarity we establish something like a domination of the intellectuals. And that's why Luther already said: *sole fide*. Fideism, *sole fide*, was a revolutionary movement against the theological domination of the hierarchy of the Catholic Church. When seen from the Catholic position it is of course a heresy, but it is a democratic heresy, it is a revolutionary heresy. I don't practice heresy myself but I try to describe certain moments that want to erase theology as such, as a way to revolutionize and democratize religion. You can agree with that or not, but that's what's happening under our eyes today.

Audience: In the beginning Mr Groys talked about freedom of faith, and about the location of faith in the private lives of people and the common agreement that nobody is actually allowed to impose his or her private faith onto public life. And that this position, this place of religion in private life, is analogous to the place art has in this society. I am not prepared to accept that art doesn't have a public role or doesn't belong to a language we created to be able to deal in the public sphere. So that's a question for you. And to Terry Eagleton, talking about how you ended your lecture, how you built it up to an analysis of civilization versus culture: we have civilization, they have culture. But who's got art in this story? So basically, my question is: Where is art in these two constellations you presented?

Boris Groys: Of course art has a role in contemporary society, has a public function. But art also gives a promise of transcending every kind of society. We are looking now at the Egyptian mummies not from the perspective of their function in ancient Egypt. This old Egypt doesn't exist anymore but we still look at the Egyptian mummies – we see them as art. Here you have a certain kind of private perspective that brings you beyond your death, beyond the death of your society, and gives you a possibility of eternal repetition. This is of course also the ultimate artistic dream.

Terry Eagleton: With the onset of modernity three things became part of the private sphere rather than the public. One is, indeed, religion, which is now just a matter between you and God. The whole social dimension of religion is lost. Secondly, the work of art no longer serves much of a public function anymore. And one way of rationalizing that is by saying: well, don't you see, the whole point of art is to be gloriously pointless. The third thing that got privatized is sexuality. Of course now, the police aren't breaking into your bedroom or telling you what to write or how to worship. There's an enormous gain in freedom. Marxists are those people who have an undying admiration for liberalism, for emancipation. At the same time, religion, art and sexuality don't matter very much. They're like hobbies, sex becomes like playing with Plasticine. I think Marxism is the only discourse left that simultaneously says that modernity is an enthralling tale of emancipation, an advance against all the Jeremiahs and backward looking people, and that it is a totally tragic catastrophe. The point about what happens to art is that culture shifts from being a primarily artistic phenomenon to being a primarily social, collective one. At a certain point, the very idea of culture undergoes a mutation. It still means art, but it now has to mean more if it is going to do the job.

W.J.T. Mitchell - Cloning Terror

Sean Snyder - Marriott Hotel Islamabad

Art & Theory

TIME

9/11

Often the terrorist attacks that took place on 11 September 2001 and their political and military aftermath are interpreted as an appeal to artists to leave their ivory towers and produce engaged works that deal with the social and political impact of these developments. Artists question the war on terror, the crucial role played by the media in influencing popular opinion and the introduction of rigid national immigration policies and rise of an 'economy of fear'. At the same time, the issue of freedom of speech is high on the agenda, both in the social and in the artistic realm, where a fear for Muslim fundamentalist aggression threatens the artist's autonomous position outside of the political arena. Artistic autonomy is a position treasured in troubled times, as it offers space for critical reflection and counter voices. In other words: the post 9/11 art world hovers between engagement and autonomy, showing that one cannot exist without the other.

Another crucial element in the academic and artistic dealing with 9/11 and its aftermath is the meaning of the image in our contemporary society. The day after the attack Karlheinz Stockhausen called the televisual spectacle that 9/11 generated 'the ultimate artwork': the crashing planes, massive explosions, falling men, collapsing buildings and ruined cityscapes are horrible and repulsive but beautiful and attractive at the same time. This ambivalence might explain the endless repetition of this visual material in and outside the world of art. And we should not forget that it is not the first time we have seen these images: they were preceded by a vast amount of Hollywood movies in which similar disasters were represented, turning 9/11 into a remake, copy or, as Derrida called it, an example of the 'hyperreal'.

In his essay iconologist W.J.T. Mitchell speaks of an 'image war', not only referring to the impact of the WTC explosions that still float around in our (virtual) worlds but also to the endless streams of related visual material such as the pictures of the captured Saddam Hussein, the video messages of Osama Bin Laden, the instruction video's or suicide messages of Muslim terrorists and the Abu Ghraib torture pictures. The question of why these images are so powerful is answered by Mitchell by laying bare the synchronicity with the complex social debate on genetic cloning. In his visual/verbal contribution artist Sean Snyder also focuses on the (post) 9/11 image production, investigating the global circulation of information and the process of translation from one ideological system to another.

W.J.T. Mitchell (USA) is professor of English and art history at the University of Chicago. Mitchell is a noted scholar in the field of media, the visual arts and literature, well known for his theories on iconology and different modes of visual and textual representation within the context of social and politic issues. His publications include *Iconology* (1986), *Picture Theory* (1996) and *What Do Pictures Want?* (2005). In addition to this, Mitchell is an editor for the journal *Critical Inquiry*. He is currently working on a new book, entitled *Cloning Terror: The War of Images, 9-11 to Abu Ghraib*, on the violence of images in the new millennium.

Sean Snyder (USA) is a visual artist based in Berlin and Tokyo. His work centres on the global circulation of information and the process of translation from one ideological system to another. Snyder works in various media, ranging from videos and photographs to text-based works and installation. His art has been exhibited in various museums and art shows, among which the Stedelijk Museum in Amsterdam, Palais de Tokyo in Paris, New Museum of Contemporary Art in New York and the Istanbul Biennial.

Cloning Terror

The War of Images 2001-2004

W.J.T. Mitchell

Cloning Terror

We are in the midst of a double revolution, one involving the mutation of political violence into international terrorism (and the 'war on terror'), the other based in technical innovations in the biological sciences. The convergence of these two revolutions is what I call 'cloning terror', by which I mean 1) the paradoxical process by which the war on terror has the effect of producing more terror, 'cloning' more terrorists in the very act of trying to destroy them, and 2) the horror or terror of cloning itself, which presents a spectacle of unleashed forces of biological reproduction and simulation that activates some of our most archaic phobias about image-making. Cloning and terror converge, in other words, at the level of images understood as life-forms – the biopicture.

The terrorist and the clone, then, are mutually constitutive figures in our time. That is why the terrorist is often portrayed as a clone, a headless or at least faceless automaton, masked and anonymous, a mindless, pathological and suicidal life form comparable to a virus, a cancer, or a sleeper cell that 'incubates' inside the body of its host, turning the body's defences against itself in what Jacques Derrida has diagnosed as a sociopolitical form of autoimmune disorder.[1] The clone, in turn, embodies a host of ethical, religious and aesthetic horrors: the reduction of human beings to mere instrumentalities or commodities (what Giorgio Agamben calls 'bare life'); the impious effort to 'play God' with technology; the spectre of reproduction without sexual difference which leads quickly to fantasies of unleashed homosexual reproduction; the figure of the macho gay male (popularly known as a 'clone') who subverts the reassuring stereotype of the sissy;[2] the spectre of abortion raised by the technique of cloning, which

1. Jacques Derrida, 'Autoimmunity', in: Giovanna Borradori, *Philosophy in a Time of Terror: Dialogues with Jürgen Habermas and Jacques Derrida* (Chicago: University of Chicago Press, 2003).

2. 'Clones symbolize modern homosexuality', notes Martin P. Levine, in: *Gay Macho: The Life and Death of the Homosexual Clone* (New York: NYU Press, 1998); see also Roger Edmondson, *Clone: The Life and Legacy of Al Parker, Gay Superstar* (Los Angeles: Alyson Publications, 2000).

involves the destruction of what some regard as an embryonic organism in order to create a new life form; the spectre of the 'monstrous double' or 'evil twin' who perfectly simulates the 'donor' or 'parent' organism, and threatens to replace it with a new race of aliens, mutants or replicants.

The real horror of the hooded suicide bombers, then, is not that there is some monstrous face concealed under the mask, but that when the mask is taken off, the face might be that of a perfectly ordinary person who could mingle among us, turning us against ourselves. The figure of Dolly the Cloned Sheep is not frightening because she is a wolf in sheep's clothing, but because she is a *sheep* in sheep's clothing, impossible to distinguish from the 'real thing' by visual, or even genetic examination. The clone represents an even deeper threat than easily profiled aliens or 'racial others' who 'all look alike', as the racist stereotype would have it. The clones do not necessarily look like each other (thus, no profiling stereotypes are available), but they may very well look exactly like *us*, and thus be indistinguishable and unclassifiable. Like terror, cloning takes the logic of the image as figure of resemblance, similitude and copying to the limit of virulence, toxicity and insidious invisibility.

Since 9/11, an intense new epoch has opened up, a 'war on terror' triggered by and waged against images. To call this a war of or on images is in no way to deny its reality or to minimize the real physical suffering it entails. It is, rather, to take a realistic view of terrorism as a form of psychological warfare, specifically a use of images, and especially images of destruction, to traumatize the collective nervous system via mass media and turn the imagination against itself. It is also to take a realistic view of the 'war on terror' as quite literally a war against an *emotion* (like 'pity' or 'love' or 'hate'). It is thus a war on a projected spectre or phantasm, a war against an elusive, invisible, unlocatable enemy, a war that continually misses its target, striking out blindly with conventional means and waging massive destruction on innocent people in the process. The aim of terrorism is, in fact, precisely to provoke this overreaction, to lure the 'immune system' of the social body (its military and police powers) into responses that will have the effect of increasing the power of the terrorists, in effect 'cloning terror' in the process of trying to destroy it.[3]

3. See Derrida, 'Autoimmunity', op. cit. (note 1).

If terrorism is primarily a war of images, however, we must ask what images are and what they are becoming in our time, when the biodigital picture has emerged at the technical frontier of image production and circulation. This necessarily involves a moment of aestheticization of the images loosed upon the world since 9/11, a consideration of their formal, sensuous, affective properties within the epoch they have come to define. The moment has evidently passed when the image repertoire of the war on terror (the whole sequence, from the attacks of 11 September through the Abu Ghraib photos) can have an immediate political impact. In fact, for many months leading up to the November 2004 Presidential election, it was widely believed that these images were revealing the naked, awful truth about the futility and horror of the 'war on terror', and that they would have enough power to bring down the Bush administration. Now that their immediate political urgency is behind us, the moment has arrived for a more considered analysis of what these images mean, even as the historical epoch they marked fades in memory.

2001 to 2004 was an epoch marked and defined by unforgettable and traumatic pictures, from the destruction of the World Trade Center to the photographs of torture taken in Abu Ghraib prison. I want to trace a pattern in these images which expresses the logic of the biopicture. I have in mind, first, the obvious fact of a new, virulent life afforded to images with the invention of the Internet and digital photography, the way images 'clone' themselves and circulate with incredible rapidity, sometimes reversing their meaning and coming back to haunt their producers. I also have in mind the figure of the terrorist as clone in the sense of 'double', twin or mirror image of his opponent; the spectacle of terror as iconoclasm, the destruction and mutilation of images (especially the image of the human body) as itself an artificially 'produced' image, or 'photo op'; the recurrence of the headless, faceless and hooded figure, or what Jean Baudrillard has called the 'acephalic clone', a mindless repository of 'spare parts' or an automaton without will or agency; the reduction of the human form to 'bare life', and the (usually futile) attempt to censor, prohibit and contain these reductive images. I will conclude, finally, with a meditation on the Abu Ghraib photographs, which I believe define a certain kind of end to this epoch, though its consequences are still unfolding for us as I write.

The War of Images

Twin Towers

As though architecture . . . was now merely a product of cloning.
Jean Baudrillard

The destruction of the World Trade Center in New York has provided the most memorable image of the twenty-first century so far, destined to join the iconic mushroom cloud as the principal emblem of war and terror in our time, leaving behind it a space known as 'Ground Zero', a label that links it (quite inaccurately) to a nuclear bomb. The 'twin-ness' of the towers and their destruction has frequently been noted: the initial doubling of the image of destruction by the two moments of impact and the two moments of collapse, followed then by the indefinite doubling and redoubling of every detail, every conceivable angle of perspective on the disaster. The towers themselves were, of course, understood as iconic forms in their identical twin-ness and their

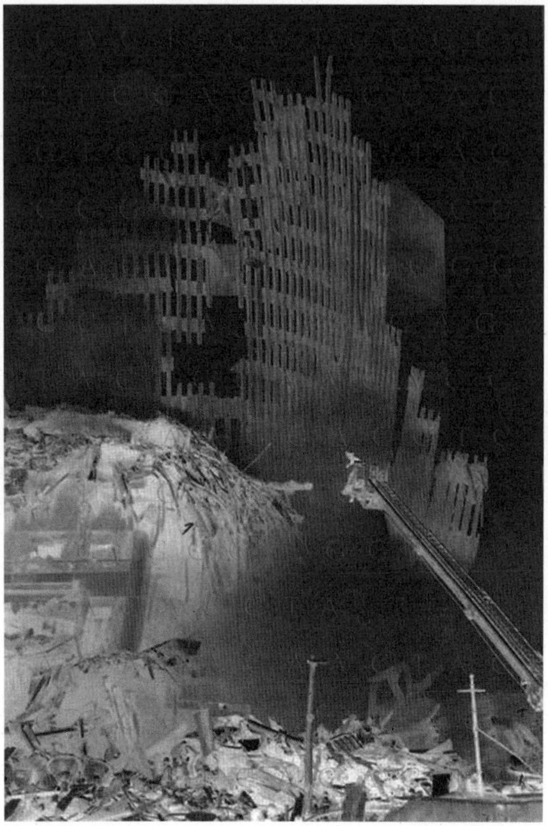

Kevin Clarke, *Dust to DNA*, 2001. © Kevin Clarke and Michael Collarone.

mutual facelessness. Jean Baudrillard compared them to bearers of digital information, the 'punch card and the statistical graph', 'as though architecture, like the system, was now merely a product of cloning, and of a changeless genetic code'.[4] The World Trade Center was already a global symbol, a 'world picture' in its own right as well as an epitome of the 'biodigital' moment of the pictorial turn. Its destruction had been foretold since the moment of its building, staged repeatedly in disaster films, and even attempted in the early 1990s.

4. Jean Baudrillard, *The Spirit of Terrorism*, translated by Chris Turner (New York: Verso, 2002), 38, 40.

The destruction of the twin towers was a classic act of iconoclasm (the destruction of the 'idol of the other') as the creation of a counter-icon, one that has become, in its way, much more powerful as an idol than the secular icon it displaced. The site was immediately declared 'hallowed ground', the victims apotheosized as heroes and martyrs. This is a process similar to the elevation of the Final Solution from a hideous extermination programme into a 'Holocaust', a sacred sacrifice, technically, a 'burnt offering'. The monumentalization of the holy place has proceeded with similar grandiosity, most notably in Daniel Liebeskind's proposed 'Freedom Tower' which, exactly 1776 feet high, and with features such as the 'Park of Heroes', the 'Garden of the World' and 'Memory's Eternal Foundations', will surpass even his Jewish Museum in

Berlin as a coercively allegorical contribution to the trauma industry.[5]

A more open and evocative memorial was provided by the Kevin Clarke/Mikey Flowers photo collage *Dust to DNA* of the ruins overlaid by the dust-filled scrim inscribed with the DNA code.[6] Flowers, an Emergency Medical Technician, took the pictures of the smouldering ruins in the days immediately following 11 September, and Clarke (an artist who also lives in lower Manhattan) overlaid the image with the letters of the DNA code (a practice he had been using for a number of years to create what I would call 'deep portraits' or 'biopictures' of human subjects). This image evokes the longing for traces and relics of the victims that was so vividly evident in innumerable informal memorials that attached themselves to the site, and throughout lower Manhattan. But it recodes this longing as a desire for literal biological reanimation, just the reverse of the funerary liturgy, 'ashes to ashes, dust to dust'. The logic of *Dust to DNA*, by contrast, leads on to 'from DNA to cloned resurrection'. Or if not resurrection, at least identification of the particular victim whose dust has been reclaimed. The Clarke/Flowers image is also perhaps a reminder of the biodigital picture that was already inscribed in the twin towers, their monumental flaunting of doubleness, twin-ness and architectural cloning, and hints at the ironic coincidence of cloning and terror in the summer of 2001. While the men of Al Qaeda were making their final plans, while Richard Clarke, the head of US counter-terrorism, was vainly trying to get the attention of the White House to warn them of the impending threat, the Bush administration was preoccupied with stopping the dangerous acceleration of biomedical research in cloning.

5. See David Simpson, *9-11 and the Culture of Commemoration* (Chicago: University of Chicago Press, 2005), for a critique of the 'memory industry' around September 11.

6. See Kevin Clarke's website for a discussion of this image: http://www.kevinclarke.com.

Uncle Osama: The Uncanny Double

We have met the enemy and he is us.
Walt Kelly, Pogo

'Only when modeled, shaped, or even cloned from those interacting with them can terrorists become terrorists,' notes sociologist Vincenzo Ruggiero.[7] The mimetic symmetry between the sovereign and the terrorist is vividly displayed by the TomPaine.com anti-war cartoon of 'Uncle Osama', a graphic clone of Uncle Sam. Uncle Osama hails American recruits with the message: 'I WANT YOU to invade Iraq.' Why? As a recruitment device for Al Qaeda. The image illustrates perfectly the assessment of counter-terrorism expert Richard Clarke: 'The ingredients Al Qaeda dreamed of for propagating its movement were a Christian government attacking a weaker Muslim region, allowing the new terrorist group to rally jihadists from many countries to come to the aid of the religious brethren.'[8] The war in Iraq was a double blessing to bin Laden, and a double mistake by the USA. It turned attention away from him and towards Saddam Hussein, who was easily

7. Vincenzo Ruggiero, 'Terrorism: Cloning the Enemy', *International Journal of the Sociology of Law*, no. 31 (2003), 23-34; 33.

8. Richard Clarke, *Against All Enemies* (New York: Free Press, 2004), 138.

rendered as a symbolic substitute. And it served as a recruiting device for jihadists. The problem is that the irony of this image was evidently lost on many viewers. Its mimicry of the prevailing fantasy was a bit too literal. After all, when George W. Bush took his 'Mission Accomplished' bow on the deck of an aircraft carrier, he explicitly linked the war in Iraq to 11 September himself. Uncle Osama could have morphed into Bush at that moment, urging young men to sacrifice their lives on both sides, calling for the Iraqi resistance to 'bring it on'.[9]

9. The photo opportunity of Bush's 'Mission Accomplished' speech was, of course, quickly disavowed by the White House when it became evident that this image was becoming the subject of parody, and had even been cloned as an 'action figure'.

Hoodwinking Saddam

Wars of images are clone wars. They require a mirroring of the faceless enemy and his acts. Even better is the *headless* enemy, what Jean Baudrillard calls the 'acephalic clone': 'On the other side of the Atlantic Ocean, headless frogs and mice are being cloned in private laboratories, in preparation for the cloning of headless human bodies that will serve as reservoirs for organ donation. Why bodies without heads? As the head is considered the site of consciousness, it is thought that bodies with heads would pose ethical and psychological problems.'[10]

10. Jean Baudrillard, *The Vital Illusion* (New York: Columbia University Press, 2000), 4.

If one cannot remove the head, however, hooding it is almost as good as a way of eliminating the 'ethical and psychological problems' presented by the sight of a human face. The so-called 'interrogation hoods' made famous by the images propagated at Abu Ghraib prison have served this double purpose: the hoods serve as torture instruments, rendering the victim helplessly blind and vulnerable to smothering and unpredictable blows, while protecting the torturers own anonymity, and from the possibility of human identification or empathy. The hoods have the effect of stifling the cries of pain, and render the victim faceless and anonymous.

No surprise, then, that the preferred photo op of the American army on entering Baghdad was the hooding of Saddam Hussein's statue with an American flag. In a moment of temporary sanity, however, it was apparently realized that this image would not suggest liberation from tyranny to most Iraqis or the rest of the world, but would look like a triumphal emblem of American imperial occupation. The hood was quickly removed (but not before it was photographed and circulated throughout the world). The more traditional iconoclastic tactic was then deployed, and Saddam's statue was pulled down. If the aim was to produce a mimesis of the destruction of the World Trade Center, laying low the phallic verticality of the enemy's monumental erection, it was something of a botched job. Saddam's statue turned out to be difficult to pull down, and it leaned over at a semi-tumescent angle before the engineers were able to complete the job.[11]

11. See the film, *Control Room*, for al Jazeera's television coverage of this event, denounced by the Pentagon for aiding the enemy. Al Jazeera's reporters noticed that the crowd assembled to celebrate the destruction of Saddam's statues was quite tiny, and contained very few Iraqis. Evidently it was mustered by the US military to produce the proper backdrop to this photo op.

Saddam's Dental Examination

The hooding of the head, and especially of the 'head of state', is an ideal strategy for humiliating the enemy in a war of images. But an even more inventive treatment of the 'head' was afforded by the actual capture of Saddam Hussein in December 2003. The once-powerful tyrant had to be paraded for the cameras in a scene of abjection and humiliation, but not one that would suggest cruelty or torture. Some inspired genius in the Pentagon's media liaison team must have come up with the idea for what became the iconic photo op of Saddam's capture: his dental examination. This image is, in a very precise sense, an inversion of the hooding of the head in that it penetrates the head, goes inside it to illuminate its dark interiors. A video loop of the dental examination, with a tiny flashlight being inserted into Saddam's mouth, lighting up his cheeks from within, was run repeatedly in the hours and days after his capture.

The sheer repetition of this image rivalled the repetition of the images of destruction of the Twin Towers, rendering it the single most memorable image of the whole capture episode. Other images, like the removal of lice from Saddam's hair, or shots of the dark interior of the 'spider hole' where he had been hiding, were simply not formally compelling enough to sustain interest. But the dental examination had the virtue of adding several symbolic components to the primary effect of humiliating the 'head of state' in the most literal possible manner. First, it defused any hint of cruelty by staging Saddam's captors as looking after his health, perhaps determining whether he had developed any cavities or abscesses during his underground existence, or preventing him from committing suicide with a cyanide capsule embedded in one of his teeth. Second, it suggested that the US military had finally achieved the elusive objective of total victory, since now it had penetrated 'inside the head' of the head of state. Any remaining secrets would now come to light, and it did not take long, in fact, for the image to be reproduced with a new caption: 'Looking for weapons of mass destruction.' Third, the real purpose of the dental examination may well have been to extract a DNA sample from Saddam's mouth, to determine with certainty that the man in US custody was not one of Saddam's many notorious doubles. Of course, if the captured Saddam was a clone, then even a DNA test would be unable to differentiate the original from a copy.

Cloning Bodies

The human body is the best picture of the human soul.
Ludwig Wittgenstein[12]

We don't do body counts.
General Tommy Franks

Until Spring 2004, the war of images was mainly running in favour of the USA. Inconvenient images of Iraqi civilian casualties had been successfully censored. The American army had made it

12. Ludwig Wittgenstein, *Philosophical Investigations*, translated by G.E.M. Anscombe (Blackwell: Oxford, 1953), 178.

clear that the Powell doctrine of 'no body counts' (either of 'enemies' or 'innocent bystanders') would be continued. The only bodies counted, the only bodies that *counted*, were those of American troops. Then, in May 2004, images of bodies began to proliferate in the mass media, and a new kind of photo op emerges: atrocity photographs and videos of the beheading of American hostages; the dismemberment of American contractors and the display of their mutilated bodies on a bridge outside the city of Fallujah; the flag-draped coffins of American soldiers; and the scandalous torture photographs from Abu Ghraib prison. The first two groups of images were photo ops deliberately staged by the enemy, the Iraqi resistance. The second two were produced by Americans themselves. Let's start with the 'enemy images'.

Horrible as they are, the images of decapitation betray a kind of symmetry with the hooding of Saddam's statue and the dental examination. The justice of an eye for an eye escalates to a head for a head, and a symbolic decapitation is trumped by the staging of the real thing. Although these images were immediately declared 'barbaric' and 'savage', decapitation was a standard (and literal) form of 'capital' punishment in European nations up to and including the French Revolution, which invented the guillotine as a 'humane' form of quick and easy execution, and it is still the legal form of capital punishment in Saudi Arabia today. The 'clinical' treatment of Saddam's head was answered, in other words, by the 'judicial' treatment of American hostages, whose beheadings were accompanied by the trappings of a legal execution, complete with the reading aloud of the charges, and the circulation of the images on the Internet to the global media.

The Fallujah photographs carried the staging of horror to a new extreme. On 31 March 2004, the bodies of four American contractors ambushed and killed outside Fallujah were set on fire, mutilated horribly in a kind of echo of the European practice of 'drawing and quartering', and then the remains of two of them were strung up as trophies for display from a bridge over the Euphrates River. The behaviour of the crowd of Iraqis before the camera made it clear that the photographs were not merely the spontaneous recordings of a passing journalist, but staged photo ops meant to outrage the eyes of the enemy.[13] Like the bystanders and participants in American lynching photographs from the early twentieth century, the assembled crowd expressed unabashed delight in the spectacle they were creating for the camera, and held up signs declaring Fallujah to be a graveyard for Americans. In contrast to the decapitations, there is no attempt to stage these photo ops as records of judicial proceedings. They portray the rough, anarchic 'frontier' justice carried out by an angry (and exultant) mob, a spontaneous act of violence meant to express the collective will of the city of Fallujah to be 'the graveyard of the Americans'. One sensed from the moment that these photographs appeared that this message would be taken literally

13. Or alternatively, 'the presence of photographers may have inflamed the crowd's passions,' according to David Klatell, dean of Columbia University's Graduate School of Journalism. *Chicago Tribune*, 2 April 2004, 11.

by the Americans, that the city of Fallujah was doomed, and that collective punishment would be carried out sooner or later. The siege and destruction of Fallujah, a city of 300,000 people, was duly executed by American forces right after the American Presidential election in the autumn of 2004.

A corpse is the primeval form of what I have been calling a biopicture. It is 'only an image' – a still, dead, motionless image – of what was once a living form. And yet it is still alive, taboo, uncanny. The mutilation of a corpse is, from a rational perspective, a futile exercise. The person, the subjective consciousness, who was or once inhabited the corpse cannot feel the wounds. And in fact, the wounds are not meant to inflict pain on the actual victim. They are meant to be transmitted in images designed to terrorize the enemy.[14] They are not images *of* trauma, but images designed to traumatize the viewer, especially those who identify with the victim. When propagated by digital reproduction and global circulation they produce a kind of effect quite different from modern(ist) 'shock', which had its therapeutic, defamiliarizing aspect. There is nothing like 'shock therapy' in the realm of trauma.[15] These images are designed to overwhelm the viewer's defences, and that is why many of the news services that carried them on 1 April 2004 elected to *blur* them, rendering their contents almost unreadable.[16]

The mutilation of a corpse is thus the mutilation of an image, an act of iconoclasm that is reproduced as an image in another medium – in verbal reports and rumours, in the memory of an impression, in photographs that can be propagated indefinitely. But this is a form of iconoclasm that goes well beyond the prohibition on images shared by Islamic, Jewish and Christian versions of the second commandment. If the human body is created 'in the image of God', and is the sacred handiwork of God, then its mutilation – even as a corpse – is an act of desecration. One of the leading clerics of Fallujah accordingly declared that the mutilation of the contractors' bodies was a 'desecration', and a violation of Islamic law.[17] From a Christian point of view, the mutilations were a double outrage, triggering not only the tribalistic reaction to the treatment of a 'member' of the social body, but also constituting a theological outrage, a crime against God – or the *imago dei* – himself ('desecration' in the fullest sense). The mutilations added force, in other words, to the sense that the USA is engaged in a Christian 'crusade' in the Middle East, not just an effort to bring secular democracy to the region. The images were perfectly designed to stoke the passions of a holy war.

Modern warfare is often portrayed as a de-realized spectacle, a mere simulacrum on the order of a video game. And indeed, that is the way the American media and its political minders would like to portray it: a war of faceless enemies marching in anonymous ranks to be vaporized by superior weapons from a safe distance. But television also has the capacity, as Edward R. Murrow pointed out long ago, to present the 'little picture', up

14. See Michael Taussig's discussion of symbolic mutilations in Columbia, 'The Language of Flowers', *Critical Inquiry*, no. 1, vol. 30 (Autumn 2003).

15. The distinction between modernist 'shock' and postmodern 'trauma' is discussed by Tanya Fernando in her PhD dissertation, *Shock Treatments*, University of Chicago, 2005.

16. 'Powerful Images Debated', *Chicago Tribune*, 2 April 2004, 11.

17. Sheik Farzi Nameq 'condemned the mutilations of the four Americans' as 'un-Islamic desecrations'. He also warned that this would bring destruction to the city. 'Cleric in Fallujah Decries Mutilations', *Chicago Tribune*, 3 April 2004, 3. It seems unlikely that this declaration was based on any notion of human body as an *imago dei*. That is a doctrine more attuned with Christian theology, and especially with the incarnation and the Catholic doctrine of the resurrection of the body. From an Islamic point of view, mutilation of the dead body is primarily a *social* sin, explicitly defined as such by the prophet himself, one to be avoided because of its capacity to mobilize revenge from the enemy. I am grateful to Abdolkarim Soroush for his advice on Islamic prohibitions on mutilation.

close and personal. And it can reduce our distance from events, even as it seems to distance us. Marshall McLuhan's vision of a 'global village' has come to pass, not as the idyllic utopia that is often (wrongly) attributed to him, but as the terrifying *immediacy* of viscerally intimate violence portrayed in real time. Archaic forms of tribal violence designed to elicit the tribalistic reactions of the American public can make the global village a very dangerous place, especially when the full force of American military power is mobilized in reaction to a local provocation. And thanks to the invention of digital media, these spectacles, the violent dismemberments of the biopicture, can be cloned indefinitely and circulated globally. They are the poisonous 'gift that keeps on giving', taking on a perverse life of their own in the world's nervous system.

Cloning Jesus

The God of Islam is an idol.
William Boykin

The most vivid example of the global circulation is the image that has now become iconic of the entire Abu Ghraib scandal, and perhaps of the whole 'war on terror'. That is the famous 'Hooded Man' with a black cloak standing on a box of C-rations with electrical wires connected to his hands and genitals. It has been obvious since the first appearance of this image that there was something special about it, something that differentiated it from the degrading, pornographic spectacles of enforced nakedness and humiliation that characterized the other Abu Ghraib photographs. The image is, to begin with, formally simple and memorable, quite unlike the chaotic, almost unreadable piles of naked bodies with their air-brushed genitalia. It achieves an instant recognizability that is easily reproduced in other media. There is also a curious air of dignity about the image, a suggestion of poise and balance under severe stress, that invites the viewer to empathize and identify with the figure despite (or is it because of?) its hooded anonymity. If one tries to project oneself into the experience of the figure, one must imagine being blinded and stifled by the hood, and then terrified with the warning that, if one falls off the precarious pedestal, one will be electrocuted. A few carefully administered electric shocks to sensitive areas of the body would make this seem far from an idle threat.

The Hooded Man has clearly been transformed into a 'Christ-figure'. It seems very unlikely that this was anyone's intention, though some of the other torture images (a naked, excrement-smeared Iraqi compelled to stand in a cruciform posture with his legs crossed) make one wonder. If the pornographic images seem to record a homophobic ritual of 'fraternity initiation', this one registers an even more profound transformation of the (suspected)

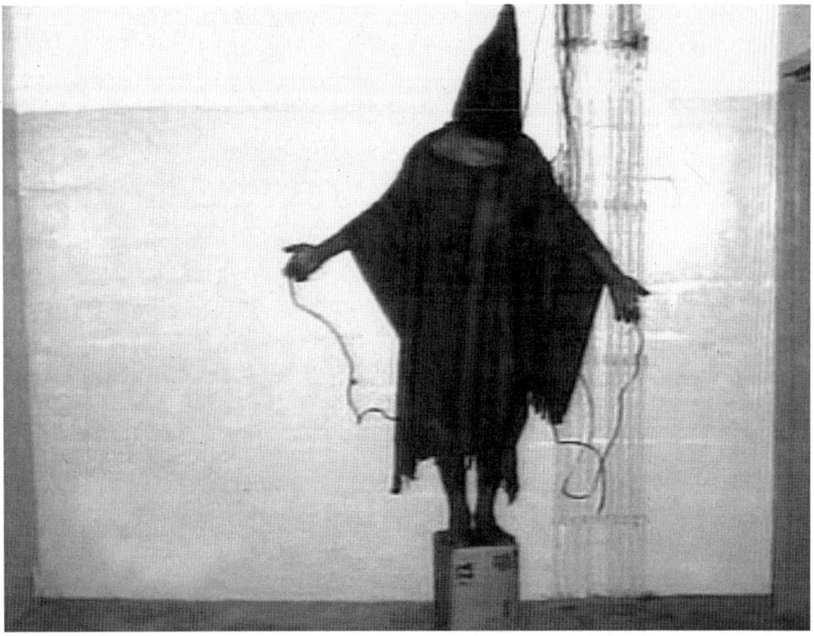

A hooded Iraqi prisoner at Abu Ghraib prison, Iraq, 2004. Courtesy of Rex – Features Hollandse Hoogte.

terrorist, the tool of Satan, into the avatar of the Christian 'son of god' himself. The figure of the (supposed) Islamic martyr, a warrior prepared to sacrifice himself in holy jihad, is converted into the Christian martyr, the patient 'suffering servant' who endures terrible pain and humiliation without protest, as an expiation for the sins of mankind.[18]

Look at this image through the eyes of an iconologist, and you will see something even more specific, and that is the particular stages of the passion narrative that are echoed by the Man with the Hood. This is clearly not a crucifixion: the arms are at the wrong angle. It is, rather, a synthesis of three distinct moments from the iconography of the passion of Christ: the first is the Mocking of Christ (which usually shows him blindfolded); second, the Ecce Homo ('behold the man') when Jesus is presented to the crowd as a mock 'king', wearing the Crown of Thorns, sometimes standing on a pedestal; and third, the Man of Sorrows, a non-narrative image that shows Jesus taken down from the cross, his body washed, and often displayed with his arms out at four and eight o'clock. It also evokes certain treatments of the resurrected Christ, arms extended in a gesture of welcome and blessing. Although the Abu Ghraib image is generally reproduced as a singular, isolated iconic form, it implies an address to and relation to others that is a central feature of the tortured and dying *imago dei* in Christian iconography. We know that the torturers are not far away, and we know from the pornographic images that they were having a good time, giving the 'thumbs-up' sign to the camera as they gloated over their victims. But this, too, is a central feature of the photographs, which, like canonical scenes

18. Actually, the man under the hood was suspected of nothing more than car theft, and (like most of the prisoners at Abu Ghraib) probably had nothing to do with the resistance. It now appears that he was a minor Baath Party official who managed a parking lot near Baghdad. He has since become an advocate for victims of American occupation forces, and says that he forgives the people who tortured him. See Hassan M. Fattah, 'Symbol of Abu Ghraib Seeks to Spare Others His Nightmare', *New York Times*, 11 March 2006, A1, A7.

of the passion of Christ, incorporate the torturers as an essential part of their iconography. Did Lynndie Englund know that a frequent motif in scenes of the mocking of Christ is the leading of him on a leash? Certainly not. These tableaux are not to be taken as expressions of the intentions of the torturers, but symptoms of the 'system behind the system' that brought them into the world.

It seems only fitting that, in May 2004, just at the moment that American Christians were wallowing in Mel Gibson's sadistic portrayal of torture in *The Passion of Christ*, an image should surface in the mass media that synthesizes the phases of the passion into a single memorable icon as a kind of summary of everything accomplished by the American crusade in Iraq. On the one hand, the image is a kind of ideological X-ray, exposing that mission as a Christian crusade that aims to 'convert' the Muslims into Christian martyrs. On the other hand, it provides (like the Uncle Osama poster) a kind of mirror reversal of its intended purpose. Instead of eliciting useful intelligence about the Iraqi resistance, it had the effect of intensifying that resistance, serving as a recruiting poster for jihadists throughout the world, and destroying the last, threadbare alibi for the American occupation of Iraq. By this point in that war, all the pretexts for pre-emptive war – the weapons of mass destruction, the notion of Iraq as a haven for

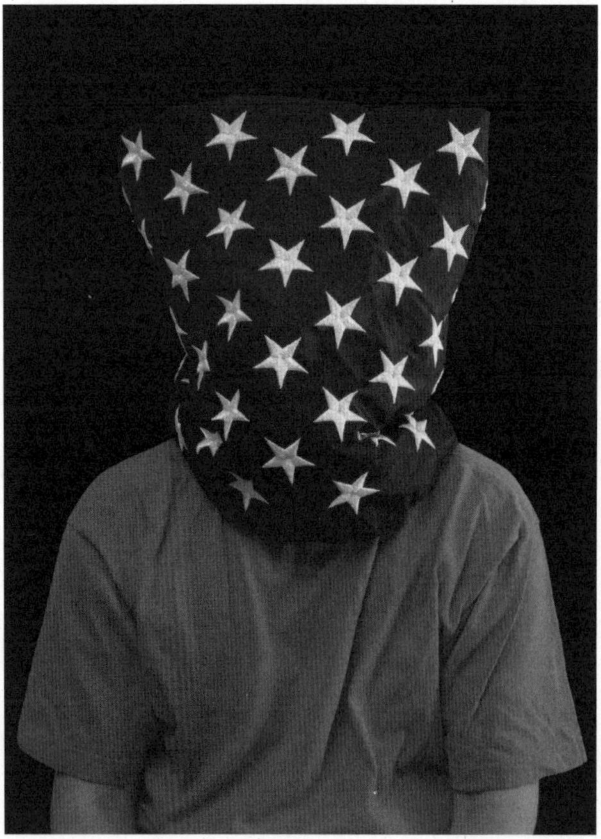

Hans Haacke, *Stargazing*, 2004. © Hans Haacke / VG Bild-Kunst, courtesy of the Paula Cooper Gallery.

terrorists, the linkage of Saddam Hussein with 9/11– had been shown to be utter illusions, if not outright fabrications. The only *casus belli* remaining was the moral crusade of 'liberating Iraq' from tyranny and bringing democracy there, a pretext that was rather effectively undermined by the Abu Ghraib photos, especially this one.

If ever an image has been 'cloned' in the circuits of the mass media, this one was, both in the sense of indefinite duplication, and in the further sense of taking on 'a life of its own' that eludes and even reverses the intentions of its producers. The Man with the Hood appeared throughout the world, on television, over the Internet, in protest posters, and in murals, graffiti and works of art from Baghdad to Berkeley. It became so ubiquitous and recognizable that it could insinuate itself subtly into commercial advertisements for the iPod in New York subways, where it merged almost subliminally the figures of 'wired' dancers wearing iPod headphones, and the Man on the Box with his wired genitals.

Let Hans Haacke have the final word in his stunning image, *Stargazing*, which shows a man in an orange jump suit with a star-spangled blue hood over his head. This image summarizes perfectly the whole complex of biopictures we have been exploring, from the 'acephalic clone' to the hooded terrorist or torturer to the hooded terror suspect transformed into a torture victim. The hood as an instrument to produce the faceless anonymity and blindness of the torture victim has been synthesized with the emblem of American sovereignty, summarizing the American 'war on terror' as the self-destructive process it has been.[19] The curious mirroring of the torturer and the victim is eloquently expressed by a subtle ambiguity about the location of agency in the figure. On the one hand, the star-spangled hood stages this figure (like the hooded Man on the Box, or the statue of Saddam Hussein) as the passive, suffering trophy of American power. On the other hand, the man's white skin and relaxed arms (no 'stress positions' here) and the title of *Stargazing* hint that this man has pulled the hood over his head all by himself. Stargazing Americans have indeed hoodwinked themselves with a peculiar combination of ignorance and idealism, blindness and innocence, a refusal to understand the consequences of their invasion and occupation of Iraq, coupled with the utopian rhetoric of freedom and democratization that has been employed throughout this war. So Haacke's image may also be suggesting that the wearer of this hood is capable of removing it and seeing things as they are. Whether the American people are ready to look without blinking at this and the other images of the war on terror, to face what they have done to Iraq, to themselves and to the world order, is quite another question.

19. Another image that resonates with Haacke's *Stargazing* is the cover of the leading German magazine *Der Spiegel*, immediately after the Presidential election of November 2004. The cover shows the Statue of Liberty blindfolded by the American flag, accompanied by the caption, 'Augen zu und durch' (Close your eyes and plunge forward). A less literal, but more poetic translation, is offered by title of Stanley Kubrick's last film, *Eyes Wide Shut*.

Postscript

This essay has been repeated and reprinted on various occasions and in various organizations around the world. I am particularly happy to contribute another clone-version for this project as I'm pleased to see a phrase like 'Now Is the Time' coming back. It strikes me as a sign that perhaps modernism and modernity is not dead after all. The era of postmodernism was one in which the slogan was 'now is *not* the time'. It was a time when we thought that 'now' just didn't work. Postmodernism felt it was too late, that the time of the now was passed. Or perhaps it was not yet, it was a time to come, as Derrida often put it.

So why does 'now is the time' seem somehow appropriate, right for this moment? There are several reasons. The most important one being that the Bush administration has come to an end. I feel like the war on terror, which was launched by 9/11, is now, if not over, fading as something that can be invoked without resistance which conquers all opponents. 9/11 meant the end of irony and scepticism; we knew that the world was divided into the good and the evil, into the saved and the damned, and we knew which side we were on and anybody who was with us, was with us, and anybody who was not with us, was against us. This rhetoric has been the dominant rhetoric in American politics for the past years, but it seems to be on the wane. I would say we are at the threshold at the end of this epoch. And the moment when 9/11 could be invoked as a talisman to justify anything, to justify for instance invading a country that didn't attack you, has passed. Obama recognizes that historical moments, moments when people are saying 'now is the time', are punctuated by images. He has used this awareness in his campaign and will use it now, now that it is his time.

© Tate 2008, *The Life and Death of Images: Exchanges on Art and Culture* (Tate Publishing, 2008). Reproduced by permission of Tate Trustees.

Marriott Hotel Islamabad

September 20, 2008

Sean Snyder

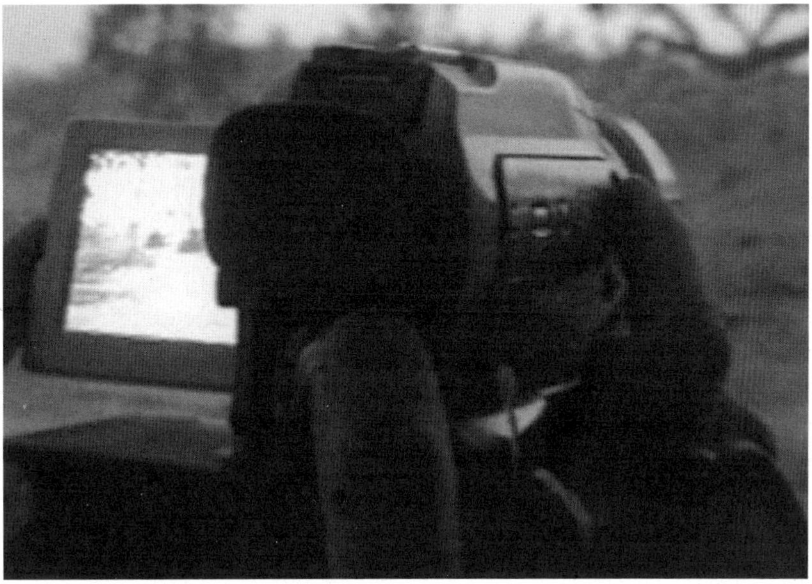

'It's just like in a movie' is a much-heard cliché about the images of the 9/11 attack on the World Trade Center. But this is only partly true, and increasingly less so. The effects are like in a movie, the images are not. Most Hollywood films are shot on 35 mm film or HD video; but many of the now familiar iconic images of the 9/11 attack were captured by amateurs and television news bureaus overlooking the skyline of New York City. In addition, the images were viewed and distributed on television and later the Internet, not on the big screen.

Hollywood has, of course, long been associated with apocalyptic images and, on more than one occasion, has even been accused of contributing to the events of 9/11. Today amateurs continue to edit and reproduce the dramatic impact of those images into existing footage, in some instances resulting in 'new' videos that generate re-readings and re-interpretation of the events of 9/11. The cumulative effort of amateur post-production posted on video sharing sites such as YouTube reconnects memory and time, while in the process potentially constructing false recollections.

I would like to emphasize that I am not directly addressing the politics of images, but rather want to engage in a subjective analysis of the visual surfaces ideology produces. As an artist I am currently working with the malleability of images and the technical mechanics of their production. As images replace textual information – taking the temporal nature of those images into consideration – they must be increasingly unconventional to have an impact. Not to say that we are entirely desensitized to spectacular acts of terror, but we are somehow conditioned to read the various subtexts for meaning. That is to say, we search for what distinguishes these images from our familiar environment and cognition.

While watching YouTube I was reminded of the Cold War-era film *Red Dawn*. Set in a small Midwestern American town under Soviet and Cuban occupation, the film *enacts* the unthinkable under détente. Playing on the ominous threat of nuclear warfare, the film depicts an unconventional invasion initiated by disguised commercial airliners followed by ground troops. Local teenagers form a guerrilla resistance to fight in an act of self-preservation and patriotism. In this case the narrative seems to obliquely

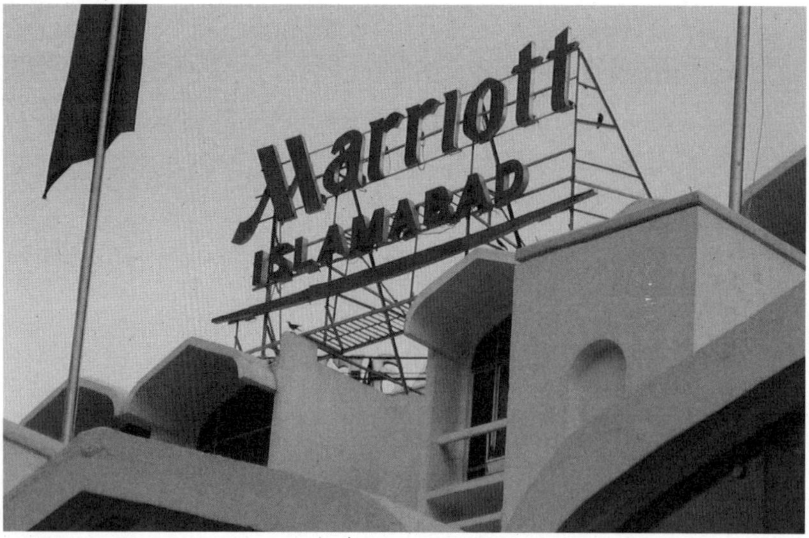

resemble the method used by the terrorists on 9/11, with no option, however, for heroics on the part of the citizens with the planes themselves being the weapons.

After the bombing of a Marriott hotel in Islamabad on 20 September 2008, the first thing that came to mind was: Why would there be a Mormon hotel chain in Pakistan anyway? One could raise the same question with regards to the Marriott hotel in communist Warsaw, but there, so I learned, Mormon missionaries were active during the Cold War and the Marriott was already in planning before the collapse of communism. However, this seemed unlikely to be the case in Pakistan. Regardless of the specifics, the Marriott was most likely targeted as a symbol of Western capitalism. Following the attack, the media images of the CCTV cameras fixed on the entrance gate of the hotel showed the event in an unspectacular way: we see guards moving around trying to figure out what to do with the large truck loaded with bombs until the screen goes blank. But it's the image of the large Marriot sign and the flames that engulfed the building below that most likely will persist.

Shortly following the events of 9/11 we were exposed to a number of vivid descriptions of everyday life in Afghanistan under the Taliban regime invoked by the Western media: hanging televisions, trees draped in videotape pulled from cassettes and 'executed computers' in the streets of Kabul, alluding to the unthinkable actions of 'the other'.

For years following 9/11, the Western media often referred to the jihadists' release of 'videotapes', implying their use of archaic or inferior technology in the production of their messages. It seems doubtful, however, that at a certain point any traditional audiotape, videotape or film was used in the production or distribution of Al Qaeda's materials (for instance by As Sahab, Al Qaeda's media wing).

We were constantly told by unknown 'experts' and well-known agencies what we were seeing or should be seeing. Take, for example, the continued mention of the specific positioning of Osama Bin Laden's watch on his wrist indicating 'further attacks'. In other words, experts are supposed to create a narrative, to construct a certain meaning of the image. However, there is a common and quite limited rhetoric, which could be extracted from an expert's discourse; it shows how our notion of credibility is based not on the old idea that 'seeing is believing', but rather on abstracted constructions of meaning.

A few years ago I worked on a project which entailed comparing the image production of the US Department of Defense to that of Al Qaeda. I will outline a series of speculative interpretations based on this research, exploring some aspects of these 'complicated constructions' of meaning that have to do with the amateur video production that Al Qaeda tactically implemented in its propaganda strategies.

As a side note: in 2008 there was a remarkable decrease in the release of videos by Al Qaeda which seems to imply that they don't intend to produce sequels.

A short scene from a 2005 Al Qaeda release includes footage of the operation of a video camera recorded by a second camera. Once slowed down, the camera being filmed appeared to be a Sony model, incidentally similar to one I purchased in Hong Kong in the late 1990s. After enlarging and printing out a series of still images of the camera and comparing its make to a number of similar Sony camcorders, I was able to identify the specific model as a Sony DCR PC-120E.

It turned out that this exact high-end consumer model was the first to be brought on the market with Bluetooth technology, giving the possibility, among other things, to upload video from anywhere via mobile phone. A Sony press release states the camera's capacity to transmit MPEG format data with a resolution of 240 x 320 pixels. On a television screen the image quality would appear equivalent to the resolution of VHS format videotape.

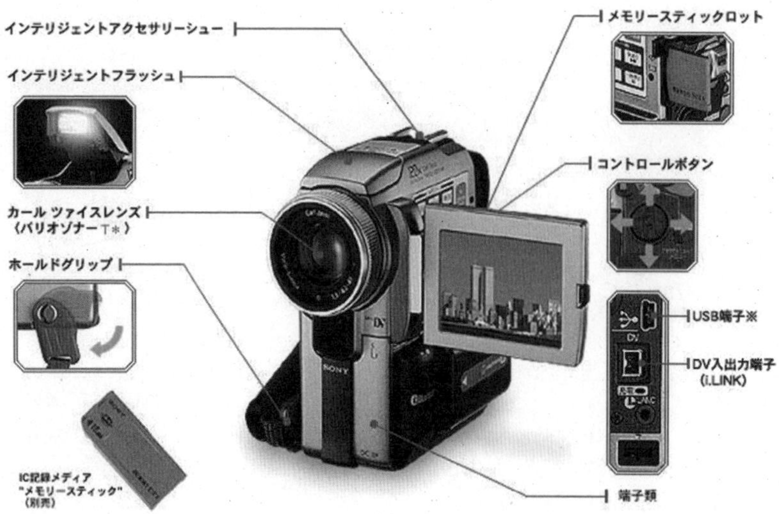

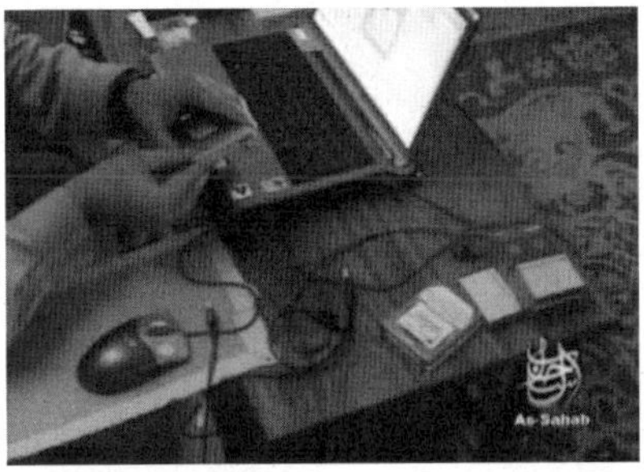
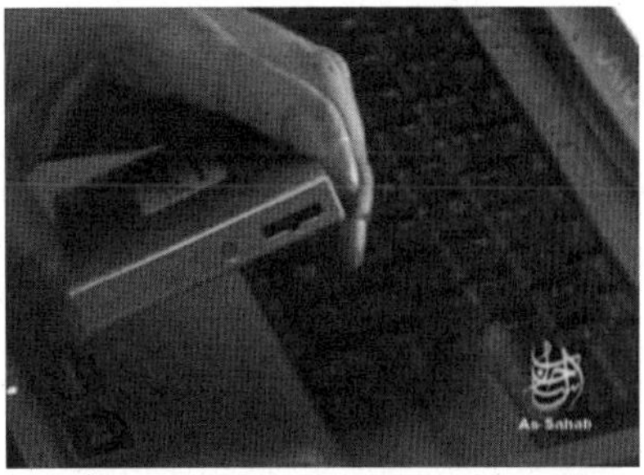
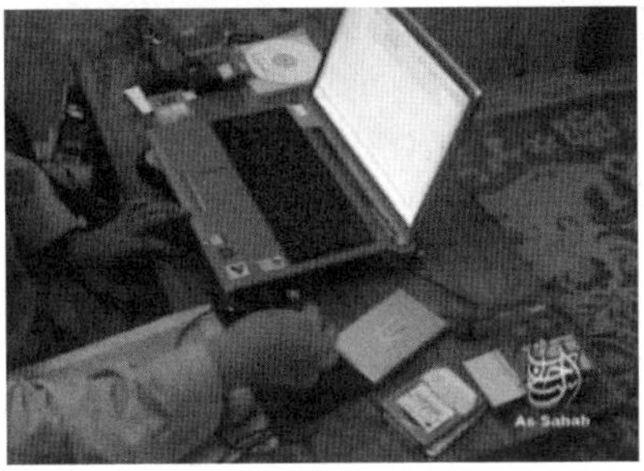
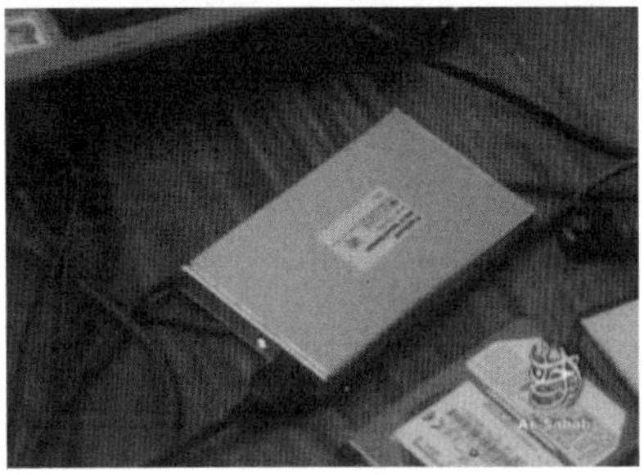

Another sequence from a 2004 Al Qaeda release shows the transference of a captured US forces' computer hard-drive and an operative using a (Sony Vaio model) computer to open a PDF file containing information about their own (that is, Al Qaeda's) tactics, underlining the jihadists' use of consumer technology as a tactical weapon.

Using do-it-yourself montage techniques, jihadist video editors employ graphics, animations and the dramatic use of sound to disseminate their message. Often assembled like music videos, their seduction is achieved by the merging of sound and image, alluding to the editors' fluency. The superimposed graphic elements and the repetition of clips from previous videos create 'iconic' moments, often including American media footage from the attacks on 9/11.

What makes a moment iconic, how does it work? It would be my hypothesis that image producers, jihadist videographers included, use common visual techniques informed by popular visual culture that constitute a similar vocabulary to that of any other YouTube contributor.

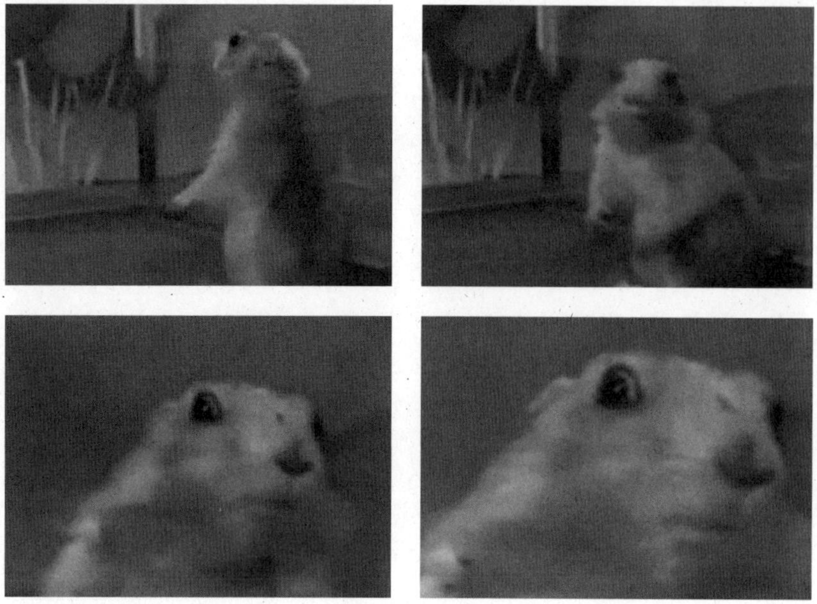

I'll somewhat arbitrarily take the popular clip 'Dramatic Chipmunk' or the 'Drama Prairie Dog' as it is also called as an innocuous/innocent subject. Currently having more than 11 million hits, the most popular version of the sequence is only 5 seconds in duration and it is simply an isolated detail from a typical Japanese television programme. I don't know the exact genealogy, but like the TV original, which I think was also a five second version zoomed in and set to music, the clip became popular, and then all possible permutations were made using various editing techniques and soundtracks from films.

If the iconic moment is something almost universal in the production, and the dissemination of imagery is part of the current imaginary, it goes beyond our visual faculty with its grounding principle of singling out and repeating the most dramatic effect. However, that aside, the iconic moment is not necessarily only visual but a kind of constructed point of dramatic intensity. There are other tendencies in the current popular visual vocabulary, which, following the slogan of a new American Television channel 'True-TV – Not Reality, Actuality', have to do with an amateurish quality opposed to professionalism. This quite established visual trend of attributing truth as actuality to the amateurs 'poor' quality (from certain films, or many on-line videos) refers not only to the changing technology but also to changing sensibility (in the visual field). This trend seems to work very well and in fact is one of the interpretative frames of the Western perception of media imagery after 9/11.

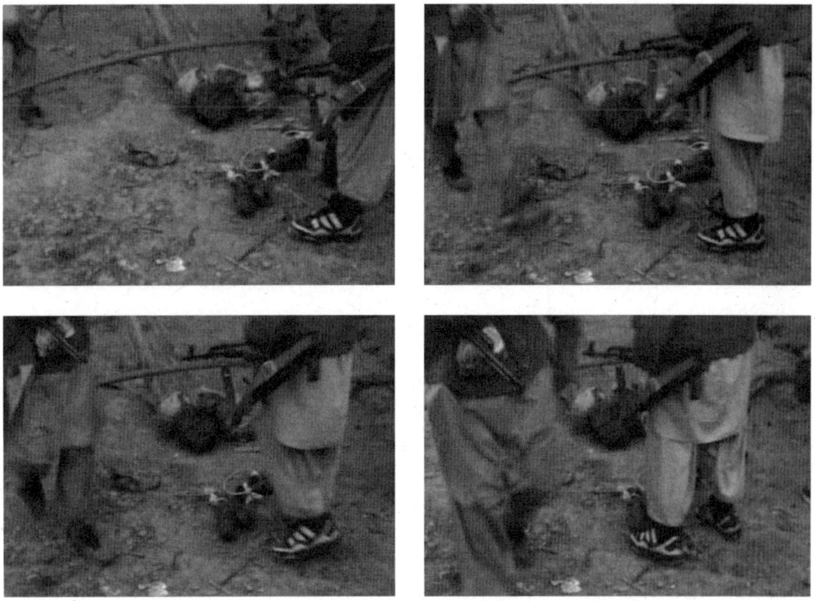

In the visual strategies of As Sahab over the last few years, the same tendency can be seen – the effectiveness of the conveyance of messages lies in the notion of verisimilitude, which depends less on the high level of technology and professionalism than on a certain emotive trust on the side of the subject/viewer. Furthermore, it could be said that the underlying aesthetics of current imaging techniques play a role in establishing a sense of authenticity. Data compression, resulting in the disintegration of image quality, gives the effect of actuality – an imaginary quality, which in respect to its rhetorical effects seems more valuable.

Many of the Al Qaeda videos not only provide a spectacular image of war, but are also designed to give an 'actual' view into the banal and everyday routines that lead up to the implementation of an operation. A video from 2005 follows the regiment of an operation in Afghanistan, including details of everyday life: cooking, their living quarters, instruction classes, bomb-making and field activities. The 60-minute video suggests the implementation of war as an ingenious and methodical craft. These images might equate to the antithesis of the representations of American military power and technology, say that of the Stealth bomber or the Apache helicopter.

In many of the As Sahab videos, the technical functions of the camera are fully implemented: the infrared night-shot function illuminates operations in the dark, the zoom lens extended to its maximum focal length traces the movements of the enemy in

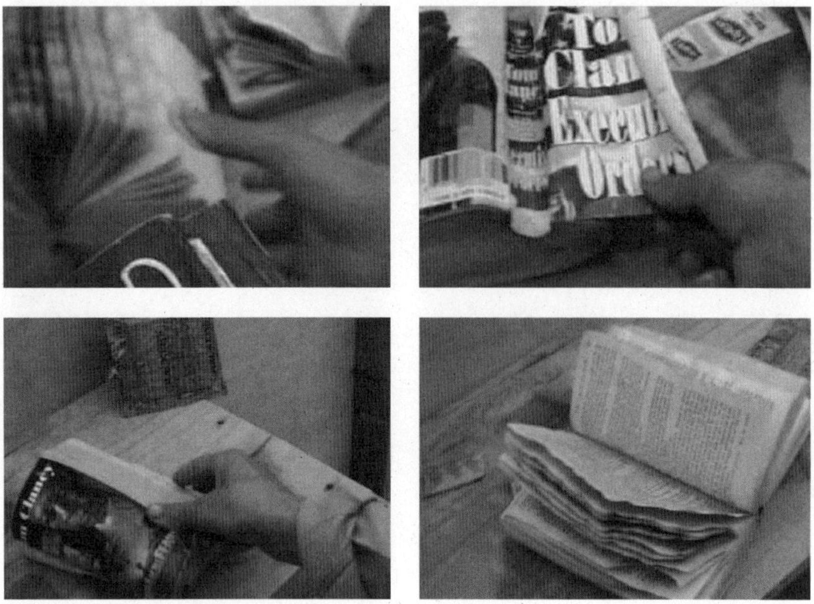

pursuit, and Bluetooth is possibly even used to upload video data. Perhaps this exploitation of the capabilities of the camera makes Al Qaeda's videographers the ultimate consumers.

The Arabic subtitling of one scene in an As Sahab video from 2005 locates an operation in an abandoned American base in Afghanistan. The jihadists wander around the site documenting their occupation of the space. A short incidental shot focuses on some paperback books on a table, presumably left behind by the US soldiers. Once slowed down and the image data enlarged, the titles of a few Tom Clancy paperback novels become legible. The plot of one of the books, *Executive Orders* written in 1997, revolves around a terrorist attack on the US Capitol using an airliner, the unleashing of a virus on the American public, and a presidential sex scandal. A coincidental identification or not, fiction and reality here come full circle.

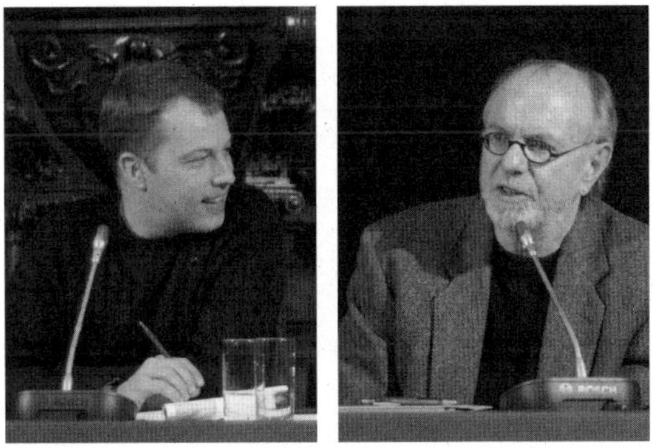

Jaap Kooijman and W.J.T. Mitchell.

Discussion

The discussion was moderated by Jaap Kooijman, assistant professor at the Department of Media and Culture at the University of Amsterdam.

Audience: It seems to me that there's a shift in the role of the artist, maybe since 9/11, from the production of images to the investigation of the image production of others. And I wonder whether that is really the task of today's artists?

W.J.T. Mitchell: Well, I don't have any simple or singular answer to that. I think artists actually don't create images, I think they've always worked with the image as a kind of ready-made that is there in language, in the environment, in culture. And what they do is to reframe them, and to help us see them. To see something more clearly that perhaps wasn't apparent to us before. I realize that artists cannot intervene in the economy the way bankers can, or governments, but what they can do is make us understand the strange effect of images, to give us a kind of secondary reflection on them. To show us when we're in the grip of a powerful image, as for instance with the 'war on terror' which is a kind of image itself, a metaphor. And revealing how it's been rendered as something quite literal and physical. So I don't know exactly what artists can do in relation to major crises such as the war on terror, the environment or the economy. However, I think one of the strategies is to work on pictures, to refunction them, expose them to new kinds of understandings.

Sean Snyder: I'm thinking maybe I'm talking about and working on images too much. On the other hand, my work often deals with the we way we look, watch and rewatch. What interests me at this moment is how the mechanics of different editing techniques are part of this endless reiteration and different perpetuations of image. Producing an image is a constant shifting, and that is what I try to make visible in some kind of form. I do that in an art context but it could happen in any other context as well.

W.J.T. Mitchell: Let me just add one thing, a kind of a failure of imagination that's been very conspicuous in the aftermath of 9/11 and that's the failure to come to terms with it in the form of some sort of monumentalization. You would think this would be one of the things that would have been done by now, but is hasn't. I think that the side-symptoms of the war on terror are that it is a war without a front and a war without an end. So this produced a kind of melancholia around 9/11, a failure of mourning, to put it in a straightforward Freudian sense. The work of Kevin Clark that I mention in my paper is a very beautiful image of the failure to produce a monument, or the inability to produce it. Overlaying the smoking ruins of the World Trade Center with the four letters of the DNA code makes us understand what the war on terror has been about: it expresses partly the longing for the ability to genetically recapture the lost lives, but also the sense in which the lost lives are the core or the melancholia of losing loved ones. One thing about 9/11, I think the one that's fed the war on terror, is that melancholia, the inability to bury the dead, the feeling that they're still floating in the air, wishing for a place to rest. In South-Africa, during the Truth and Reconciliation Commission, they asked people: 'Why do you want to hear these terrible torturers and murderers spill their guts about what they did, and how can you forgive them?' The answer was: 'We don't forgive them, but we want to know where the bodies are buried, so that we can take care of our dead.' And that I think is what has fed the melancholia underlying the war on terror, made it so hard to overcome.

Moderator: One question about that, to what extent is that an American experience? Is the image of 9/11 stronger then the reality or materiality of the victims? Is the terror of the image not the image itself?

W.J.T. Mitchell: Definitely, the image was excessive in several senses. One, it was immediately sacralised, turned into a sign of hallowed ground. The sight of the World Trade Center was referred to as Ground Zero, which turned it into, metaphorically, a nuclear attack, using that figure from the nuclear era. And it was turned into this kind of unprecedented world historical trauma. I think the British have a much more realistic attitude about terror, even though Tony Blair sadly went along with Bush's war. But having gone through the major siege of a city, the battle of Britain and the firebombing of London . . . I think Europeans also understand, it was the destruction of one building, with terrible loss of life, but hurricane Katrina destroyed an entire city. Very little is left of New Orleans, just a kind of theme park at the centre of it, Bourbon Street, the French Quarter and Garden District. So there's a complete lack of proportion, a sense of 'how bad was this?' It was as if we had been invaded, but that's a fantasy. I think, as you point out, that it is a very American thing, the idea that somebody could violate our borders this way. And it was treated as the equivalent to Pearl Harbour – that was the other great analogy that was built. And I think it inflated it into, as I said, a talisman, all you had to do is say: 'Well, after 9/11, now we know. We know what we're up against.'

Julian Stallabrass - The Fracturing of Globalization

Hou Hanru - Acting Out in the City

Art & Theory

TIME

Globalization

The world of today is constantly being redefined by the process of globalization, and although the bubble of this 'new world order' dominated by global capital, consumer culture and neoliberal economy has burst, its effects are irreversibly and intricately integrated into every aspect of our lives. In the arts the most visible manifestation of this process is probably the increasing number of international biennials and triennials. These manifestations have not only grown to spectacular proportions, they have also become instrumental in the rise of the art world as market place.

In his contribution Julian Stallabrass critically analyses how the effects of neoliberal politics and economic policies are reflected in the art world of today, taking the rise of the biennial as a key example. He evaluates the liberal ideals that lie at the heart of these events and shows their uneasy, conflicting relation with what has now become the economic basis of the art world. Furthermore, he examines the growing fractures in this new global art economy, caused by 9/11 and the recent financial crisis.

Besides money, the art-theoretical debate on globalization also focuses on the meaning of the local and the production of new localities, especially within the contexts of the many biennials where international artists are invited to create site-specific works. In his contribution Hou Hanru, curator of many large-scale exhibitions and biennials that deal with the transformations of public space in the age of globalization and neoliberal politics, reflects on the urban and social conditions which his curatorial practice draws upon. One of the questions he explores is: Can art activate resistance or reclaim a public space that is increasingly becoming an urban spectacle invaded by global capital through, for example, large gentrification projects? Hanru provides his readers with an illustrated account of the changes caused by globalization on an urban scale, of how these changes affect our private lives and of how small acts of resistance can have a large impact.

Julian Stallabrass (UK) is reader in modern and contemporary art history at the Courtauld Institute of Art, London. Aside from focussing on recent developments in British art, new media art and the history of photography, Stallabrass researches the political aspect of the globalized contemporary art world. His most recent publication, *Art Incorporated* (2004), inquires into the connection of contemporary art with neoliberalism. Other publications include *Internet Art: The Online Clash of Culture and Commerce* (2003) and *High Art Lite: British Art in the 1990s* (1999). Furthermore, Stallabrass curated the Brighton Photo Biennial on the theme of the representation of war in 2008.

Hou Hanru (CHN/FR/USA) is an internationally renowned curator and art critic, based in San Francisco and Paris. At the moment Hanru is director of exhibitions and public programs and chair of exhibition and museum studies at the San Francisco Art Institute. He is best known for his critical engagement with the effects of globalization on migration, urbanization and modernization in developing countries, as well as with the international redistribution of labour. He curated a number of exhibitions that addressed these issues, for example *Z.O.U. Zone of Urgency* (Venice Biennale, 2003), *Not Only Possible, But Also Necessary – Optimism in the Age of Global War* (The 10th Istanbul Biennial, 2007) and *Trans(ient) City and Global Multitude* (Luxembourg, 2007).

The Fracturing of Globalization

Julian Stallabrass

The World

The art world really became a world following the collapse of Eastern European communism from 1989 onwards. Biennials sprouted in new markets across the globe, artists from Asia, Africa and South America began to appear in major exhibitions in significant numbers, contemporary art scenes evolved outside the USA, Japan and Europe, and it became plausible to conceive of the art world less as a constellation of fixed centres and more as a series of flows from one locale to another, accompanied by flocks of private jets. Yet lately, the comfortingly multicultural scene that emerged has been subject to serious political and economic stresses, which have already sufficiently disturbed that world to have produced within it some very strange phenomena, and which threaten to break it apart entirely.

'Globalization' is, of course, a complex and much contested term, but for our purposes it can be taken to mean the consequences of the freer circulation of money, investment and goods (but not, at least officially, of labour), and of the unequal international trade and legal agreements that regulated that freedom. Space seemed to shrink as rapid travel became cheaper, and especially through the wider availability of data communication systems, phones and the Internet. In its much-publicized utopian moment, the globe became a universal play-area for the rich and for multinational capital. But globalization also encompasses the multicultural slums of the world's mega-cities; the trade in human and animal bodies, and in pollution; the increasingly widespread ruination of the environment; and indentured or even slave labour. So it encompasses the greatest freedom and the greatest oppression, each structurally bound to its opposite.

The emergence of globalization was also aligned with neoliberal politics and economics (this despite the nationalist rhetoric

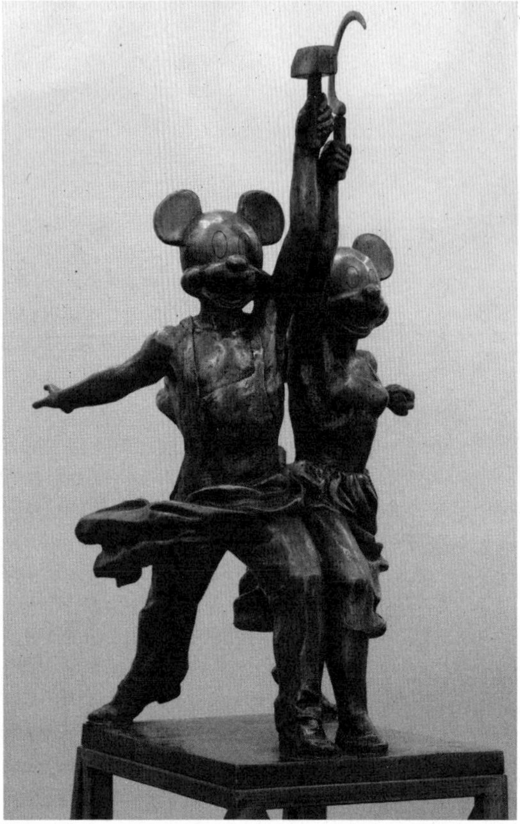

Alexander Kosolapov, *Mickey and Minnie: The Worker and the Kolkhoz Woman*, 2004.
© Alexander Kosolapov.

of the pioneering neoliberal governments – of Thatcher, Reagan and Pinochet – which was a mask for the radical erosion of national economies and cultures). So globalization in part caused, and was accompanied by, the familiar effects of neoliberal political and economic policies: the elevation of finance and service economies over industry, rising inequality, the decline of the labour movements, and the emergence of a large and structural mass of the under- and unemployed.

Until recently, there were good reasons to think that the globalization of the art world had its limits and did not fully reflect the general globalization of the economy. The dominance of the New York art scene was one factor here: while many artists from China, Brazil, South Africa, Russia and Cuba became prominent, many of them also ended up living and working in New York. The USA, and New York in particular, dominated the buying and selling of contemporary art, and as a consequence much of the language and terms of its reception.[1]

In the last few years, however, there have been profound and very rapid commercial changes, particularly in the rise of Chinese, Indian and Russian art, and with it of indigenous markets. There has been a five-fold increase in the size of the Indian contemporary art market in a few years; and a ten-fold increase in average

1. For a fuller account, see my book *Art Incorporated* (Oxford: Oxford University Press, 2004), chapter 2.

auction prices achieved for Indian art between 2004 and 2008.[2] Of the top ten auction prices for contemporary art in 2007-2008, three went to Chinese artists – Cai Guo-Qiang, Zeng Fanzhi and Liu Xiaodong. Data on the best prices achieved in first sales at auction in 2007 (thus focusing on young artists) show that nearly three-quarters of the top 50 are Chinese, and (in a sense, more importantly) that over half their sales were made in China.[3] As remarkably, in the annual turnover of contemporary art at auction, in 2007-2008, China came within a hair's breadth of overtaking the UK, for long the second-largest market. This development has taken place with breathtaking rapidity. The comparative dominance of the USA has declined, in line with its deeply troubled economy and the decreasing global hold of its ideological model. In the remarkable speculative fever that gripped the contemporary art world in the last five years, the promise of globalization was finally reflected in the market: successful artists could live (at least for some of the time) in Havana, Mumbai or Beijing and their works were purchased by domestic speculators and collectors. Those who wished to follow the developments in that world had to fly further and more often.

2. *Le Marché de l'Art Contemporain 2007/8* (Saint-Romain-au-Mont-d'Or: Artprice.com SA, 2008), 126.

3. Ibid., 133.

The longer-term globalization of the art world has in large part been propagated by the rise of the biennial. Here, ideally at least, the virtues of cultural hybridity and mobility are promoted through works of art and acts of curation that should erode fixed values and ideals, including national political attachments and Enlightenment principles (given their haunting by colonialism, the Holocaust and the Gulag). Indeed, there is suspicion of any firm identification, lest it yield some abuse of the Other. Much of the work shown at biennials exploits the charge produced by cultural splicing – socialist realism meets Disney, for instance, though the examples could be effortlessly multiplied. The positive message of the biennial, again ideally, gestures towards the emergence, through the intermixing of cultures, of a global consciousness in which all voices can be heard.

The hybrid art itself, like the spread of pigeons or rats, forces the local species into narrow and insecure ecological niches. In its shuffling of familiar post-conceptual devices and readily recognizable national symbols and concerns into an endless parade of novel combinations, it remains identified with its nation of origin. Fredric Jameson's well-known remarks about Third World literature being condemned to appear as an allegory of nation still applies to its art, but also to that of post-communist states, and increasingly to the art of the 'developed' world, too, when it is seized on by marketers for whom national identification is used as a convenient pre-existing brand.[4] Even when the work is not manifestly national-allegorical, it often gets read as such, urged along by interpretation material that insists on national identification, including those labels for works that include the artist's nation of origin. At first sight, this insistence on nation-labelling

4. Fredric Jameson 'Third-World Literature in the Era of Multinational Capitalism', *Social Text*, vol. 15 (1986), 65-88.

may appear to cut against the ideals of hybridity, but it celebrates the broadening ambit of neoliberal hybridity, the induction of culture after culture into the realm of free exchange, where a new set of cultural tokens becomes available for combination and trade.

That the process is far from complete was the point of a work by Antonio Muntadas for the Venice Biennale of 2005, entitled *Giardini*: a double-sided lightbox, it showed on one face photographs of all the Biennale's national pavilions, and on the reverse, a list – rather extensive – of all of the nations that do not show at Venice. There is, incidentally, a remarkable overlap between Muntadas' list of absentees and another list of nations – those of the 'bottom billion' as economically defined, of that part of the 'developing world' that does not develop.[5]

5. The list of the bottom billion is compiled by Paul Collier in his book *Wars, Guns and Votes: Democracy in Dangerous Places* (London: The Bodley Head, 2009), 239-240.

While the ideals of the biennial are politically liberal, they are also economically neoliberal – the scepticism towards all ideals that might establish barriers to global exchange, the denigration of the national, and the implicit endorsement through lack of critique of the 'natural' environment of the unfettered market. In its conventional recommendation of these neoliberal virtues, the art world celebrates as freedom all that is forced upon us.[6]

6. This is one of the main arguments of my book, *Art Incorporated*, op. cit. (note 1).

Since the cultural politics of the art world is in contradiction with its economic basis (or to be more precise, the economics of its production and consumption is in contradiction with the political outlook of the large majority of its viewers, if not owners), these neoliberal virtues have to hide themselves, and this concealment leads to a good deal of obfuscation in works of art, curating and the literature that might otherwise elucidate them.

There are, however, aspects of the art-world celebration of globalization that, beyond the irreducibly contradictory nature of globalization itself, tend to undermine the idealism of the biennial, and lead the viewer to critical thinking. There is the familiar critique of the easily recognizable standard character of 'biennial art', with its spectacular inflation of size, gestures towards political themes, and fairground air – products of hasty overproduction and the courting of easy controversy. There is the paradox, analysed by Elena Filipovic, that while the biennial is supposed to celebrate the local and the contingent, the standard

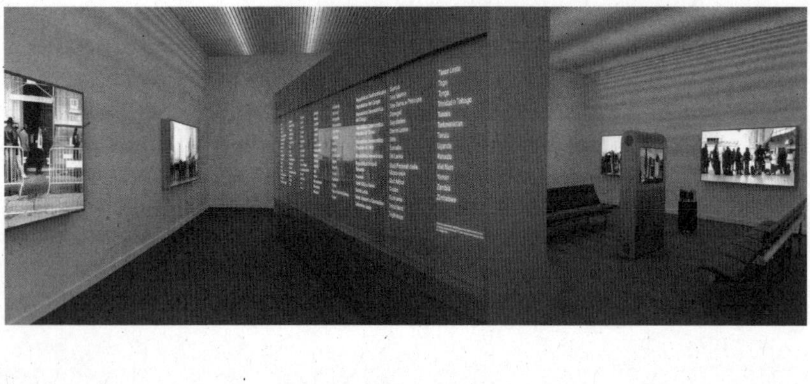

Antonio Muntadas, *On Translation: I Giardini*, 2005, Pavillion On Translation, 51st Venice Biennial.
Photo: Claudio Franzini.
© Antonio Muntadas.

international-style white cube continues to reign as the wrapping in which the various products are offered.[7] There is the often-transparent character of the biennial in boosting the fortunes of some city or region in its efforts at gentrification, and in supporting – or even establishing – the local art market. The funding of these necessarily expensive collections of shows produces further visible instrumentalism which sits uneasily with the pure ideals of the biennial, from sponsorship (branded rest areas, for example) to the merchandizing of the event itself through the sale of souvenir mugs and other knickknacks.

7. Elena Filipovic, 'The Global White Cube', in: Barbara Vanderlinden and Elena Filipovic (eds.), *The Manifesta Decade: Debates on Contemporary Art Exhibitions and Biennials in Post-Wall Europe* (Cambridge, MA: MIT Press, 2005), 63-84.

Above all, however, the lure and trap of money mocks the liberal ideal of the biennial and the globalization of the art world in general. A central aspect of neoliberalism is the rise of inequality, with the long growth in the fortunes of the wealthy and especially the super rich at the expense, not merely of the poorest, but of an increasingly large section of wage earners, whose income has been declining now for decades.[8] The art world is one arena for the global super-rich elite to pursue their conspicuous expenditure. Their increasingly extravagant ways of marking themselves out from one another with gigantic yachts, private jets and helicopters, and vast mansions are of a piece with the love a proportion of them profess for art. As Joseph Bachstein, co-ordinator of the Moscow Biennial, wrote of the rise of the Russian collector: 'What is a rich Russian? It means you must have an apartment in Moscow, a Bentley, a dacha on Rublyovka, a house in London, a villa in Sardinia, and a yacht. Then you must buy modern art.'[9]

8. See David Harvey, *A Brief History of Neoliberalism* (Oxford: Oxford University Press, 2005).

9. As quoted in Sophia Kishkovsky, 'Moscow Biennale Pokes Fun at Consumers and Politicians', *New York Times*, 10 March 2007.

Sarah Thornton describes the hundred private jets that touch down in Basel for the art fair, and the fine gradings of sociocultural rankings for those jostling for position at Venice, where for some dealers the poolside of the Cipriani is their informal office.[10] What is purchased through participation in the art world, through collecting or patronage, is not merely or even primarily things, but access to a certain social set, a type of quasi-intellectual discourse, and a social cachet in which wealth is leavened by high culture – this is Bourdieu in practice.[11] That art which has made personal interaction its metier merely formalizes this arrangement by providing the global elite (already homogenized through wealth and cosmopolitanism) with eccentric opportunities for socializing.

10. Sarah Thornton, *Seven Days in the Art World* (London: Granta, 2008), 78, 224, chapters 3 and 7.

11. See Pierre Bourdieu, *Distinction: A Social Critique of the Judgement of Taste*, translated by Richard Nice (London: Routledge, 1984).

There is another kind of tie to money, which is relatively new (and now endangered): art as a pure investment – especially as a hedge against the downward movement of other types of investment. It is this development that explains art's relative buoyancy in the downturn, and why the situation in the art world seems a little less dire than, for example, in the British property market or the US car market. There is generally a cost to owning art, which performs less well in gaining value than stocks and shares, and which is costly to insure, conserve and sell. That cost is part of the basis for its social cachet. The contemporary art bubble of the past five or so years changed that calculation, and instrumental investors moved in. One result has been the rapid lionization of young artists, since they offer the greatest opportunities for successful speculation. There was a frenzy to be in on the investment opportunity that the rising art market presented: during the run of the PS1 exhibition 'Greater New York', in 2005, which showed a large number of younger artists, those mentioned favourably in the press had queues of potential buyers outside their studios the following day.

The concerted manipulation of prices by hedge-fund traders, who have carefully chosen artists who they consider to be undervalued (whose prices are comparatively low but are held in prestigious collections and have a good critical reputation) have caused rapid and spectacular rises in the prices of some artists – Richard Prince being a model example.[12] Small groups of dealers and collectors also conspire to gather large amounts of an artist's work and drive up the price by bidding way over the odds for his or her work at auction.[13]

The art boom, now recognized as a bubble, has tended to produce a particular kind of work: spectacular objects that serve well as conversation pieces in the living rooms of billionaires. The focus on money, prestige and celebrity is in tension with the qualities of art that make it most valuable to that very elite, for it should gesture towards the higher realm of autonomous action and absolute, individual freedom, and not to the grubby world of the bottom line. (Damien Hirst, in recent works, including his notorious diamond-encrusted skull, almost makes this a theme.) Thus art may be seen as a paragon of globalized culture, in which the lingua franca is not American, and not even the English language, but simply money.

12. See Molly Concannon, *Collecting Richard Prince: Strategies of a New Type of Investor in the Contemporary Market*, MA Dissertation, University of London (Courtauld Institute of Art), 2005, passim.
13. Marc Spiegler, 'Is the Art Market the "New Economy"', in: Margriet Schavemaker and Mischa Rakier (eds.), *Right About Now: Art and Theory Since the 1990s* (Amsterdam: Valiz Publishers, 2007), 135.

The Break

The years of the art investment boom were also those of the 'war on terror'. While the excesses of the boom mocked the political ideals of cultural globalization, the war on terror – summed up in President Bush's position that you are either for us or against us – was a more direct assault. On both sides, after all, this was a way of dividing the world between terrorist and hero, religious fanatic and true believer, those who love death and those who love life. The invasions, kidnappings, beheadings, murders, torture, extra-legal imprisonment and the bombing of civilians (whether with home-made explosives or million-dollar missiles), much of it captured on photography and video for propaganda purposes, were the products of that division as it fractured the globalized ideal.

Multiculturalism itself came under attack, and the drawbacks as well as the virtues of hybrid mixing became evident. In the UK, this was illustrated graphically with British-born suicide bombers, an event that helped to bring about a volte face in state policy towards multiculturalism. There was a confrontation here with

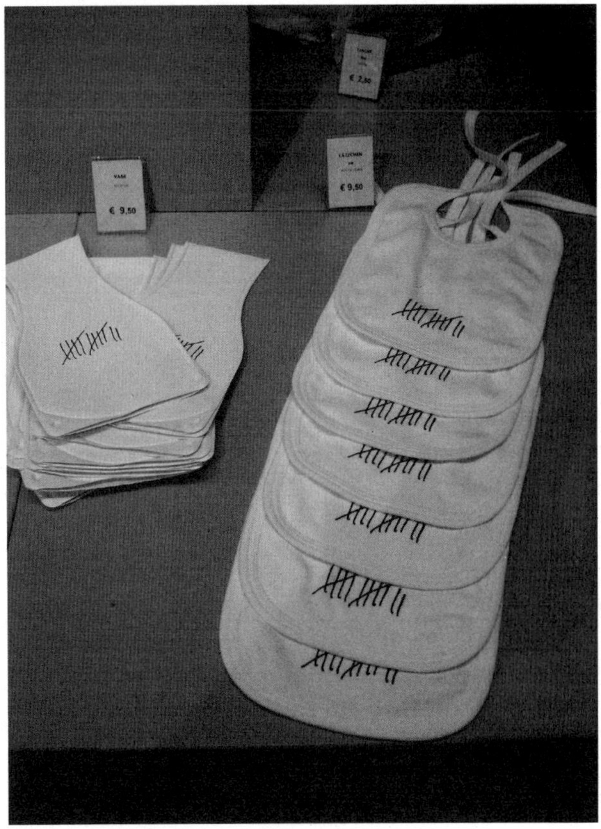

documenta 12 merchandize.
Photo: Julian Stallabrass.

others who were truly other, who were uninterested in swapping stories or recipes, and wanted only the death of apostates and the destruction of their culture.[14] With that confrontation came a widespread demonization of a broad swath of culture and religion.

At the same time, 'we' also became unrecognizable in our fundamentalism. The USA and its allies behaved in ways that were as alien to our purported values as were the acts of our enemies. Did we really have our agents snatch people from streets to be interned indefinitely in secret torture centres? Did we really imprison their children to extort information from prisoners? Even the new administration, acting on the intelligence of the whereabouts of some Al Qaida suspect, delivers a bomb to that location by pilotless drone. How is that morally different from detonating a truck bomb at a political parade?

In this, the (neo)liberal art world finds it hard to place itself: it can comfortably attack US neoconservative fundamentalism as a barrier to free flows of trade and culture, and does so often. More rarely, it can register the full extent of Western brutality. Can it also bring itself to attack Islamic fundamentalism? Or the broader cultural and religious predilections that bring it into existence? To do so would clash with one of its core values – an ethical respect for the 'other' that is the basis for free trade, free cultural

14. For the limits of liberal multiculturalism, see Slavoj Žižek, 'Multiculturalism, or, the Cultural Logic of Multinational Capitalism', *New Left Review*, no. 225 (September-October 1997), 28-51.

exchange and even tourism. More fundamentally, the danger of any oppositional art, of an art that speaks too clearly and with too radical an intent, is that it takes on too clear a use, losing its art-like character to become a part of the mundane world of politics and propaganda. In its celebration of individual autonomy, art must never tie itself to use, or must only do so in gestures that are self-evidently futile or Quixotic.

Hence the hard-to-credit claims of artists, who on the face of it appear manifestly political, and whose work appears to set out to alter a political climate of opinion, such as Santigao Sierra and Regina José Galindo, that their art is meant to have no political effect. Hence, the continual playing up in contemporary political video and photography of the mechanisms and rhetoric of representation (for instance, in the work of Omer Fast), so that thoughts about political content face continual interference from those about how politics is represented.

As the boom and the war on terror coincided, the biennial, a thermometer of art world climates, registered both, crazily. So the phenomenon of the split biennial emerged, in which the formal and the political were pushed up against each other without sufficient reflection or mediation: signal examples here include Robert Storr's Venice Biennale, and Roger Buergel and Ruth Noack's documenta 12 (both 2007). This was the high art reflection of the fracturing of globalization – in broken and deeply split biennial displays, which no longer seemed to function placidly as the mere emanation of the aesthetic tastes and ideals of the curators, but must also register, with acute discomfort, the political storm that blows beyond their walls. Sometimes the decorative and the political met in bizarre works of political entertainment and spectacle. More often, the bewildered viewer, unenlightened by confused curatorial justifications, moved from decorative abstraction and knowing kitsch to large-scale displays of documentary photographic and video work that at least referred to the most hideous and desperate human situations. In the worst cases, the political, and even terror itself, was rendered aesthetic.[15] Curatorial pretensions to coherence were lost or wilfully abandoned.

15. This is the argument of Oliver Marchat on documenta 12. See 'Schröder's Return: Documenta 12 as a German Summer-Camp of Reconciliation', in: Irene Montero (ed.), *¿Modernidad? ¡Vida! Documenta 12* (Madrid: Brumaria, 2007), 375-381.

The Crash

Plainly, since autumn 2008, things have changed again with the growth of the global financial crisis, which has had a deep effect on the economy of art. Even in October 2008, contemporary art sales in London were badly affected, with many lots bought in, and others failing to meet their estimates – including works by major artists such as Gerhard Richter and Takashi Murakami. Buying has not ceased, and occasional signal prices are reached, to much publicity, though rarely with contemporary works. Recently, the number of contemporary art lots sold has halved, as has their average price. Compared with the previous season, the overall value of the auction market for contemporary art has fallen even further by over three-quarters.[16] Hedge fund traders have been leaving the market. So the effect is already profound, and we are, most likely, at the beginning of this recession.

16. See Colin Gleadell, 'Art Sales Halved at Sotheby's and Christie's as the Recession Hits the Art Market', *The Daily Telegraph*, 19 January 2009.

I have tried to come up with a visual illustration for the crisis, along the lines of those photographs of vast numbers of new cars sitting unsold near their factories; here a bored and lonely art dealer tries to amuse herselve with papers and a laptop at the Zoo Art Fair in London last autumn.

It is too soon, of course, to say what will happen at this time of unique economic trouble. Art at a time of recession tends to become more innovative, as artists have to abandon the golden umbilical cord in their attempts to rethink their identity, exploit new technologies, and engage with issues that interest large numbers of people.

It may be that recession will lead, as it has done before, to new modes of working in which collaboration, dematerialization and the side-stepping of the market gain some traction. In a situation where the art world was split weirdly between an engagement with politics and the (rarely overlapping) gilding of the lives of the global elite, we may expect radical change when one half of the structure is suddenly chopped away. One might hope for a wave of work that is not only documentary but is also fixed on new technologies of communication, and that engages with its audience seriously in collaborative works of discourse, that, in short, takes democratic values seriously. One might even anticipate that biennials become more cogent reflections upon the extraordinary conditions of the world (political, economic, military and environmental) and the role that art plays in their propagation and critique. Yet it may be that the art world as it is currently constituted is unsuited to deliver such work, and that only a recession that is deep and long enough to change the basis

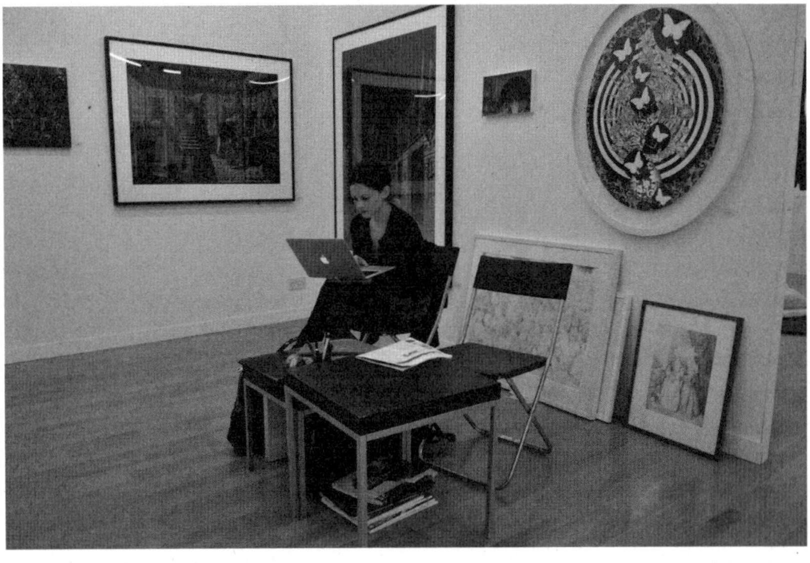

Art dealer at the Zoo Art Fair, London, October 2008. Photo: Julian Stallabrass.

of its economics, and the very conception of what an art work and an artist is, can change that.

We are, nevertheless, faced with two deep uncertainties: first, that the financial crisis is an unprecedented one – the first in the post-Cold War era to have done what previous crises threatened to do, and become global – and we have no idea of its length, depth or true character. Second, that in its unfolding, we have little notion of the shape of the power relations that will emerge in the world that follows: will this, for example, spell the end of US dominance, as many commentators have been warning for so long?[17] And, if so, where will the new centres be, and what will be the concerns of those who govern them? In that new world, it may be Europeans and North Americans who have to come to terms with the invasion of dominant alien species.

17. See, for example, Immanuel Wallerstein, *The Decline of American Power: The US in a Chaotic World* (New York: The New Press, 2003).

Acting Out in the City

Artistic Intervention as Production of Public Space

Hou Hanru

Introduction

We are living in a time of urban spectacle. Contemporary art projects, whether international biennials or urban-scale art events, are an integral part of the rapid expansion of this spectacle. Meanwhile, we are also witnessing a worldwide dramatic trend of privatization, gentrification and social division: public spaces are being increasingly reduced, while civil society and democracy are under threat by the pressure of 'liberal' global capitalism. With the complacence of various political powers, neoliberalism and its economic counterpart, global capitalism, are becoming the homogenizing and even monopolizing model of economic, cultural and social production and exchange. And as a consequence, their impact on society and our public space is undeniable. While social justice, equality and solidarity are being undermined; protest and resistance against this dominant ideological and economic system are being mounted from the bottom of society. A key element in this conflict seems to be the deconstruction of a conception of the public sphere as the physical, political and cultural guarantee for democracy and social participation, in order to make way for a new notion of public space and publicness.

How do these conflicting dynamics play out in our everyday environments? In order to start to answer this question, I will try to sketch the impact of globalization and global capital on the transformation of our cities and societies by introducing some recent examples from China. Furthermore, I would like to take a closer look at some of the fundamental questions involved with curating public art events by asking, for instance, how we can understand this new notion of public space and its relation to the private. How can artistic activities and public art events like biennials and triennials preserve or produce public spaces, providing platforms to debate or to envision imaginative solutions to the conflicts we are currently facing? What kind of new strategies of public intervention can we imagine to address and implement these issues? Confronted with the way art is being systematically absorbed into the circulating system of capitalism and privatization, we need to reconsider art's very nature and social role and its potential as a platform for resistance and as a generator of alternative social and cultural structures.

Urban Spectacle

When we talk about globalization, we talk about change: changes we need, and changes we maybe don't need. In the last decade, along with unprecedented urban growth, Asian cities are catching up with this explosive wave of spectacle and urban expansion with a tsunami-like enthusiasm, the Beijing Olympics being the most recent prominent example.

Four centuries ago, the Netherlands, a small country, had an empire around the globe and for a period it was the centre of the world. It founded New Amsterdam, which turned into New York, which became the centre of the world for the last 60 to 70 years. And today, it is the People's Republic of China – that once considered itself to be the centre of the world – that wants to reclaim that status. So in China, globalization is about claiming oneself to be the centre of the world. As we know, one effective way to do this, in part, is to organize a biennial or a triennial, but the best way is to organize the Olympic Games!

Initiating the Olympic Games in Beijing constituted the largest nationalist claim in its most global form. The country spent two billion dollars on the organization of the event, including all sorts of propaganda surrounding the event. The most inventive and magnificent spectacle was staged before the eyes of the world. An image of this world was presented as a perfect society in which a multitude of different communities coexist in peace and harmony. During the opening ceremony 56 children represented the 56 different ethnic minority groups that don't belong to the Han majority (though as it turned out, in reality all of the participating children belonged to the Han majority and were just dressed up in different ethnic costumes). In addition, the best team was put together to deliver a superbly spectacular event. Such as, for instance, artist Cai Guo Qiang, an expert on fireworks, who was contracted to assist Zhang Yimou, the art director of the opening show, who himself is a film director of Hollywood-style big productions.

In addressing some of the questions posed earlier, I want to discuss what goes on beyond this momentary staging of a public spectacle. I would like to focus on the whole project of urbanization involved with organizing the Olympics, because I believe that this process of urbanization, and gentrification, is what

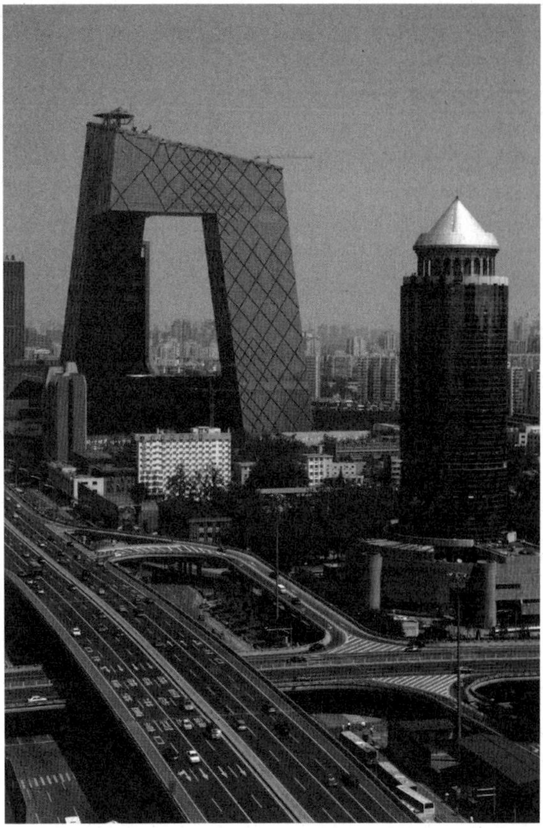

Rem Koolhaas and Ole Scheeren (Office for Metropolitan Architecture), China Central Television Headquarters building (CCTV), Beijing, 2008. © Office for Metropolitan Architecture (OMA).

constitutes the most important part of the globalization process in China today. Renowned architects from all over the world have been brought to China to create spectacular architecture: Herzog & De Meuron designed the Olympic Stadium; Paul Andreu from France did the National Grand Theatre in Beijing (which actually encountered a lot of protest from local architects and urban planners who believe it destroyed the local urban context) and Foster and Partners got Beijing Airport. Let's also not forget the Dutch architect, Rem Koolhaas, whose OMA office designed the CCTV Building. The vast majority of these structures designed by these star architects have no apparent formal relation to their surroundings and could just as easily have been constructed on a different continent. To me, this is the way in which globalization today not only operates as a powerful force in the production of (urban) spectacle, but also in the production of (urban) spaces by generating a totally new form of urbanity which is truly global – not only in terms of its aesthetic vernacular, but also its developmental process based on digital imagination and the economical logics of commercial real estate development. This urbanity is very much related to a kind of urban fiction, a fiction that is created by the combined forces of state politics and liberal capitalism. This is certainly how China, as an eager player on the world stage of globalization, is now inventing a new system for its society in which these two forces are combined in order to generate a new version of utopia to replace the obsolete Maoist one.

Global Urbanization, Gentrification and the Everyday

The quest for urban spectacle in China does not only play out on the level of political power, it also occurs in the everyday. Catering to the new middle class, project developers are building thousands of new residential and office buildings that are carbon copies of those in Western countries (but tainted with some 'national characteristics'). People are actually trying to turn themselves into global citizens by leading a life identical to their economic counterparts in the West. So in a way, what we see here is the birth of a global *nouveau riche* class, which translates in physical terms into *nouveau riche*-class architecture.

Of course these beautiful dreams have a price. Take, for instance, a neighbourhood in 'Pearl River New Town', a new district of Guangzhou dotted with high-priced residential and office buildings. In front of the neighbourhood there is a large stretch of green, a park which is supposed to be a public space to serve the population of all social classes. But the Guangzhou city planners decided to build a highway that separates the expensive high-rise apartments and the park from the rest of the city, protecting the isolation (segregation) of this high-priced lawn and effectively closing it off to the general public. In other words, a lot of money was spent to build this public park for the citizens of Guangzhou only for it to be enjoyed by those who can afford to live and work in these buildings.

Many city centres in China, like those in many Western countries, are undergoing large-scale urban regeneration projects, usually coined gentrification. 'Regeneration' seems to be a euphemism for the kicking out of the city's original inhabitants. Local governments claim the land and sell it to private developers with the excuse of upgrading the urban conditions, which of course leads to higher prices that only the rich can afford. The original communities are forced to move to less expensive areas in the city, usually on the outskirts.

The emergence of this beautifully designed and spectacular privatization of urban space is a change in our public space that we don't need. What we do need is to reclaim public space from these commercial interests driven by the forces of state politics and global capitalism. Indeed, in recent years resistance movements against gentrification have been organized by local populations across the country.

So called 'nail houses' are probably the most iconic images of this new social trend of resistance to the dominant political and economic powers and the gentrification developments that they generate. The most famous case of a 'nail house' is the following:

one family that lived in such a house, located on a construction site in Chongqing, refused to move out and sell its property to the real estate developers. Instead, the family stayed put and continued living in their house while the building activities carried on, isolating themselves in the middle of the construction site. In the end, construction was actually stopped for more than three years. The family resisted by living inside the house in these conditions and decided to go public with their cause. They put up a national flag as a statement and as a reminder of the Chinese constitution that protects the rights of its citizens. As a result, the municipal government, the project developer and other parties got involved in the negotiations. In the end, the owners of the house won a significant amount of money in compensation. This case has been widely reported on the Internet and in various national media and hailed by the public as a heroic example of the capacity of ordinary people defending their rights and standing up to the pressure of the political and economic authorities. Overnight, hundreds of similar cases were exposed and debated across the country. Some artists have even created works to celebrate their 'victory' (Jiang Zhi's photograph *Things would turn nails once they happened* (2007), rendering the 'nail house' in Chongqing angelically beautiful, is a remarkable example). This example and plenty of others across China show how individuals can resist the negative changes instigated by globalization and actually reclaim their own space. Such acts of resistance finally forced the Chinese government to face reality by submitting a law in October 2007, to be passed by the parliament, resulting in the protection of private property for the first time since the beginning of the communist era.

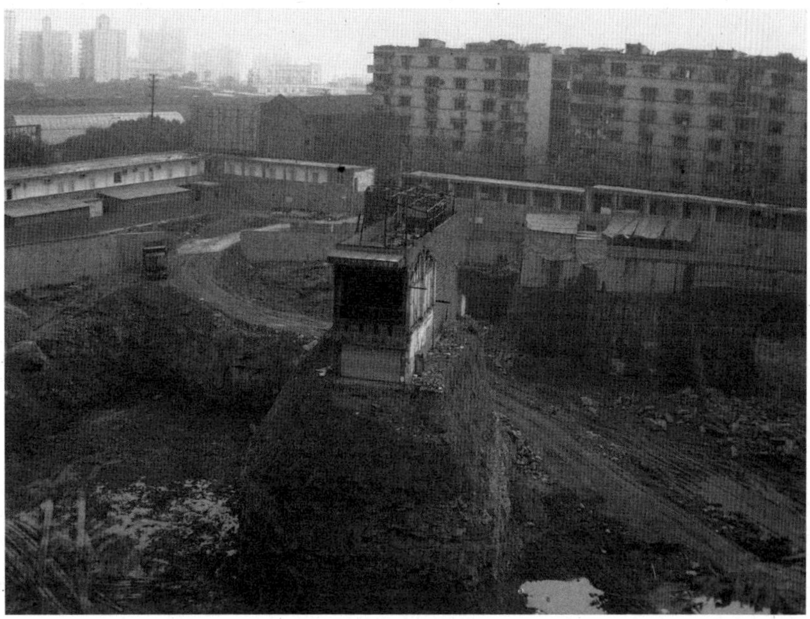

A 'Nail House', Chongqing, China, until 2007.

Acting Out in the City: Reclaiming Public Space

Once it became clear that the city of Beijing would host the Olympics, plans were immediately made to redevelop the old city centre, including the Dazhalan area, and turn it into a new cultural district for global tourists. The city authority ordered to demolish the neighbourhood and make it into a theme-park-like 'authentic old Beijing'. The original inhabitants were forced to move out of their houses. Resistances by the community were mounted. Violent confrontations between the inhabitants and the authorities occurred, and intellectuals and artists got engaged. Ou Ning, Cao Fei and their research group started working on a documentary about this process of demolition. And again they encountered some people who refused to leave their houses and put up a national flag as a sign of protest. Ou Ning and Cao Fei's work points to an interesting element of these dynamics of resistance, which is the powerful role of the camera. They handed one of the protesters a camera to document the negotiations and confrontations with the police, and when the demolition team arrived and he started to film it, suddenly the police decided to stop everything . . .

These gentrification processes inform many of the conditions that artists and curators alike are confronted with when they enter public space, while also becoming an important source of inspiration for their work. Talking about biennials today means talking about how to negotiate the place of art, or artistic intervention, in terms of the negotiation of a public space, which is constantly transformed by the forces of politics and global capital. For this paper, I selected three large-scale urban projects which I curated in the new millennium and which all address the issues I outlined earlier. One project is situated in China, one in Europe and one, in-between, in Istanbul. And for each of these social and spatial situations I will introduce one or two works that, in my opinion, critically engage with the urban transformations we are facing in the age of globalization.

One of these works, included in the 2007 Istanbul Biennial, entitled *Not Only Possible, But Also Necessary: Optimism in the Age of Global War*, is the research project entitled *Manufactured Sites* (2007) by San Diego-based architect Teddy Cruz. For the last ten years, Cruz has done research along the border between San Diego and Tijuana – between California and Mexico. In one of his projects he ran 30 miles into Mexican territory and 30 miles into American territory to find out how, in the process of globalization, these two different economic systems left their marks on the different typologies of urban organization on both sides of the frontier. He then tried to develop a new architectural system, transporting recycled materials from the USA to Mexico, in an effort to help people improve the conditions of their lives.

I included this project as part of the Istanbul Biennial, as the city there is going through a very spectacular urbanization process. Take the Sulukule quarter, a famous, traditional, Ottoman-style area located next to an old Roman city wall, with a predominantly Romani population that has lived there for hundreds of years. Recently, the neighbourhood has become a very important target for urban developers and the city government to invest in and gentrify, which naturally will lead to the relocation of the existing inhabitants. As a consequence Sulukule has become an important battleground between, on the one side, the intellectuals, architects and other social activists in Istanbul who struggle to conserve historic heritages and the lifestyle of local communities, and on the other the city authorities and developers who try to impose a *nouveau riche* style of urban transformation. This situation became an important context for my 2007 biennial.

The first question that needs to be asked before starting to curate any biennial should be: 'Why does this place need a biennial?' A biennial in such an urban context must be a space for creation and it must start from the desire and utopian possibility to bring in new energy. It must consider the most efficient and effective means to engage artistic activities within the given social reality and to provide innovative visions for change. For me, by bringing both local and international artists together, and by encouraging them to carry out dialogues with the local community, a biennial produces a space where global-local negotiations can take place. Ultimately, it is a continuous process to produce new and ever-changing localities as a part of the constantly restructuring global and artistic order.

In Istanbul, the artist Wong Hoy Cheong from Malaysia decided to explore this situation in Sulukule and engaged in a project with the local population. The Romani community of Sulukule is part of a long line of Roma who arrived in the Byzantine capital over a thousand years ago. Music and dance not only form an integral part of Romani tradition and culture, but also make up their profession and economy. However, in 1991 the state shut down most of their taverns, taking away a large part of their

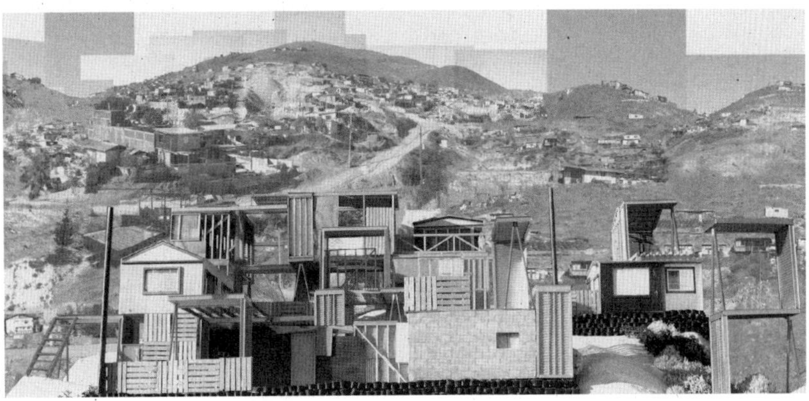

A housing urbanism made waste: Southern California's first ring of suburbanization (Levittown) is being dismantled as new and large Mac-mansions fill the new periphery while Levittown's debris is recycled to build the new suburbs of Tijuana. © Teddy Cruz.

income. On top of that, there are now plans to demolish the houses, relocate the community and gentrify the neighbourhood. Wong Hoy Cheong collaborated with a group of kids from the Romani community and let them participate in informal fieldtrips, play, drawing, photography, video and performance that resulted in an experimental documentary offering insight into the everyday issues these kids are concerned with and the way they deal with their uncertain future, while showing their determination and resistance to the imminent gentrification.

The project I did in 2003 in Shenzhen was called *The Fifth System: Public Art in the Age of Post-Planning*. To start the project, I did some research in the city, discovering that Shenzhen used to be a village on the border between China and Hong Kong. In 1980, it was appointed a Special Economic Zone where the introduction of foreign investment and new industrial development made it a model of urbanization experiments in China. Shenzhen was ultimately transformed into one of the biggest cities in the country, with an official population of seven million and an unofficial one of twice that number. One high-end, high-brow residential area there is built around one the first theme parks in China. It consists of two parts: 'Beautiful China' and 'Window of the World'. Hotels and offices were also built in the area. They borrow their looks from Venice, for instance, invoking memories of Las Vegas. Together they form a district called 'Overseas Chinese Town'. Interestingly, and different from its American counterparts, there is a museum in the theme park that tries to deal with rather experimental art projects, The Xiangning Art Museum. The existence of such a museum derives from a model plan for urban development in which residences are mixed with 'entertainment' and cultural infrastructures for the benefit of the new middle class. This same model grounded the sculpture biennial, from which a programme of large structures all around the city radiated.

Working on this biennial together with co-curator Pi Li, in our research we basically discerned four different types of interesting urban systems which were defined by four typologies of buildings. Included in these typologies were the theme park itself, high-rise residential buildings, middle-sized office buildings and the road system. All of these four systems are quite fixed, forced together, resulting in a relatively isolated area – a private or gated community. We decided to try to bring other things into the area, something alien to this system, to encourage exchange and dialogue and even to instigate conflict among the inhabitants and people from outside. We called this intervention 'The Fifth System', a sort of mobile, open system that could project new possibilities on urban life. One of the more classic highlights of our project was a pavilion by Olafur Eliasson which was 16 m high and thus very spectacular. This pavilion started to function as a meeting point for people in the centre of the area.

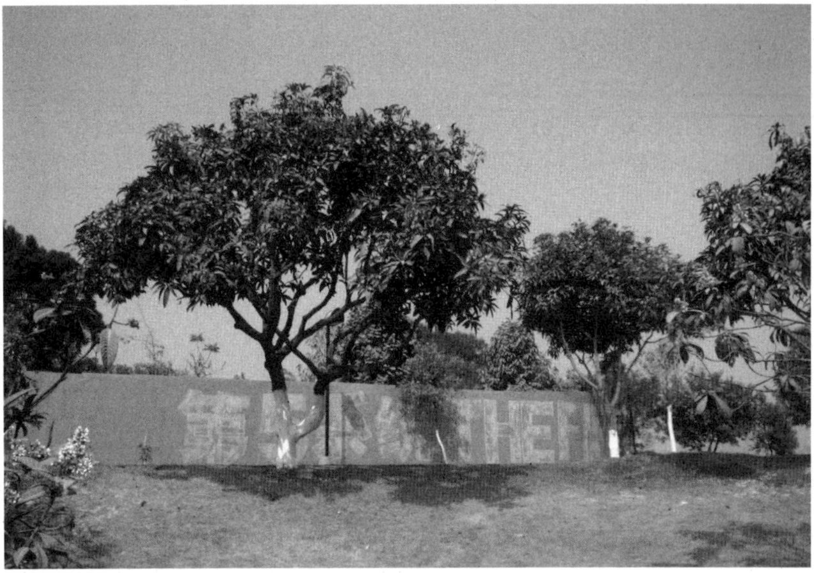

Yan Lei, project for *The Fifth System: Public Art in the Age of Post-Planning*, 5th Shenzhen Contemporary Sculpture Exhibition, He Xiangning Art Museum, Shenzhen, 2003. Photo: Hou Hanru.

Other projects went deeper into the history of the city's recent economic boom. On an existing architectural structure in the central plaza, Yang Jiechang lined up plates with the names of industries and companies that originally existed in this little town. Many of them were now closed and gone. They looked liked a memorial of the history of this somehow sad story of industrialization. A concert with a folklore band singing rock'n'roll-like songs telling the stories of these companies was held in the opening. Yan Lei focused on a park in the middle of the city, or rather a piece of abandoned land the size of an Olympic stadium, waiting to be sold by the city for further development. In the name of art, the artist convinced the city government to give him temporary ownership of this piece of land for two years and he then closed it off with a fence with the slogan-like text 'The Fifth System' painted on the surface, and left it undeveloped. It actually meant an important financial deficit for the city, since the city was forced to wait to develop the terrain, and the artist managed to keep the lot empty in the middle of a boomtown, somehow predicting the logic of the nail house family.

In Luxembourg, for the event of European Capital of Culture in 2007, I realized *Trans(ient) City*. Occupying public spaces across various areas of the city, this project of urban interventions consisted of three different parts: 'Urban Lab', 'Urban Landmarks' and 'Community Life'. The project aimed to demonstrate the dynamics of Luxembourg City as a hub of transitions among different European nations and the necessity to re-energize its public spaces with diverse forms of artistic, architectural and cultural interventions, including the participation of the multicultural urban communities. This leads us to further debates on the future of public spheres in Europe in the time of privatization of urban space. 'Urban Lab' started with a research laboratory on Luxembourg City's historical urban landscape, intending to provide an opportunity for people to foresee the city's future, with the participation of several European schools of architecture, design and cultural management and internationally renowned architecture and town planning agencies. 'Urban Landmarks' saw the birth of architectural artistic projects integrated into urban areas, created as reference points to show off key city sites, such as the projects realized by Olaf Nicolai, Carl Michael von Hausswolff and Périphériques Architectes. Finally, 'Community Life' comprised projects created to revitalize isolated or abandoned urban spaces, giving different communities an opportunity to participate in the development of their cultural imagination, such as the project by Jung Yeondoo.

The *Trans(ient) City* project referred not only to transient art and artists, but the city itself was taken as a site of transience as it expanded and contracted on a daily basis, as a place people passed through to work, and then evacuated in the evenings. The works in public space also occupied itinerant positions – karaoke and tango competitions on specially constructed dance floors, fight clubs and one-euro market stalls were among the strategies employed by the artists.

With all of these examples I hope to have made clear that such curatorial strategies can actually reveal a critical counterforce against the large-scale and money-driven urban transformations happening throughout the current global scene.

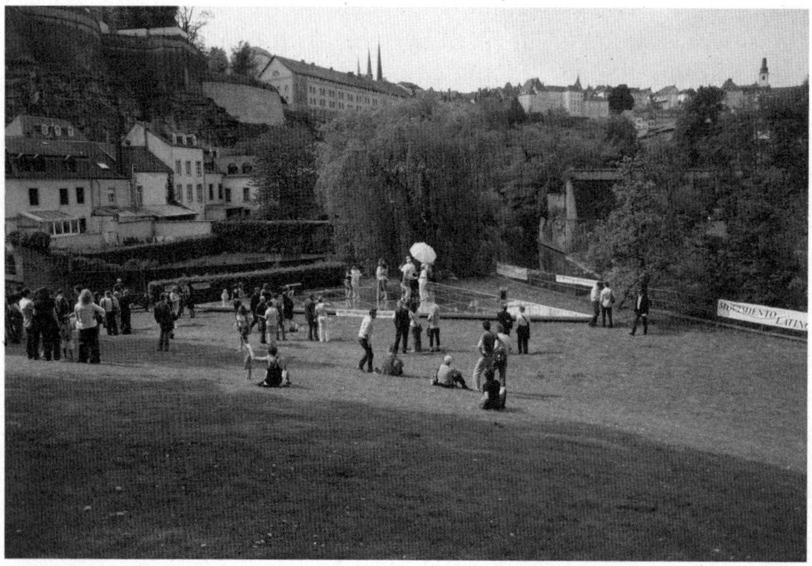

Yeondoo Jung, project for *Trans(cient) City*, Luxembourg, 2007. Photo: Hou Hanru.

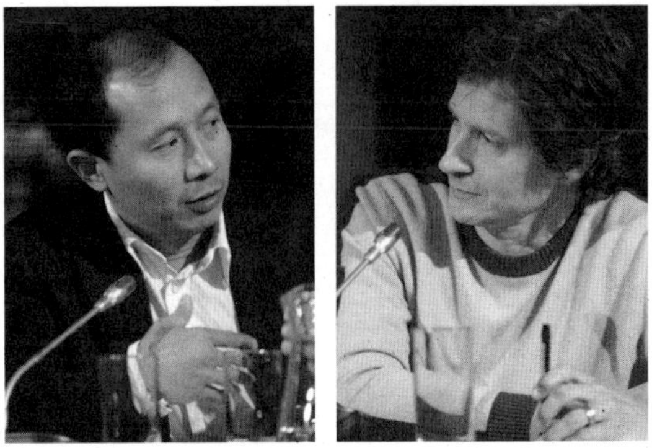

Hou Hanru and Julian Stallabrass.

Discussion

The discussion was moderated by Deborah Cherry, Chair of the Department of Modern Art of the University of Amsterdam and editor of Art History Journal.

Moderator: Both of you focussed on biennials, triennials, Olympics; the magnificent spectacular events of our expansive and extensively spectacular 21st century globalized world. So my first question is: does globalization equal visual spectacle, or are there other, maybe less visible, narratives that run underneath your papers; narratives about different kinds of local engagements, different kinds of interventions in cities and public space? And so my second question is: how can art negotiate, activate, identify and work with local as well as a global politics to engage us as spectators?

Julian Stallabrass: It depends on what you mean by 'spectacle'. If used in the Debordian way, the commercialization of social life, then yes, it covers quite a bit, but not everything. The extraordinary architectural and urban global spectacle Hou was talking about is definitely part of it, but there are many, many aspects to globalization that are invisible or at least need to be made visible. One invidious example of a globalized network is the secret CIA rendition flights, and to answer your question as to how art can work with these phenomena, this particular 'non-spectacular' globalized network is just one of many which various artists, notably Trevor Paglen, have chosen to render visible. There are many complex forces that operate under the radar and are hard to represent but should find representation.

Hou Hanru: I believe globalization is a very complex system working gradually over time and on many different levels, almost every level of our life. I would like to differentiate between an external and an internal globalization, one that is very visible, or spectacular if you wish, and one that is not so visible. The latter is a direct effect of the emergence of a global economy and production system that completely changes the structure of a society's population. A typical example of this is migrant workers in Third World countries that came from agricultural areas to work in the so-called new factories of the First World. This movement changes not only the psychological but also the social structures of a society. At the same time, I believe that globalization also happens on the body of one person. Another important moment is when the spectacle is being brought into the individual life, privatized life, such as the sample I mentioned of Mr Chang, who is living in this old house trying to defend himself against the demolition of his house in order to make way for a grand-scale urbanization project, and he happens to pick up a video camera and record the event, as a kind of witness to the process of this violent gentrification. To me this signifies a very important moment of what I call internal globalization: on the one hand the recognition of the power of the mediatized spectacle, and on the other hand the transformation of the identity of this person and his community. So on one side we see the emergence of a global city through gentrification and all the changes it brings that we don't need, and on the other side the prosperity provided by this new technology which would not happen if there was no globalization.

Moderator: Could I just take up what you've been saying about migration? Hou, you stated that globalization is about change and one of the largest changes associated with globalization has been migration, many forms of migration. Generally we think of the migration of people, but there is also the migration of forms, technology, capital, knowledge and movement, and of art. Could you expand a bit on the ways in which art has engaged migration?

Hou Hanru: Again, migration has a very important impact on art. Firstly, today you see more and more artists from different cultures living in major international cities. They actually play increasingly important roles in the transformation of the art scene of that city. Secondly, when we move from migration to questions of integration and transformation, this sometimes happens in a very radical way, remember for example the violent upheavals in the Parisian suburbs, and these events raise many questions about a society that for a lot of artists, including so-called non-Western artists, are a starting point in their projects when they work in these contexts. They try to bring in the artistic intervention not only as a kind of social service to help people, but also to bring up a sort of self-awareness, even self-critique, to help this community re-invent its own future.

Audience: I heard Mr Hanru and Mr Stallabrass propose two different models of curating: Mr Hanru essentially proposes a methodology that, for me, has to do with navigating forces in real life, or as you phrased it, navigating between the change that we need and the change that we don't need, while Mr Stallabrass seems to advocate in a way a form of resistance curating, which I feel is more about resisting certain mechanisms of the art world and the art market rather than challenging forces in reality. How would you describe your curatorial practice?

Julian Stallabrass: The art world is part of reality! It might like to think of itself as separate but it's absolutely connected, and I think the art world is actually quite an important aspect of the ideology of neoliberalism and of capitalism in general. So I do think that to make visible, or more visible, its operations and open it up to critique is in itself valuable.

Hou Hanru: For me really, the role of the curator evolves even more quickly and is more complicated in the context of today's globalized societies. It's not that simple anymore to identify what the changes are that we need and the ones we don't need, I think it's all about engaging with change itself. So what is needed would be generated over time, during the process. I think making exhibitions or artistic interventions, organizing or imagining, producing this kind of events, is all about making proposals for the next step of change, envisioning the next threshold.

Robert S. Nelson - Canons of Art in the Spaces of our Desire

Ruth Noack - Canons and Publics

Art & Theory

TIME

Canon

Within the field of art and art history, the art-historical survey is probably the most familiar expression of a canon. From the nineteenth century onwards, the modern perspective on art determined the canon of art, setting the Western parameters according to which artists, artworks and events were included or excluded from its narrative. However, from the 1970s onwards the hegemony of the West has been contested and artists as well as curators and art theoreticians have engaged in 'differentiating the canon' which resulted in an array of new and alternative versions that included artists and artworks previously overlooked by the mainstream. Today, a new global art history is developing as a response to post-colonial critiques of nationalisms, and art historians and curators alike are facing the utopian challenge to write a global art canon. Yet with new orientations come new omissions. Is it possible to imagine a positive, all-inclusive canon? Can any canon ever be representative of a shared national or cultural identity? Or maybe the crucial question is whether the idea of a proscriptive canon has become obsolete in a society that embraces democracy, participation and interactivity across all layers.

In his essay Robert S. Nelson offers an insightful analysis into the utopian nature of the canon, the authority attached to its narrative, and its different manifestations in the symbolic spaces of our society, especially museums. According to Nelson, any canon constitutes a form of utopia, an ideal place that does not exist, in other words that is never complete; yet each history needs a canon. To assess the future of the canon and its utopian potential in our world of today, Nelson proposes to reverse the terms of the debate and instead of asking 'what canons of art do to people', pose the question 'what do people do with canons of art?' thereby introducing the issue of agency. In a similar vein, Ruth Noack explores how the canon-building process involved with curating an international survey exhibition such as the documenta 12 can lead to a revision of the canon in which the public plays a central role. Can the inevitable gaps that each new canon possesses be made productive and can the audience play a vital role by filling in these gaps from their own experience and knowledge?

Robert S. Nelson (USA) is professor of art history at Yale University. He specializes in medieval art, particularly in the Eastern Mediterranean, and the history and methods of art history. Nelson was co-editor of *Critical Terms for Art History* (1996-2003) and co-curator of *Holy Image, Hallowed Ground: Icons from Sinai* at the J. Paul Getty Museum (2006-2007). He is the author of *Hagia Sophia 1850-1950: Holy Wisdom Modern Monument* (2004), and the eminent essay, 'The Map of Art History' (1997).

Ruth Noack (GER) is an art historian, critic and exhibition maker. She was curator of documenta 12 in 2007. Other exhibitions include: *Scenes of a Theory* (Vienna 1995), *Things, we don't understand* (Vienna 2000), *Organisational Form* (Lüneburg, Ljubljana, Leipzig, 2002-2003), *The Government* (Lüneburg, Miami, Vienna, Rotterdam, 2003-2005). From 2000 to 2009 she has taught courses on film, contemporary art and curating at art schools and universities in Vienna, Lüneburg and Kassel. Her numerous texts and lectures comprise feminist theory and contemporary art. She is currently working on a book on Sanja Ivekovic and doing research on translocal museums.

Canons of Art in the Spaces of our Desire

Robert S. Nelson

In October 2008, *The Times* of London published its list of the top universities in the world, and that same fall, visitors to the Van Gogh Museum in Amsterdam were invited to pick the top three works of art given to the country by the Rembrandt Foundation. Each year, *Capital*, the German financial and business magazine, publishes a list of the top contemporary artists, arranged like financial tables and dependent upon sale prices. None of these lists, however, is a canon, whose definition has instead a proscriptive quality: 'A body of literary works traditionally regarded as the most important, significant, and worthy of study.'[1] With characteristic clarity, Ernst Gombrich elucidated the meaning of canon in published correspondence with the English critic Quentin Bell. Gombrich argued that a ranking is to a canon as the 'Top Ten' is to the 'First Eleven'.[2] Both are popular culture references. The Top Ten are the most popular hit songs, as determined by marketing firms or radio stations.

The 'First Eleven' is a different concept. It refers to the eleven players on a sports team – cricket or football (in America, soccer). The First Eleven are the best team sent into a crucial match. The Top 10 refers to the past, the First Eleven to the future. They represent the coach's best estimate of the most skilled players for the forthcoming contest. They are the ideal. In an article in *The Spectator*, sports reporter Michael Henderson described his First Eleven of composers as the best 'team to take on all-comers over five days in some celestial field'.[3] That particular First Eleven comprised Haydn, Beethoven, Schubert, Brahms, etcetera. Such is a canon, personally derived, dependent upon a set of values, derived from the past, but hortative, predicative or instructive for the future. As Gombrich put it: 'The social scientist can always tell us which are the top ten; he [or she] cannot commit . . . to picking a first eleven.'[4] The Top Ten belongs to the realm

1. *Oxford English Dictionary*, Draft Additions June 2002 (accessed March 10, 2009). I thank Tim Barringer and Margaret Olin for their help in the preparation of this essay.

2. E.H. Gombrich, 'Canons and Values: A Correspondence with Quentin Bell', in: E.H. Gombrich, *Ideas and Idols: Essays on Values in History and in Art* (Oxford: Phaidon, 1979), 155-156.

3. M. Henderson, 'My first Eleven', *The Spectator* (21 September 1996), 58.

4. Gombrich, 'Canos and Values', op. cit. (note 2), 155.

of science or social science, because it is based upon evidence derived from a repeatable experiment conducted over a defined audience in a specific location. *The Spectator's* First Eleven are literally not of this world; they play on a 'celestial field'. Such a canon, like all canons, is imaginary and constitutes a form of utopia, an important concept for what follows.

A visual example of a canon is Raphael's representation of the luminaries of Greece led by Plato and Aristotle in the centre. The image needs no illustration, because all art historians know the *School of Athens* – it is canonical. It also is utopian. As Louis Marin has explained, the word utopia is a neologism coined by Sir Thomas More in the early sixteenth century. Its meaning lies in its Greek etymology. A utopia is a place of perfection and a place that does not exist, a perfect place and no place.[5] The *School of Athens* portrays the sages of ancient Greece arrayed beneath a High Renaissance version of ancient architecture. Even in its prime, Athens never possessed such soaring Roman vaults, and Raphael never went to Athens, then an impoverished, provincial Ottoman village. His perfect place is no place.

Studies of artistic canons have taken several forms. Older accounts documented the changing fortunes of specific artists or artistic cultures. More recently, the utopian nature of the canon has been questioned and found, not surprisingly, to be subject to mundane social forces of wealth, power, nationalism and gender. From the 1970s, the artist Hans Haacke created installations that critiqued the association of wealth and power with museum exhibitions and declared that 'the canon is an agreement by people with cultural power at a certain time. It has no universal validity'.[6] In a similar vein, art historians Linda Nochlin and Griselda Pollock wrote about the patriarchal bias of the canons of art during the 1980s and 1990s.[7]

These and other similar efforts rely on a hermeneutics of suspicion, an approach associated most profoundly with Michel Foucault and one that I employed in an article, titled 'The Map of Art History', about disciplinary knowledges that were more local than universal.[8] Such critiques continue in the recent collection of essays titled *Partisan Canons*,[9] and some argue that contemporary art has no canon, or that it continually attacks the very possibility of a canon.[10] Yet in so doing, it contributes to the canon's continuation, which many deem inevitable. To paraphrase Harold Bloom and Claude Levi-Strauss, canons are myths we think with.[11] For Steven Nelson, 'there is no way to practice a canon-free art history'.[12] As Marlite Halbertsma put it, art history without a canon is like theology without God.[13] The gods of art history, however, can be investigated by believers and non-believers. A hermeneutics of suspicion poses the basic question: What do canons of art do to people?

Reversing the terms of the debate suggests another approach less commonly taken: what do people do with canons of art? Both

5. L. Marin, *Utopics: The Semiological Play of Textual Spaces* (Amherst, NY: Humanity Books, 1984), xiii.
6. W. Grasskamp, M. Nesbit and J. Bird, *Hans Haacke* (New York: Phaidon, 2004), 15-16.
7. L. Nochlin, 'Why Have There Been No Great Women Artists?', in: *Women, Art, and Power and Other Essays*, (New York: Harper & Row, 1988), 145-178; G. Pollock, 'Firing the Canon', in: *Differencing the Canon: Feminist Desire and the Writing of Art's Histories* (New York: Routledge, 1999), 3-38.
8. R.S. Nelson, 'The Map of Art History', *The Art Bulletin*, no. 79 (1997), 28-40.
9. A. Brzyski (ed.), *Partisan Canons* (Durham: Duke University Press, 2007).
10. T. Smith: 'Contemporary art does meet many of the conditions of canonicity . . . But certainty, even a degree of confidence, in the widespread valiance of judgment and in continuity of valuing is gone. As to the fate of canons [of contemporary art] . . . we can perhaps guess that, while attempts will continue to affirm them, reconstruct them, and readjust them, these efforts will meet with increasingly diminished, isolated and futile returns.' 'Coda: Canons and Contemporaneity', in: Brzyski, *Partisan Canons*, op. cit. (note 9), 324-325. Similarly, Carol Armstrong: 'We live in an art-historical moment in which the canon has been deconstructed, destroyed, blown to bits; and yet, at the same time, the canon has been expanded to infinity, to include anything and everything, to let every comer in. Either way, the canon becomes a nonsense, its categories baseless, while the exercise of aesthetic judgment has been ruled a thing of the past and/or a matter of indefensible personal taste without any common cultural basis. These attitudes are found nowhere more so than in that beast called contemporary art, which has from the start taken canon-busting as one of its main briefs.' C. Armstrong, 'Canon Fodder: On the Whitney Museum and Tate Modern Collections', *ArtForum*, no. 45 (November 2006), 113.
11. C.B. Steiner, 'Can the Canon Burst?', *The Art Bulletin*, no. 78 (1996), 213.
12. S. Nelson, 'Turning Green into Black, or How I Learned to Live with the Canon', in:

questions are related, of course, but they are not symmetrical, and they lead in different directions. The hermeneutics of agency has complex theoretical ancestry that lately includes the English anthropologist Alfred Gell[14] and has mainly focused on the power or effectiveness of individuals. Yet, the concept can just as well be employed more broadly for social groups, where agency might refer to 'the ability to transform the world'.[15] This approach interests me more at present, and I agree with sociologists and anthropologists who stress that in order to understand the valence and significance of a cultural or religious phenomenon, we must bracket or suspend suspicion, distaste, or lack of belief and proceed with 'a sympathetic engagement [and] a prejudice toward understanding'.[16]

Such an approach might examine, for example, how art displays suggest canonicity. At the Art Institute of Chicago in recent years, the curators have hung Gustave Caillebotte's painting, 'Paris Street Rainy Day' so that its elegantly dressed couple interacts with viewers, processing to and from galleries at the rear. The central location of the painting and even that certain marker of prestige, the suspended rope in front, signal that this is an important work of art and encourage the embodiment of its canonicity. The technique, well known to museum designers, is demonstrated most magnificently in the placement of the Nike of Samothrace at the top of a long flight of stairs at the Louvre, as if alighting to honour not an ancient victor but virtuous tourists. The power of such installations has been the special concern of the German photographer Thomas Struth.[17]

The art historical canon of art, however, involves more than the choice and display of art. It also implies a narrative, order and thus a history of art. For two centuries now, canons of art have been communicated through the art lecture and the sequences and narratives that it imparts. In the nineteenth century, artists and art historians lectured in front of works of art or provided simulations in the form of drawings or casts. Museums documented the canon by means of plaster casts. With the invention of photography and the electric light came the illustrated slide lecture that continued many aspects of prior stagings.[18] In the space of the art lecture, the temporal combination of word and image constructed a narrative by, about and through canons of art. That canon relied upon governing theories of the period (for instance modernism, nationalism, gender) and also upon the set of objects that could be reproduced through the evolving forms of photographic reproduction. Changing technology permitted and encouraged new canons, because the performative history of art can only be the history of what can be put before audiences. Fast changing digital modes of reproduction are currently transforming discipline and canon once again.

For many people, their first sustained encounter with the art lecture takes place at the university, where professors hold forth

E.C. Mansfield (ed.), *Making Art History: A Changing Discipline and its Institutions* (New York: Routledge, 2007), 55.

13. M. Halbertsma, 'The Call of the Canon: Why Art History Cannot Do Without', in: Mansfield, *Making Art History*, op. cit. (note 12), 28.

14. I take this formulation from an overview of work on ritual: E. Collins, 'Reflections on Ritual and on Theorizing about Ritual', *Journal of Ritual Studies*, no. 12 (1998), 3.

15. W.S. Sax, 'Agency', in: J. Kreinath, et al. (ed.), *Theorizing Rituals: Issues, Topics, Approaches, Concepts* (Boston: Brill, 2006), 474.

16. K. Flanagan, *Sociology and Liturgy: Re-presentations of the Holy* (New York: St. Martin's Press, 1991), 9.

17. H. Belting, et al., *Thomas Struth: Museum Photographs* (Munich: Schirmer/Mosel, 1993).

18. R.S. Nelson, 'The Slide Lecture, or the Work of Art *History* in the Age of Mechanical Reproduction', *Critical Inquiry*, no. 26 (Spring 2000), 414-434.

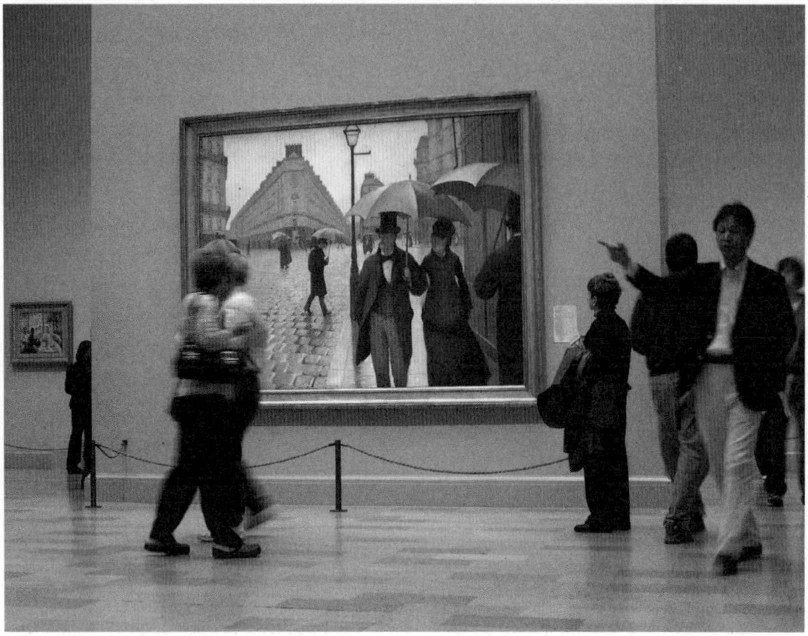

Caillebotte in Chicago, with homage to Thomas Struth. Photo: Robert S. Nelson.

about the great works of art and in so doing make and remake a canon of art. All lecturers know that only a certain number of works of art can be shown in any course and that hard choices have to be made. Each year thousands of such lectures take place in Europe and America, but few leave traces that a historian of canons might follow. However, general courses do use textbooks, and these can be used to document canons of art over time.

Since the first general history of art, the *Handbuch der Kunstgeschichte* of 1842 by Franz Kugler, such accounts have described the rise of the art of Western Europe and marginalized other areas through segregation by place and time. The result is a history that ends in the present-day triumph of Western Europe and North America and thereby validates the peoples and nation states of those regions.[19] Johannes Fabian had much to say about such temporal marginalizations in his classic *Time and the Other: How Anthropology Makes its Object*, an example of the Foucauldian hermeneutics of suspicion.[20] Today in many places, a new global art history is developing in response to post-colonial criticisms of national parochialisms and as a result of the changing global economy.

One important manifestation of this scholarship is David Summer's *Real Spaces: World Art History and the Rise of Western Modernism* of 2003.[21] Eschewing traditional Eurocentric narratives, it discusses the world's art by means of general conceptual categories. At its conclusion, the book moves to the present and 'The Conditions of Modernism' and ends with the Rothko Chapel in Houston. The reviews of *Real Spaces* in major journals that normally ignore survey books attest to the increased interest in a

19. Nelson, 'The Map of Art History', op. cit. (note 8).

20. J. Fabian, *Time and the Other: How Anthropology Makes its Object* (New York: Columbia University Press, 1983).

21. David Summer, *Real Spaces: World Art History and the Rise of Western Modernism* (London: Phaidon, 2003).

globalized canon of art.[22] James Elkins begins his assessment of the book with an arresting, if perhaps hyperbolic claim: 'Far and away the most pressing problem facing the discipline of art history is the prospect of world art history.'[23]

In 2007, this approach to art history, much simplified, reached the basic textbook: *Mirror of the World: A New History of Art*.[24] The author is Julian Bell, the son of Quentin Bell and the grandson of Clive Bell, the famous art critic of the Bloomsbury group and friend of Virginia Wolff and Roger Fry. In his book, Julian Bell treats the arts of diverse parts of the world and arranges the material chronologically, not topically. Some chapters are more successful than others, and at one point he is forced to title a section 'Unrelated Images', because they are just that.[25] The last chapter he correctly calls 'Foreground', presumably because the present or near present is what we see first when we look to the past. Here Bell breaks down that old narrative about the rise of New York as the pre-eminent art centre after the Second World War and rejects this self-serving story of triumph propagated by museums, dealers and critics living in New York City, a sure example of what people do with canons and the subject of a book by Serge Guilbaut.[26] In the process, Bell goes beyond Summer's high modernist conclusion and opens the history of art to global developments.

With Bell's book, we are near the point of view expressed in documenta 12, held in Kassel in 2006-2007. In their introduction, the curators Roger Buergel and Ruth Noack explain an unusual aspect of a contemporary exhibition: 'With our choice of works we have moved deeply into the past. Although this might look odd considering that documenta is an exhibition of contemporary art, we believe that it is necessary because most forms and formats come with rather a long history. They may also extend well into the future.'[27]

The catalogue includes historical works of art, beginning with a fourteenth-century Persian drawing of a dark landscape. The entry about the drawing joins it to the exhibition that follows: 'A certain form, permanent and changeable, continues to live, transferred to another horizon. That is its fate.'[28] The term 'horizon' recalls a second metaphor advanced in the catalogue's introduction: 'Exhibitions are only worth looking at if we manage to dispense with preordained categories and arrive at a plateau where art communicates itself and on its own terms. This is aesthetic experience in its true sense: The exhibition becomes a medium in its own right and can thus hope to involve its audience in its compositional moves.'[29]

'Horizon' and 'plateau' are places, distant from us, ideal and imaginary and thus utopian. 'Horizon' and 'plateau' are also metaphors, as is the first word in the title of Bell's book, *Mirror of the World*. Like all metaphors, they impose the real world on what they transform; hence their inherent contradiction. No mirror gives a perfect reflection, Bell's included. Since we understand the

22. D. Carrier in *Caa.reviews*, no. 91 (2003).

23. J. Elkins in *The Art Bulletin*, no. 86 (2004), 373. See also J. Elkins (ed.), *Is Art History Global?* (New York: Routledge, 2007).

24. Julian Bell, *Mirror of the World: A New History of Art* (London: Thames & Hudson, 2007).

25. Julian Bell, 'Unrelated Images', in: ibid., 85-90.

26. Ibid., 413-466. S. Guilbaut, *How New York Stole the Idea of Modern art: Abstract Expressionism, Freedom, and the Cold War* (Chicago: University of Chicago Press, 1983).

27. R.M. Buergel and R. Noack, *Documenta Kassel 12 16/06 - 23/09, 2007* (Cologne: Taschen, 2007), 12.

28. Ibid., 16.

29. Ibid., 11-12.

play of metaphors, we do not regard his book as an actual mirror, although we may accept that its contents may be transformed by metaphoric predication. Similarly, the declaration that documenta 12 is a 'plateau where art communicates itself and on its own terms' metaphorically alters the space and experience of the exhibition, even though we do not expect to find art installed on an actual plateau. Both the book and the exhibition are partial utopias.

There are many varieties of quasi utopian structures in our world, and for them Foucault invented the word heterotopia, or other place, a term that is crude and undifferentiated but useful nonetheless. His examples of heterotopias are cemeteries, theatres, gardens, museums, vacation resorts, model towns and cruise ships. These are places that are a part of, but also separated from society, spaces that though applied, enacted and real are utopian in operation. 'The ship,' he writes, 'is the heterotopia par excellence. In civilizations without boats, dreams dry up.'[30] A heterotopia is a place and means to dream, create, invent and remember. It makes possible the productive juxtaposition of objects, people, places, periods, causes and aspirations that could never exist in one place in the actual world. Foucault aptly described the museum as a place for 'indefinitely accumulating time'.[31] Although an actual building, the museum is also partially imaginary, a place where past and present coincide and time is arrested, arranged, condensed and inverted. To use Summer's terms, the museum and the art history survey book are real spaces that take us to virtual spaces.

30. M. Foucault, 'Of Other Places', *Diacritics*, no. 1, vol. 16 (Spring 1986), 27.

31. Ibid., 26.

No museum possesses the complete canon of art, although great dictators, like Napoleon and Hitler, tried and ultimately failed to assemble as perfect a canon as possible. What they possessed or wished to possess, nineteenth-century museums inscribed on their façades in the case of the Rijksmuseum in Amsterdam or the Kunsthistorisches Museum in Vienna. A chronological series of artists' names also encircles the entrance pavilion of the Art Institute of Chicago from the late nineteenth century. The first set of names ends with Leonardo, Dürer, Michelangelo and Raphael, or the acme of the High Renaissance. After the central gable, the canon resumes with Titian and proceeds through European painters of the sixteenth, seventeenth and eighteenth centuries down to Turner, the sole single nineteenth-century artist, and one Japanese artist, Kanaoka. The latter, an isolated but prescient exception to the Eurocentric model, was a consequence of the local regard for Japanese art. The Art Institute when built had no collection. It never has had and never will have a painting by Leonardo or Michelangelo. The façade inscriptions, therefore, describe the ideal, not the actual contents of the museum and hence are an art historical utopia.

If museums are manifestations of imaginary canons and containers for 'indefinitely accumulating time', their physical limits are neither imaginary nor indefinite, a problem for nineteenth-century museums with their classicizing designs and symmetrical plans. Additions have usually taken the form of new wings or separate museums of modern or contemporary art, institutions that instantiate the increasingly problematic modern myth of their break with the past. Although the architectural signifiers of status change over time, the modern museum remains a hetero-topic container of the utopic. As Brian O'Doherty once described, in the modern gallery: 'The outside world must not come in, so windows are usually sealed off. Walls are painted white. The ceiling becomes the source of light . . . Art exists in a kind of eternity of display . . . there is no time.[32] These are the visual properties of a utopia, that 'discursive expression of neutral,' which 'stages . . . an imaginary (or fictional) solution to [a] contradiction,' as Marin put it.[33]

32. B. O'Doherty, *Inside the White Cube: The Ideology of the Gallery Space* (Berkeley: University of California Press, 1986), 15.
33. Marin, *Utopics*, op. cit. (note 5),xiii.

Like utopias, museums effect imaginary and fictional solutions to the contradictions of contemporary life. Some are more successful than others. As a coda to my paper, I want to introduce counterexamples of the canonical Agency, or lack thereof, in museological heterotopias. In 1997 the city of Thessaloniki, Greece, was a European Capital of Culture, and with the support of the European Union it renovated its historical monuments

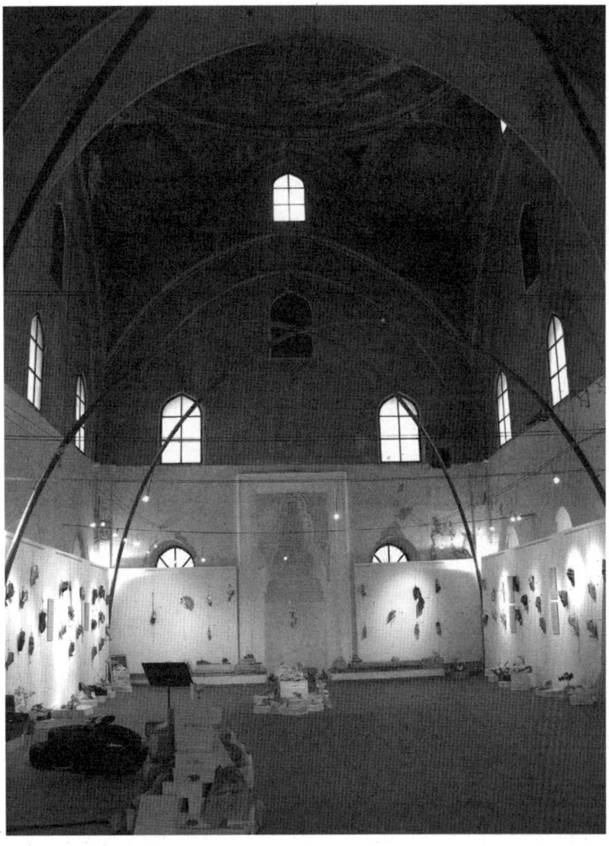

Alatza Imaret Camii, Thessaloniki, 1484.
Photo: Robert S. Nelson.

and defined a local canon, preserving and publicizing that which was deemed worth saving and ignoring the rest. Certain abandoned nineteenth century mansions were restored and turned into museums or galleries, as were Ottoman mosques whose utility had disappeared following the exchange of populations between Greece and Turkey in 1923. An important early mosque in the city, the Alatza Imaret Camii of 1484, was carefully restored by the Greek Archeological Service and converted to museum space for changing exhibitions by local artists.

One presentation caught my attention when I visited the city in the fall of 2008. Temporary white exhibition panels had been carefully installed inside the mosque, so as not to harm the mosque walls and their Arabic inscriptions. An exhibition by the local Greek artist Katefenia Zafeiriadou displayed shoes that she had artfully crafted and richly decorated with more than a hint of surrealism. Like the installation of the Caillebotte at the Art Institute, the positioning of the art works attempted to associate objects and viewer, although with less success. All seemed familiar here and no different from local exhibitions in many cities in Europe and America, until I noticed that one of the shoes hung in the centre of the mihrab, the most sacred place of a mosque. At that moment, the heterotopia of the historic monument and the modern gallery clashed, and utopic space and neutral stage dissolved, because even the most casual visitor knows of the prohibition against shoes in a mosque. No longer were the white walls of this and art turned into ideology.

The seamless merger of past and present also collapsed for me when I visited Thessaloniki's Museum of Byzantine Culture, an excellent institution and the winner of the 2005 Council of Europe's Museum Prize, 'awarded annually since 1977 to a museum judged to have made a significant contribution to the understanding of European cultural heritage'.[34] In addition to being a first-rate introduction to Byzantine art and culture, the museum endeavours to associate Byzantium with modern Greece, the same strategy employed by the city's Byzantine revival architecture built after a devastating fire in 1917.[35] That fire and the subsequent rebuilding displaced Thessaloniki's significant Jewish population. The location of the museum was problematic for similar reasons.

It and the nearby buildings of the University of Thessaloniki occupy the site of the large Jewish cemetery that had been located outside the walls of the mediaeval city. The cemetery held the remains of a half million inhabitants of one of the largest Jewish communities in the Mediterranean, descendants of the Sephardic Jews who fled Spain in 1492.[36] Virtually all perished in 1943. On one wall of the Byzantine museum was a quotation in English: 'The past is a foreign country from which we come.' The source was the historian David Lowenthal and his important book about attitudes towards the past and cultural patrimony.[37] However, in

34. http://www.mbp.gr/html/en/nea_vraveio.htm (accessed 10 March 2009).

35. M. Mazower, *Salonica, City of Ghosts: Christians, Muslims, and Jews, 1430-1950* (New York: Alfred A. Knopf, 2005), 305.

36. According to Mazower, the location of that Jewish cemetery remains unacknowledged at the university, despite pleas by many professors: ibid., 438.

37. D. Lowenthal, *The Past is a Foreign Country* (New York: Cambridge University Press, 1985).

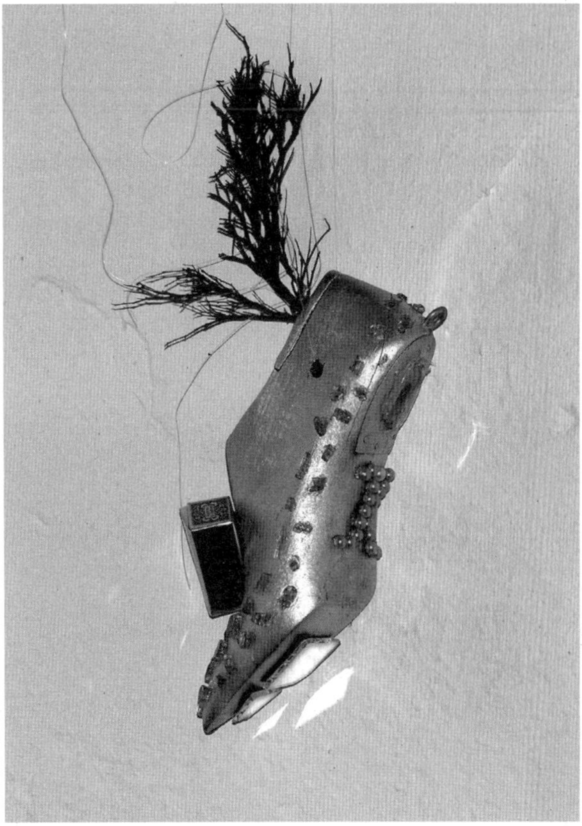

Katefenia Zafeiriadou, decorated shoe in mihrab, 2008. Photo: Robert S. Nelson.

this particular physical setting, these words took on new, fraught meanings for they reminded me of how much Thessaloniki had changed from the nineteenth century, when its population had been more or less equally Jewish, Muslim and Christian. The 'we' of 2008 is not the 'we' of 1908 or 908.

But museums – historical, art historical or otherwise – are canonical or ideal before they are historical or real. They attempt to direct the present and the future by means of the past. Yet their agency has limits. Only because we continue to regard them as heterotopian do we expect that the monuments and museums of Thessaloniki should be sites for healing religious trauma and resolving social conflict. As fugitive, ephemeral and fictive as museums may seem, the enduring power of their agency derives from their audiences, who continue to believe in them. Canons and their instantiation are one way that groups of people attempt to live together in peace. When civil discord becomes too great, however, museums and canons are among the first victims, as seen in Iraq recently or in Europe during the Second World War. Reinstating and enabling heterotopias in Thessaloniki and elsewhere is one sign of peace. If only there were white walls powerful enough to contain and neutralize the antagonisms in Palestine and wherever canons and cannons clash.[38]

38. Cf. an exhibition of 'Israeli and Palestinian contemporary art and material culture' about notions of homeland that opened at the Spertus Museum in Chicago on 2 May 2008. The catalogue *Imaginary Coordinates* (Chicago: Spertus Press, 2008), edited by R. Rosen, 'is a manifesto more than it is a description or pendant to an exhibition. It is a proposal for what an exhibition in a Jewish museum in a postethnic world might look like.' The exhibition was deemed offensive to Israel and canceled months early, as *The Guardian* reported: http://www.guardian.co.uk/commentisfree/2008/jul/10/art.israelandthepalestinians (accessed 10 March 2009).

Canons and Publics

Ruth Noack

I

It is a strange time to be dealing with the topic of the canon. On a theoretical level, the canon has long been recognized as a tool of institutional power. By way of inclusion into and exclusion from a canon, power structures forge identity and become fossilized in the process. We all know that this process works for individuals as well as for people inhabiting a common territory, resulting in a unified subject or a unified nation. It also works for the field of art, creating a system in which the production and reception of works of art are stratified in such a way as to create the disciplines of art history and criticism, as well as to determine the positions of experts and laypersons alike. And whereas the fight for inclusion in the canon is probably as old as the idea of the canon itself, by the end of the twentieth century the focus had shifted to an analysis and critique of the structure, resulting in calls for the rereading, differentiation or dissolution of canonicity.[1]

It is a strange time to be dealing with the topic of the canon. On a practical level, canons continue to shape what we conceive of as worthy subjects of intellectual discourse and public debate. With respect to art, they influence the private and public collection, conservation, study and display of certain works, as well as forms of communication involved in these activities. A prime example of the practice of a canon is the newly established 'Canon of Dutch History'.[2] To an outsider such as I am, this endeavour is truly baffling, mainly because hegemony does not always operate so overtly. In fact, one might claim that outspoken canons are much less pernicious than implied ones. Although the 'Canon of Dutch History' can and must be criticized, particularly for its depolitization of subjects pertaining to Dutch power structures – themselves under the nebulous cover of culture and diversity – in view of advancing global changes it remains but a pitiful tool of governmentality.[3] The world is changing rapidly, and with it Western canons are rightfully eroding; in fact, I am not so sure that we will need to bother much longer with a critique of Western hegemony. It's a situation in keeping with history, as canons

1. See, among others, Griselda Pollock, *Differencing the Canon: Feminist Desire and the Writing of Art's Histories* (London: Routledge, 1999).
2. See http://entoen.nu.
3. Presumably, there is a lively debate on the content and aim of the Dutch canon, yet I refer only to the website, where, it seems, the primary mode of representation is one that names areas of conflict in the most innocuous way possible. Examples include the relationship between the Netherlands and Indonesia, as well as the cultural role of migrants. Even the harmless topic of 'feminism' is represented in an apolitical way by means of only one subject rather than by discourse on the women's movement as such. Any inclusion based on the traditional 'polder' model – one that allows topics and cultural players to appear next to one another as equals, while disregarding the actual, often conflictive power relations between them – might be defined as 'diversity'. This kind of diversity does not allow, however, for a process aimed at a fairer society, because it assumes, as a given, that which still needs to be established. Thus the question of who is to name what and whom, and of who gets to represent the status quo, remains a contentious issue.

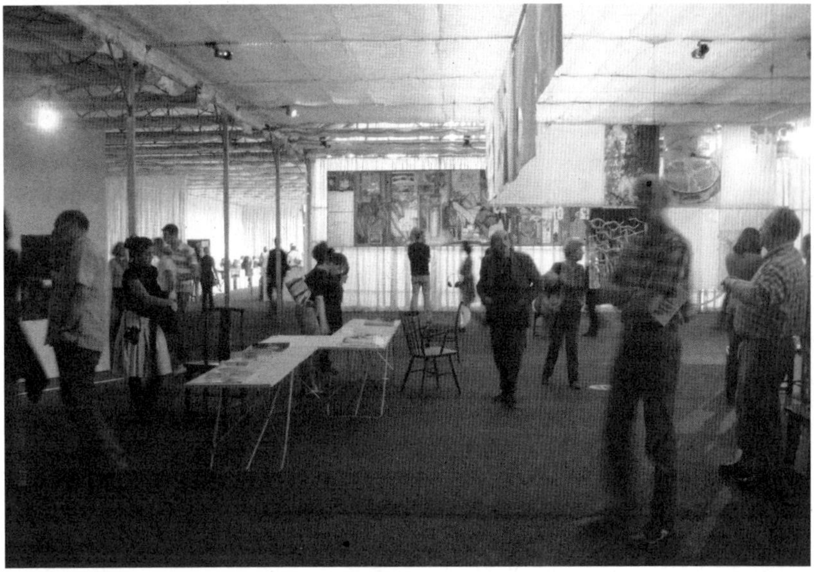

Installation view, Aue Pavillion, documenta 12, Kassel, 2007. Photo: Ruth Noack. Courtesy of Genevieve Fraisse.

are always in the process of being formed and reformed. Only in terms of sedimentation as a result of the passing of time does it truly make sense to speak of a fixed canon, and even then histories can be revised.

Why then, one might ask, bother with canons at all? Three answers come to mind. To begin with, we are all part of a network of material and immaterial relationships in which power sustains itself at any given moment. I'd rather position myself reflexively and become as active as possible in the process of negotiating the revision of canons than contribute inadvertently to established yet unjust practices. If this is a personal political stance, my second answer concerns a public matter. It seems to me that a public debate on canons might be one of several possible and necessary ways to discuss how we want to live together. In this respect, rather than taking an existing canon or an existing community as our point of departure, we might engage in canon-building and in the formation of provisional consensus in a way that leaves room for conflict and dissent. Obviously, such a debate is fruitless unless we question the 'we' so generously used in this essay. To my mind, questions of canon or community cannot remain local (or national); they must be asked translocally. In other words, we have to come up with ways of communicating with one another that do not take for granted a global or local given. The basis of this negotiation can be neither a predefined, though perhaps somewhat fuzzy, national or cultural identity nor an assumed universality, because each person's position within time and space differs *and* matters. Thus the only possible basis is one that integrates the desire, interest and necessity of personal change for the purpose of coming together. And here I arrive at my third answer, which argues for combining the political with the personal by means of

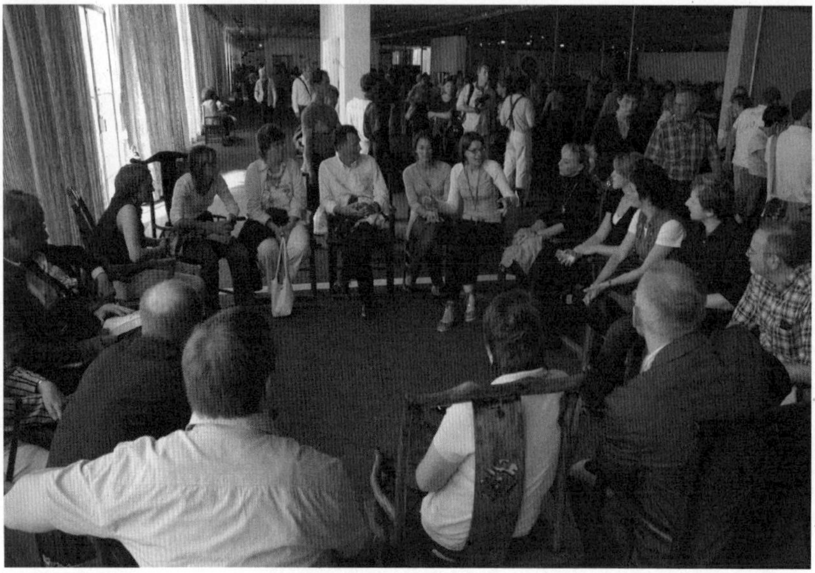

Sitting and talking, Aue Pavillion, documenta 12, Kassel, 2007. Photo: Ruth Noack. Courtesy of documenta 12.

the aesthetic: I propose that good art, and a good exhibition, can articulate the relationship between 'self' and 'other' on a level of complexity that I consider a prerequisite for any change worthy of the name. I'd rather see good art than bad art be researched, preserved, presented and debated. And this statement is nothing other than a claim to a canon.

II

At documenta 12, an exhibition held for 100 days in 2007 in Kassel, Germany, and visited by over 750,000 people, our attempt was to shift the gaze away from Western centricity and to revise the canon of contemporary art in such a way as to form another kind of coherence than the one issuing from a system of star players or key themes. Such a revision entails more than merely mounting different works on the wall or moving those that have been marginalized to centre stage. It requires an examination and critique of the organizing principles of an exhibition all the way down to the conventions of the display. It is clear that curators alone cannot achieve the desired shift. It needs a viewer who is willing to make sense of the presentation. In Kassel, where the public was our focal point, we saw visitors as an entity previously unconnected to the exhibition but capable of engaging with the art on display and drawing sustenance from this engagement. In other words, we thought the meaning of the exhibition would have to be negotiated, and that the negotiation process would involve the art, its display and the audience in an experience with an outcome we would be unable to control.

What we *could* control were the material components and, to some extent, the discursive input. To give an example of the latter: for two years prior to the show, we met monthly with forty residents of Kassel, including teachers, unionists, architects and social workers. Our discursive input was to suggest that we discuss the three leitmotifs of the exhibition – modernity, basic life, education – in relation to the city. We also invited artists to present their work at these meetings. We did not control the form or function of the group, which influenced the exhibition both intellectually and pragmatically by revealing to us the hidden social fabric of the city, in part through links forged with the people and informal institutions of Kassel. The choice of the Bergpark, the castle at Willhelmshöhe and the Schlachthof cultural centre as venues for the exhibition was based on information gathered at our meetings with the 'local board of "documenta 12"'. Gradually, the group evolved into a force that organized local activities (independent of the exhibition but shielded by its symbolic power) and directed the programme of free-lunch lectures that took place at the documenta Halle each day.

Soon after starting to work on the exhibition, we realized that a negotiation of the canon would also involve fundamental questions about the environment in which art is shown and observed. The visitor's attitude towards art is determined not only by the display of individual works but also by the building in which they are exhibited: an architectural structure has a cultural tradition of built-in viewing habits. As part of the eighteenth-century Enlightenment project, the Fridericianum was designed to house one of the first public museums; in this case, the viewer was envisioned as a scientific researcher. The cabinet structure of the nineteenth-century Neue Galerie ties into the ideal of the bourgeois connoisseur. And the modernist documenta Halle finds a metaphor for the assumed transparency of the public sphere in its glass façade. Each of these buildings creates problems for a contemporary exhibition, and we approached each in a different way, allowing viewers to experience what it means to look at a particular work within a specific environment. We abandoned all pretence of the pseudo-neutral white cube, feeling that if we were to start rethinking a given canon, we'd have to do it in a space less associated with the Cold War, Western-centric model of display. Contemplating the masses of people who would be milling around the exhibition every day, we wanted a situation in which it would be possible to concentrate on an individual work while being aware of participating in a larger event. We wanted one building to allow individual reflection as well as group discussion, to combine viewing art with sitting, relaxing, talking with friends or attending a workshop. For this purpose we built the temporary, 10,000-m^2 Aue Pavilion, a structure based on greenhouse architecture, and opted for plenty of space around the art on display. The artist Ai WeiWei let us use part of his work, 1000 old Chinese wooden chairs, for people to sit on in an arrangement we called *Circles of Enlightenment*.[4] Apart from the chairs, the space offered visitors a very loose *parcours* of works, which allowed them

4. *Circles of Enlightenment* was our English term for the circles of chairs that we saw as one arena for audience interaction. The term was chosen to provoke a discussion on the relationship between aesthetic experience and discourse.

to link one piece with another and forge connections as they walked through the exhibition as one might walk through a forest. During a break, we introduced yet another mode of display with an unofficial title: 'Art Fair on LSD'. Presented in a cul-de-sac at the very end of the building was Zoe Leonard's *Analogue* (1998-2007), a research project featuring the journey of second-hand clothes from Leonard's New York neighbourhood to places elsewhere on the planet. Leonard's photos display the problematic passage of what begins as the residue of Western consumerism into a commodity that threatens local clothing industries. We thought it fitting to show this work in the only place at documenta 12 that references the white cube.

The Aue Pavilion was probably the exhibition space that best enabled visitors to experience, intellectually and physically, what we called 'migration of form', which entails the display of art – with an eye to stratification and the creation of associations – that works both thematically and aesthetically on varying levels of complexity. Although it is a historically proven fact that forms have migrated, and although the exhibition showed instances of such long-term globalization – in which Europe seems to be almost an afterthought – we chose to emphasize ambivalence and speculation, and to open multifaceted doors into singular works of art, while providing condensed constellations of what were at times very diverse pieces. Where we had more than one work by an artist, for example, we distributed the various items throughout the exhibition, allowing people to stumble across them like old acquaintances and, at the same time, to see them under new circumstances. We felt it was important to offer a sense of the more recent history of contemporary art, as well as of globalization, by means of juxtaposition. But it seemed even more vital to have people discover for themselves holes in the research and

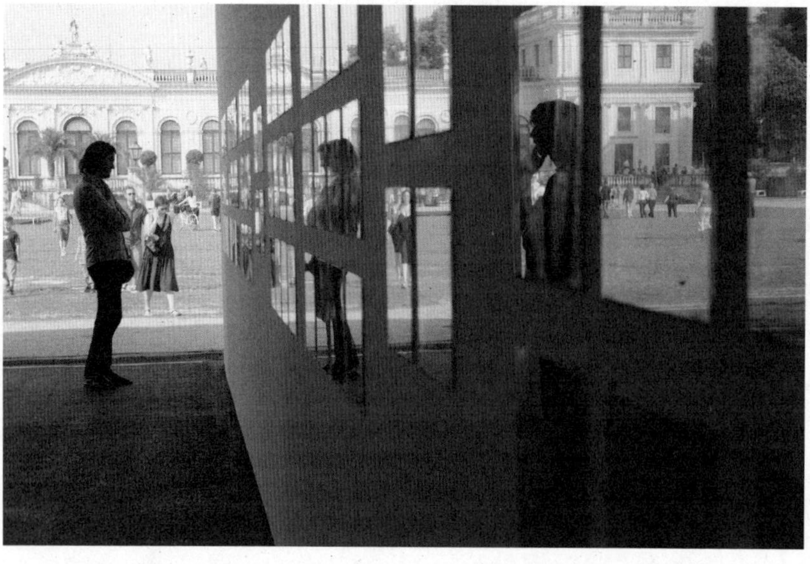

Installation view (white cube), Aue Pavillion, documenta 12, Kassel, 2007. Photo: Ruth Noack. Courtesy of Genevieve Fraisse.

a lack of knowledge about artistic practices worldwide, matters often covered up by means of categorization and national canons for the purpose of creating a seamless narrative. The display served at times to accentuate the function of an art show as a way of generating the meaning of art; in other words, the exhibition apparatus was exhibited alongside the works themselves. This made it easier for viewers to understand what was being done and, perhaps, to realize their role in the scenario. The sometimes highly subjective manner of showing or combining objects allowed aspects of the work to surface that might not have been noticed had we used the prevailing framework of interpretation. We took the risk in recognition of the irrationality of aesthetic experience.

III

Form need not be thought of as an essential attribute of an object; an observer can also relate to a work of art either contextually *or* phantasmatically. It must suffice here to point out that a development of this argument leads to aesthetic theory.[5] I do want to emphasize, though, that the aesthetic quality of the relationship between a viewer and a work of art, which critical theory discusses under the heading 'aesthetic experience', can and should be thought of as a phenomenon connected to both the contextuality of the individual experience and the psyche of the viewing subject. In other words, both the meaning of the work and the relevance of its reception depend on who, where, when and why – not to mention the viewer's prior experience.

5. Kaja Silverman, *World Spectators* (Stanford: Stanford University Press, 2000); Leo Bersani and Ulysse Dutoit, *Forms of Being: Cinema, Aesthetics, Subjectivity* (London: British Film Institute, 2004).

At documenta 12, a difference in aesthetic experience emerged from the varied reactions of diverse segments of the audience. While many experts chose not to enter into the experiment proposed by the exhibition, local visitors, particularly laypeople who visited the show several times, eventually looked for, found and discussed relationships linking the various works, most of which we had not considered and many of which made good sense. Over the course of the 100 days, it became obvious – at lunch lectures and during the many formal and informal discussions conducted by the 'documenta 12' team, as well as mediators, educators and guides – that these people were searching actively, on their own, for what they felt were the missing facts, in order to create a canon. We knew no way to lend form to this new information, other than the conventional methods of audience research and documentation of certain discursive formats. Thus what could be thought of as a new form of multivalency remained ephemeral. Then, too, although in theory the notion of a canon that exists only because and during the process involved in its creation does sound like a good idea, there is a problem: as long as the structures of discourse within the public sphere are dominated by so-called expert opinions, the discourse of the audience remains private, at least to some extent. What could become a fairer and more impartial way to determine what a society deems worthy of interest and debate is thus relegated to individual change and growth.

Negotiation, of course, is one way to approach the problem. And negotiation demands time, which would suggest that the solution lies not in exhibitions but in the hands of institutions. I propose, however, the need for intelligent ways of lending form to a canon created by the public – please note that I do not mean simply representatives of the public – within the medium of the exhibition itself. We have to bring the canon back into the sphere of the aesthetic in order to address the viewer's idea of what it means to occupy and define a common space.

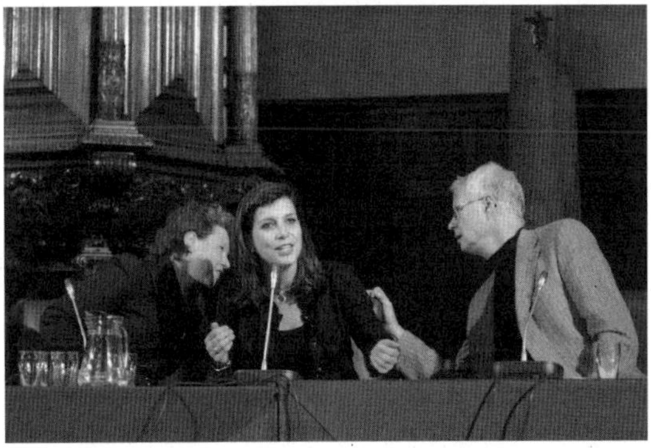

Ruth Noack, Margriet Schavemaker and Robert S. Nelson.

Discussion

The discussion was moderated by Margriet Schavemaker, Head of Collections, Stedelijk Museum Amsterdam.

Moderator: Both of you addressed issues of hegemony, power and authority intrinsic to the phenomenon of canon and canon building. Also in each of your papers you referred to the deconstruction of the Western-centric canon and you explored alternative ways of canon-building that maybe more suitable to our present times. In doing so each of you brought up the topic of agency: the agency of the canon and the agency of the public. But where, or better with whom exactly does this agency lie? Do you believe the future of the canon might be that it is user generated? One could even stay with the popular term UGC (short for User Generated Content) as it could also refer to User Generated Canon.

Robert Nelson: A canon has to be made by a larger social group than one person. Although I am all in favour of democracy and freedom of choice, a canon is not the same as interactive television where you choose what programme you want to watch or which commercial. That information is useful for marketing firms when they research the demographic profiles of their commercial target groups. A canon is very much involved with politics, for better or for worse, and it is involved with the ideals of a society, ideals of knowledge, ideals of the past that should be ideals for the future. When talking about canons, I am interested in the agency of that utopian project, and in doing so I try to suspend my suspicion about the operation and the organisations that are involved in these canon-making processes and that lay claim to a certain authority. When I think about agency, the functioning of the canon, what it does and what it creates, I very much like Ruth Noack's notion of a local canon; and I like the way in which she works as a curator and allows this local canon to be assembled, re-assembled and then remade again. I believe canons are important for any society. I would even go as far as to paraphrase Harold Bloom to the effect that canons are a means by which we think.[1] Canons are one of the constitutive ways by which we function in society.

Ruth Noack: The documenta, like any other art institution, is a canon-building machine. For documenta 12 we tried to shift away from the Western-centric narrative and form another kind of coherence. Amongst other strategies, we left out the captions and other explanatory texts in the exhibition in an attempt to foreground the decontextualisation that automatically happens in every exhibition, but often remains hidden. We were heavily criticized for this and other of our strategies by many of the so called experts of the art world. It is obvious, that our purposeful shift away from the gate keepers towards the constitution of a general public caused havoc and resentment, but we thought it most important to invest in a general audience and their responses, their interaction with the works. Some of the team of mediators documented what visitors talked about, there were public discussions every day and towards the second half of the exhibition I made myself personally available for critique and comments by holding a regular sit-in in front of one of our venues. It was amazing to hear what connections and stories the lay audience discovered between the works: interpretations the experts never came up with. I still regret it that these interpretations didn't make it into a canon, because as you said: a canon is made by a large social group and it is not just done informally.

Moderator: This issue between hegemony and the public or institutions using the canon and in a way trying to suspend it, interact with it, negotiate with it, that's something you've been addressing too, Robert. Do you see a difference between what you were talking about the with regards to museums and your experiences in Greece, and what Ruth has been talking about? Could we say that museums reinforce the canon as some sort of utopian dream, whereas exhibitions like documenta 12 paradoxically still try to subvert and de-canonise albeit being canon-building machines themselves?

Robert Nelson: I think utopias are positive things, but what I am interested in as an historian, is this diffusion of utopias. If we cut away all the discussions about the branding and commercialisation of museums, the museum, as a heterotopic space, still functions. Because it remains heterotopic, it is worthwhile to some people to create a brand and to market the museum. Functionally I do not see a great difference between selection of art for a museum or for an exhibition. Contemporary artists area well aware of the power of museums to accept and thus subvert their cultural critiques.

Ruth Noack: The aspect that we are forgetting in this discussion is education. Canon building is not just about putting things on the walls and creating a kind of utopia. It is not simply about the social space in which these works interact. And education is not just about knowledge. It's also about understanding a lack of knowledge and then having the agency – as an audience – to find the space to educate oneself further. And this, I believe, is not happening enough in museums. Canon building should be done by a larger group, and its process is one way of debating how we want to live, and therefore it is a very important political project. Having or not having a canon in this respect is completely unimportant; what is important is the canon building process itself. The emphasis should be put on the dialogue with others about what is important or unimportant. And this process of canon building needs to be democratised. I believe that art can help in generating this dialogue. Potentially, people can confront themselves with their lack of knowledge. And the aesthetic experience can enable them to deal with the fact that they cannot understand – and thereby own – everything.

Robert Nelson: There is another aspect to this discussion about canons: and that is what I encountered in Thessaloniki; that is this phenomenon that cities themselves are becoming containers of canons, of monuments. Think about the committees that are involved in the elaborate political decision-making processes of nominating/qualifying something as a monument or not. I want to point out that canons – as a phenomenon that is constitutive of our society – are not just reserved to art and art history. It's a fascinating process to observe which buildings are brought into the canon and which are not. At this point, there is a building in America that before Barack Obama's victory didn't belong to any canon anywhere and now I am sure will become a canonical monument for American history. I am thinking of the building where Michelle Obama's great-grandfather lived as a slave. This is the point where, as Marx said, the past is remade by the present for the future. Michelle Obama's great-grandfather's cabin will become, I predict, a tangible physical sign in a narrative about how life in the United States of America gets better and better. But now, our job is to deconstruct, analyze, or question this canon and the story that is being formed on any given day and say: Au contraire, things aren't necessarily improving, there are still minorities that are persecuted, et cetera. That's one form agency in relation to canon. Of course, that critical perspective, that agency, is only possible because some people in society reside in and are paid by heterotopic institutions, such as my university, and are able to speak to audiences in another, this conference at the University of Amsterdam. This is the larger agency of the heterotopia/utopia. If this sounds circular, it is.

1. Harold Bloom, 'Without the Canon, We Cease to Think', in: Harold Bloom, *The Western Canon: The Books and School of the Ages* (New York, Harcourt Brace & Company, 1994), 41, quoted in Christopher B. Steiner, 'Can the Canon Burst?', *The Art Bulletin*, no. 2, vol. 78 (June 1996), 213.

NOW design

Rick Poynor - Design Thinking or Critical Design?

Camiel van Winkel - Middle Culture

Art & Theory

TIME

Design

All is design. For several years now the primacy of design has generated intense discussion in the art world. Design seems to succeed – a broad public seems to appreciate it – where art fails in the crossover with society at large. A vast group of designers move towards more autonomous projects in a desire to permeate the art world and museums, and from the 1980s onwards artists increasingly make use of and reflect upon the primacy of design in their work. How do we redefine the current relationship between design, art and mass culture? And how should one value the social relevance of design to society?

Design critic Rick Poynor counterpositions two important recent developments in design. In the business world 'design' has become synonymous with 'innovation' and 'creativity'. This rhetoric of 'design thinking' is contested by a group of critical designers. They believe that design's role in society should be broader then just serving consumption and production rates. Design practice could make a vital contribution to areas of contemporary life such as education, free exchange of information, democratic participation, sustainable living, etcetera. In his contribution Poynor analyses the different strategies designers apply to penetrate our social awareness.

What to think of the tendency of artists becoming designers, and vice versa? Culture critic Camiel van Winkel opens up the discussion by arguing that contemporary art has increasingly become a restrictive form of, what he calls, 'applied concept art'. Not only a certain group of artists has been moving towards design, but art itself in a very fundamental way has too. In this sense critical self-reflection is not only needed within design, but maybe even more so in art itself. And how should we value the social relevance of critical design, if it represents only a small critical-intellectual base, which relies for a great deal on an art context? According to Van Winkel, a true analysis of the social relevance of design cannot ignore the study of how design has permeated society via the mainstream, as a historically and inherently applied art form.

Rick Poynor (UK) writes about design, media and visual culture. He was the founding editor of *Eye* magazine, a co-founder of the *Design Observer* weblog, and contributes regular columns to *Eye* and to *Print* magazine in New York. His books include *Design Without Boundaries* (1998), *Obey the Giant: Life in the Image World* (2001), *No More Rules: Graphic Design and Postmodernism* (2003), and *Jan van Toorn: Critical Practice* (2008). In 2004 he curated the exhibition *Communicate: Independent British Graphic Design since the Sixties* at the Barbican Art Gallery, London. He is a Research Fellow at the Royal College of Art.

Camiel van Winkel (NL) is professor in visual art at the Academy for Art and Design | St. Joost in Den Bosch, the Netherlands. Based in Amsterdam, he teaches art theory at Sint Lukas School of Arts in Brussels. He is the author of *Moderne leegte: Over kunst en openbaarheid* (1999), a critical study on the theory and practices of public art. In 2005 he published *The Regime of Visibility*, a book on the dialectical relationship between art and mass culture.

Design Thinking or Critical Design?

Rick Poynor

Art's recently renewed romance with design – the reason for the subject's inclusion in this series of essays – comes at a time when design has been going through a phase of self-questioning and review. Seen from the perspective of the design world, which happens to be my own location as a writer, the art world's perception of both design and designers' motivations fails to take into account the full range of positions and stances possible in the contemporary design scene. Most telling, perhaps, is the enduring assumption that designers lack agency – that the designer, unlike the free artist, is fatally restrained by the presence of the client and the need to answer a given brief, so that any and every outcome must be compromised. The free art/un-free design dichotomy is so deeply inscribed that even experienced designers can be inclined to view design in these restrictive terms. The American designer (and artist) Milton Glaser reports that whenever he speaks to students they always ask him whether he does any work for himself. 'The presumption beneath that question is that since one works to assignment, the work is not for oneself. My view is that *all* the work I've done is for myself, and it also involves accommodating either a personality (the client) or problem that has to be solved. Such is the nature of the design profession.'[1]

1. Milton Glaser, *Drawing is Thinking* (Woodstock and New York: Overlook Duckworth, 2008), 13.

While it is certainly the case that design activity is often conceived and applied in purely instrumental ways, many designers are troubled by their role in consumer capitalism. In the last decade, there has been much discussion within design education and the more self-aware parts of practice about the social and cultural role of design, a continuation of recurrent bouts of disciplinary soul-searching that can be traced back to modernism. It is not especially surprising if the art community is unaware of this self-examination since it is confined to specialized design publications and professional events and receives barely any attention in the general media. A more questioning view of design also fails to fit the media perception of design as being essentially concerned with branding, lifestyle, shopping, cool gadgets, luxurious home makeovers, stunning restaurant interiors and hip hotels. One might add that any critique of design issuing from the art world is likely to be complicit, too, since art insiders, just like everyone else, enjoy the trappings of the designer lifestyle.

What I want to examine here are two ways in which design is now being reconsidered within the field. The first development, called design thinking, is the more widely used term. Although design thinking claims to challenge design's established practices and received ideas, it does this from the perspective of the client's business interests, while purporting to empower design's users, and it aspires to an even more focused form of instrumentality without disclosing its underlying motivation. The second development, critical design, arises from within design practice itself and has so far received much less discussion. Critical design proposes new possibilities for design as a form of speculative practice and implicitly resists design thinking's urge to subjugate designers and control the design process in the name of a dubiously imagined public good.

In 2007, *BusinessWeek* journalist Bruce Nussbaum gave a speech at Parsons, The New School for Design in New York and then published an edited version in the blog he writes for the magazine's website. His piece was headlined 'Are Designers the Enemy of Design?' and in Nussbaum's view the answer was affirmative. 'There's a big backlash against design going on today and it's because designers suck,' he writes, acknowledging his desire to provoke.[2] Designers suck, he explains, because they are arrogant, believing that only they know how to design, and because they are ignorant, knowing almost nothing about sustainability. 'The rap against designers is that they design CRAP that hurts the planet,' he declares, making it sound as though these unscrupulous polluters with bloated egos are running around at will designing harmful, unnecessary junk. He has nothing critical to say about the *BusinessWeek*-reading industrialists, managers and marketing people for whose commercial enterprises and profit margins these crimes against the planet are being perpetrated. Nussbaum's argument might lack evidence and be laughably sweeping, but it captured a growing conviction among business thinkers that design has become too important to be left to designers. He ends by reporting that business people don't like the term 'design', which sounds to them like it is concerned with dresses or drapery, and that top

2. Bruce Nussbaum, 'Are Designers the Enemy of Design?', *BusinessWeek*, 18 March 2007, found at http://www.businessweek.com/innovate/NussbaumOnDesign/archives/2007/03/are_designers_t.html.

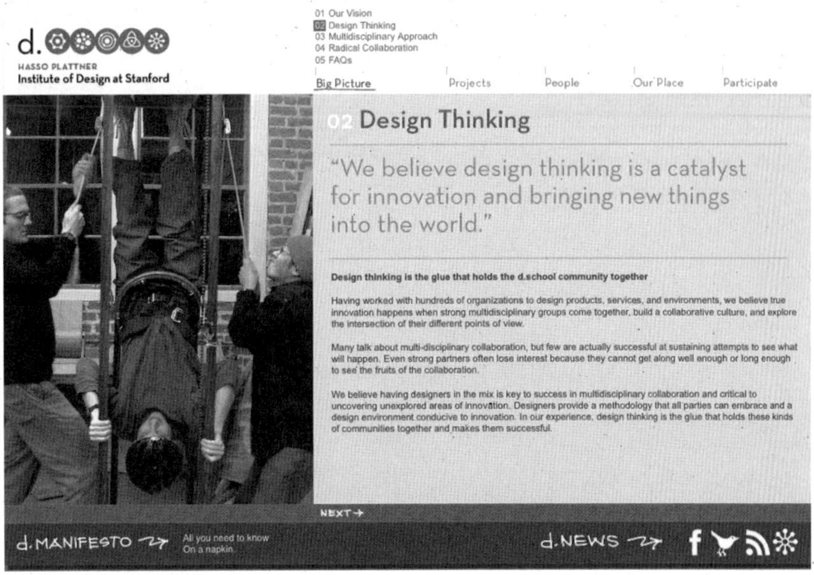

D-School website, 'Design Thinking' screen. Courtesy of Hasso Plattner Institute of Design, d-school, at Stanford University, California.

CEOs who embrace design would prefer to rename it something manly like 'innovation' – Nussbaum's calling card and the banner under which he blogs.

Roger Martin, dean of the Rotman School of Management at the University of Toronto, takes up the theme: 'Business people don't just need to understand designers better – they need to become designers,' he says.[3] The problem with the way business people think, argues Martin, is that they are over-inclined to 'crunch the numbers' and reach for formulas that have worked in previous situations. Instead, they should organize businesses so that they operate more like design studios, where life is organized around work and one project flows into the next, and they should embrace the 'mystery' of the problem with open minds, just as designers do. Business schools locked into traditional patterns of thought have failed to deliver this new breed of manager. 'We're telling students that the big bucks are made by administering linear improvements – getting better and better at doing essentially the same thing,' says Martin. 'But the real challenge lies in getting better and better at a different thing: devising clever solutions to wickedly difficult problems.'[4] Rotman's answer was to introduce the study of design principles, which it calls 'business design', into its MBA courses. 'Whether the goal is to develop new products or services, create new ways of marketing to customers or reinvent an entire business model, "design thinking" helps get bigger ideas, faster and more efficiently. We believe the mindset and methods behind great design are the same ingredients for successful Business Design. By incorporating the "design experience" into our curriculum, we offer students a unique and valuable opportunity to learn new ways to tackle complex challenges in deeper and more holistic ways.'[5]

3. Roger Martin quoted in Bill Breen, 'The Business of Design', *Fast Company*, 19 December 2007, found at http://www.fastcompany.com/magazine/93/design.html.

4. Ibid.

5. 'Business Design', Rotman School of Management, found at http://www.rotman.utoronto.ca/businessdesign/default.aspx.

Design and Innovation

'Design thinking' was given another notable boost when Stanford University launched its high-profile D-School founded on the concept. The school provides a meeting place where graduate students at Stanford from any discipline – engineering, computer science, business, medicine, humanities – can take additional courses in design. The D-School claims that only this kind of multidisciplinary interaction, with designers involved as a key part of the mix, can create the fertile conditions necessary for innovation. Today, the Internet abounds with attempts to define design thinking. Tim Brown, president of IDEO, based in Palo Alto, a highly successful design company in the forefront of the movement, uses the term as the title of his blog.[6] 'Design thinking is inherently about creating new choices, about divergence,' Brown told the *New York Times*. 'Most business processes are about making choices from a set of existing alternatives. Clearly, if all your competition is doing the same, then differentiation is tough. In order to innovate, we have to have new alternatives and new solutions to problems, and that is what design can do.'[7] Even YouTube has a short film about design thinking, offering a series of brief definitions. Among other things, we learn that design thinking is: 'Developing understanding and solutions through modelling and conceptual play'; 'Finding new insights into the familiar'; 'Imagining the as yet unimagined'; and 'Seeing and making connections'.[8]

When design thinking is summarized like this, it is hard to see what the fuss is about. There are no startling revelations here. Artists have always thought in this way and so have designers. There is an inescapable feeling with much of this rhetoric that business theorists, having belatedly woken up to the vital role played by design, are now trying to bottle, re-label and peddle to credulous clients – as though it were something new – intuitive modes of investigation that were always intrinsic to visual thinking. In essence, it is not much more than sales talk, a jazzy way of restating the obvious. Designers have always hoped to collaborate with clients open to design's possibilities and they have always had to deal with clients that thought they knew better, often leading to concepts and finished projects that were compromised. On one level, the new rhetoric of design thinking simply codifies and validates a longstanding reluctance, in some quarters, to trust the designer's unquantifiable expertise. It is hardly surprising that some designers are suspicious of recent attempts by business people to 'become designers', especially when the motivations of this supposedly 'human-centred' design thinking trend are so murky. If design has suddenly become human-centred, as the design thinkers assert – it's a favourite term – then what was design before: human-opposed? Designers have always visualized their task as being to improve the quality of everyday life for people by creating better objects and environments. The frequent failure,

6. *Design Thinking: Thoughts by Tim Brown*, found at http://designthinking.ideo.com/.

7. Tim Brown quoted in Janet Rae-Dupree, 'Design is More Than Packaging', *New York Times*, 4 October 2008, found at http://www.nytimes.com/2008/10/05/business/05unbox.html?_r=2&scp=2&sq=stanford&st=cse&oref=slogin.

8. 'Design Thinking – Some Thoughts', *YouTube*, 31 January 2008, found at http://www.youtube.com/watch?v=4RjpWfVbDWA.

despite this idealism, to design products, services, visual communications, housing, public spaces and public facilities as well as they could be designed is a collective responsibility, in which short-sighted business decisions and failures of public policy-making play a considerable part. Design can only be as good as its commissioners.

This might seem to take us some distance from art theory's concerns, but as stated earlier, art's view of design is partial – in both senses of the word – and does not address design in the round. To fully understand the conditions operating in design now, and then, perhaps, interrogate design through art, a more contextually specific awareness is necessary. The most notable recent book-length examination of the relationship between art and design, Alex Coles' *DesignArt* (2005), focuses on four areas: pattern, furniture, interiors and architecture.[9] Coles examines the contributions made by artists to each field, analysing both historical and recent examples – 'from Matisse to Murakami'. Designers' involvement in the art/design interface receives no attention and the design business, as a business, falls outside Coles' field of inquiry. Meanwhile, the costly collectibles produced for the growing designart market can be seen as extreme embodiments, aimed at the wealthiest class of consumers, of the view that design is inherently concerned with the consumption of luxurious designer accessories and experiences. This misapprehension now dominates public perceptions of design.

9. Alex Coles, *DesignArt: On Art's Romance with Design* (London: Tate Publishing, 2005). See also Alex Coles (ed.), *Design and Art* (London: Whitechapel and Cambridge, MA: MIT Press, 2007).

Critical Design

By comparison with design thinking, which has the backing of wealthy universities, globally positioned, high-earning design companies and widely read business magazines, critical design is a less pushy, almost grass-roots phenomenon within the design scene. In the last two years, several exhibitions, each using the term in its title, have helped to define critical design's territory: *Designing Critical Design* (Z33 Gallery, Hasselt, Belgium, 2007); *Don't Panic: Emergent Critical Design* (Architecture Foundation, London, 2007); and *Forms of Inquiry: The Architecture of Critical Graphic Design* (Architectural Association, London, and other venues, 2007-2009). To these might be added *Wouldn't it be nice . . . wishful thinking in art and design* (Centre d'Art Contemporain Genève, and other venues, 2007-2008), which featured some of the same designers as the other shows: Jurgen Bey, Martí Guixé, Dunne & Raby, and Dexter Sinister. The catalogue briefly considers the recent emergence of critical design, noting that the exhibits are not formally attached to it (though there is no formal critical design movement or group), but suggests that there might be some overlap with critical design's concerns in the exhibition's theme of wishful thinking. 'Common to both is the business of envisaging a different scheme of things, one that is imagined in spite of, or maybe even because of, harsh realities.'[10]

10. Emily King, 'Wouldn't it be nice . . .' in Katya García-Antón, Emily King and Christian Brändle (eds.), *Wouldn't it be nice . . . wishful thinking in art and design* (Geneva: Centre d'Art Contemporain Genève, 2007), 46.

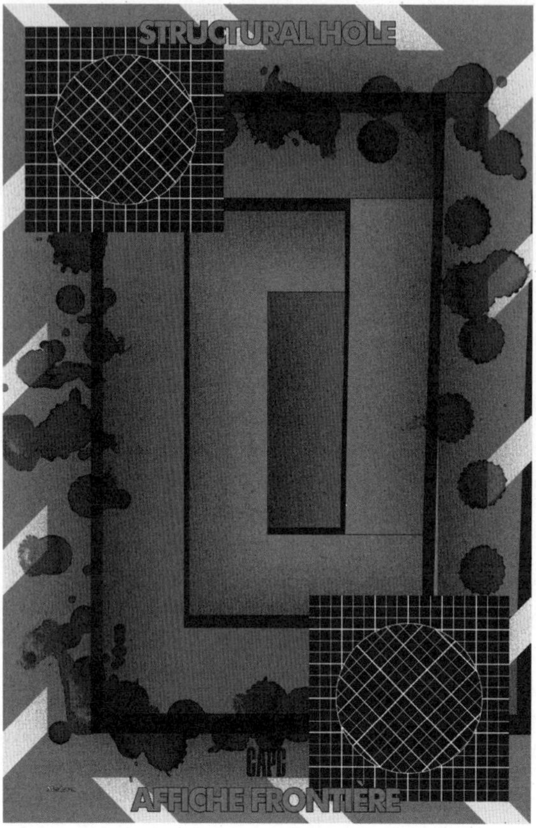

Metahaven, *Structural Hole* (poster from the series *Affiche Frontière*), 2008. © Metahaven and CAPC musée d'art contemporain de Bordeaux.

This is putting it too diffidently. Critical designers believe that design's role in society should be broader and more inquiring than simply serving the processes of manufacturing, promotion and consumption. While commerce and wealth generation are important, there are other areas of contemporary life – education, culture, health, the free exchange of information, democratic participation, sustainable living – to which design thinking (in its ordinary, non-business design sense) and design practice can make a vital contribution.

The British design duo Anthony Dunne and Fiona Raby have done most to formulate and disseminate critical design as a theoretical and operational position. Dunne used the term in the subtitle of his first book, *Hertzian Tales* (1999),[11] and Dunne & Raby's *Design Noir: The Secret Life of Electronic Objects* (2001) develops the concept. 'Critical design, or design that asks carefully crafted questions and makes us think, is just as difficult and just as important as design that solves problems or finds answers,' they write. 'Critical design takes as its medium social, psychological, cultural and economic values, in an effort to push the limits of lived experience not the medium.'[12] As pragmatically inclined theorists and committed educators, Dunne & Raby are exerting considerable influence on a new generation of critical designers

11. Anthony Dunne, *Hertzian Tales: Electronic Products, Aesthetic Experience, and Critical Design* (Cambridge, MA and London: MIT Press, 2005, second edition), 205.

12. Anthony Dunne and Fiona Raby, *Design Noir: The Secret Life of Electronic Objects* (London and Basel, August and Birkhäuser, 2001), 58.

– they teach in the Design Interactions department at the Royal College of Art, London.

For Dunne & Raby, as for other critical designers, the purpose of critical design is to stimulate discussion and debate among designers, industry and the public. Its basic tool is the speculative proposal – a design version of 'paper' or 'un-built' architecture – used to extrapolate the possibilities of design ideas that may never be realized as finished projects, or put into mass production. Proposals might take the form of plans, drawings, texts, videos or models. Using these devices, critical design has the potential to travel far beyond the usual boundaries of design conceived as an activity concerned primarily with the creation of commodities.

While a critical point of view will be the basis of any intelligent design process, it should be remembered that some designers have always taken the practice further. The stance of the early modernist artist-designers was a critical reaction – underpinned by utopian idealism – to the outdated aesthetic dogma, inefficient modes of production, and restrictive social conventions and political structures of the time. Intellectually and practically wide-ranging designers such as Charles and Ray Eames and Bruno Munari also have much in common with contemporary critical designers. 'When the objects we use every day and the surroundings we live in have become in themselves a work of art, then we shall be able to say we have achieved a balanced life,' writes Munari, a Futurist artist who later transferred his attentions to graphic and industrial design.[13] Victor Papanek's influential book *Design for the Real World* (1971) was a radical blueprint for rethinking design practice in terms of a more rational ecology. Also in the 1970s, the Italian team Superstudio mounted a sustained attack on architecture's and design's role in servicing the consumer culture. 'If design is merely an inducement to consume, then we must reject design . . . until all design activities are aimed towards meeting primary needs,' writes Superstudio member Adolfo Natalini.[14] The Dutch graphic designer Jan van Toorn, active in the 1970s and 1980s, provides another paradigm for the critically engaged practitioner. The critical designer, Van Toorn advised, should make viewers aware of the ways they are being manipulated by design by restructuring the message and making its code visible.[15]

In the 1990s, graphic design theorists, seeking greater autonomy for designers, proposed the idea of the 'designer as author', a self-motivated initiator of projects who was not content merely to carry out a client's bidding without offering a personal point of view.[16] This powerful idea has been taken on board by critically inclined industrial designers, most notably Dunne & Raby.[17] Another widely used term, representing a similar desire to reform design practice, is 'citizen designer' – an image that makes the designer's social responsibility plain.[18] As a developing category of design, critical design grows from the ideas and innovations of all these earlier design movements and tendencies.

13. Bruno Munari, *Design as Art* (London: Penguin Books, 2008, first published in 1966), 27.

14. Adolfo Natalini, 'Inventory, Catalogue, Systems of Flux . . . A Statement', in: Peter Lang and William Menking, *Superstudio: Life without Objects* (Milan: Skira Editore, 2003), 167.

15. See Rick Poynor, *Jan van Toorn: Critical Practice* (Rotterdam: 010 Publishers, 2008).

16. See Michael Roek, 'The Designer as Author', *Eye*, no. 20, vol. 5 (spring 1996), 44-53.

17. Dunne, *Hertzian Tales*, op. cit. (note 11), 75-78.

18. Steven Heller and Véronique Vienne (eds.), *Citizen Designer: Perspectives on Design Responsibility* (New York: Allworth Press, 2003).

Art and Design

Contemporary critical designers share some obvious concerns with contemporary artists. First, and most controversially, their work is often self-initiated, though this doesn't rule out working to commission for clients in the usual way. Second, the exhibition space is the primary platform for presenting their speculative projects and proposals and engaging the public. Third, some critical designers have working relationships and friendships with artists. British artist Ryan Gander, for instance, has close ties with designer-editor Stuart Bailey of Dexter Sinister – they have collaborated on a book – and both were included in the mix of artists and designers featured in *Wouldn't it be nice . . .* 'Our purpose is not to propose a destruction of the boundary [between art and design],' write the curators, 'but to create a space to investigate the divide in an environment where art asks questions of design and design asks questions of itself.'[19] Without already knowing which was which, it would have been difficult, solely on the basis of the projects presented in the exhibition, to distinguish the artists from the designers in most cases. Nevertheless, while some critical designers might indulge in wishful thinking that they could be taken seriously as artists, Dunne & Raby emphatically reject the idea that their work should be understood as art,

19. *Wouldn't it be nice . . .*, catalogue (London: Somerset House Embankment Galleries, 2008).

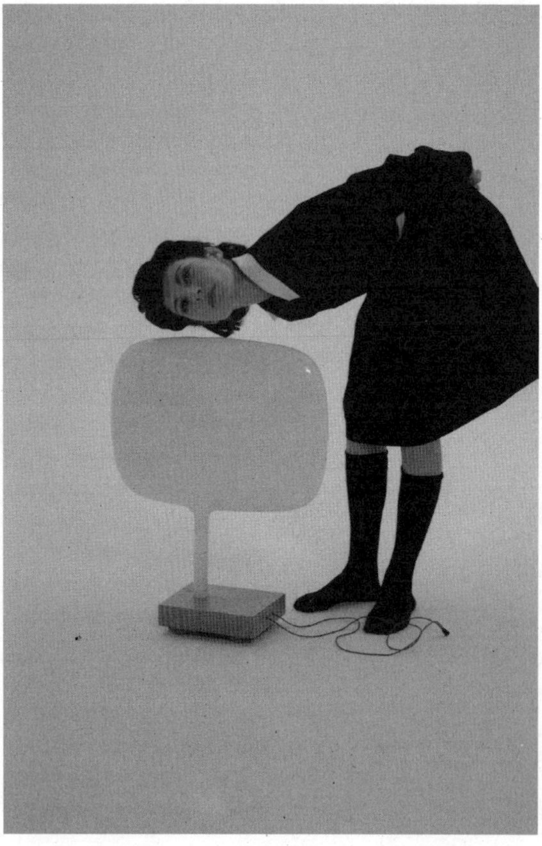

Dunne & Raby,
Robot 4: Needy one from *Technological Dreams Series: No.1, Robots*, 2007.
Photo: Per Tingleff.
© the artists.

although they dislike the separation of art and design and regard the blurring of boundaries as desirable. This is a view shared by the Dutch 'design think tank' Metahaven, founded by graphic designers Daniël van der Velden and Vinca Kruk and spatial designer Gon Zifroni, who were included – as was Bailey – in 'Forms of Inquiry'.[20] Both teams argue that the persuasive force of their projects, as visual arguments, depends on its framing and reception as design. These proposals are aimed at industry, policymakers and design's users, the public. If they were to be perceived as art, as purely fanciful constructions with no intended application, then it would be easy to dismiss them as catalysts for provoking changes in our use of design.

The ambiguous nature of critical design projects can be seen in Dunne & Raby's *Technological Dreams Series*, commissioned by curator Jan Boelen for 'Designing Critical Design' at Z33, and also shown in *Wouldn't it be nice . . .* and in *Design and the Elastic Mind* at the Museum of Modern Art (2008). The piece consists of four 'robots': Robot 1, a high-density foam ring; Robot 2, a funnel-like form; Robot 3, an angled wooden box; Robot 4, a white screen mounted on a movable wooden platform.[21] Presented only as immobile objects, these would have been un-engaging. What gives the series life and humour is a video by Noam Toran – also a critical designer – in which a young woman responds to each robot in a manner that reveals its personality. The woman, dressed with fetishistic formality in a black dress with white trimmings and long black socks, moves around the white space with studied grace and precision, circling, approaching and picking up the robots, so that her interactions take on the quality of a stylized rather than naturalistic performance. Robot 2 is described by the designers as nervous: it scans intruders with its many eyes and becomes agitated if they approach. Robot 4 is characterized as needy, fidgety and whiney. Using its own expressive electronic language, it calls the woman to encourage her to move it around, coaxing her into forming a symbiotic bond with its unfathomable machine intelligence. The robots prompt questions not only about the nature of our growing interdependence with complex forms of technology, but about the possible new relationships that might emerge as artificial intelligence evolves. In Dunne & Raby's science-fiction scenario, machines entirely lacking in human or animal attributes in their outward appearance nevertheless share emotional characteristics with children or pets that oblige human care-givers to react to their needs, demands and whims.

Technological Dreams' emotionally engaging micro-narrative works a similar effect on the viewer. Dunne & Raby might think like artists, but the cogency of their analysis comes from being situated in design. A curator asks Dunne what design must accomplish. 'The integration of poetry and everyday life,' he replies. 'A hybrid of politics and poetry . . . Design can only follow our

20. See Zak Kyes and Mark Owens (eds.), *Forms of Inquiry: The Architecture of Critical Graphic Design* (London: Architectural Association, 2007).

21. This follows the robots' numbering in Libby Hruska and Rebecca Roberts (eds.), *Design and the Elastic Mind* (New York: Museum of Modern Art, 2008), 28-29. The numbering differed elsewhere.

needs and desires, it can't create them. If our desires remain unimaginative and practical, then that is what design will be. I suppose in our projects we are hoping for a time when we will have more complex and subtle everyday needs than we do today. Our objects are designed in anticipation of that time. Patiently waiting. Maybe they are utopian.'[22] Measured against critical design's wild dreams, design thinking's rhetoric just sounds tawdry.

22. Anthony Dunne quoted in Christian Brändle, 'Dunne & Raby and Michael Anastassiades', in: King and Brändle, *Wouldn't it be nice* . . ., op. cit. (note 10), 165.

Middle Culture

Designers, Artists, Professionals

Camiel van Winkel

The opposition between high and low culture, between elite art and the culture industry, is a product of modernity. Historically the rise of mass culture must be linked to the appearance of the autonomous work of art. Each half of this pair can only be imagined in opposition to its 'other'. The split between high and low culture is more than a product or effect of modernity – you could say it is its foundation. To borrow a phrase from Boris Groys: 'Modernity is not only characterized, but even constituted by this split: in a sense modernity *is* nothing but this split.'[1] The autonomous work of art is inconceivable without its dialectical counterpart, its 'other': the heteronomous and the banal; the kitsch product; global mass entertainment. Before Beethoven and Balzac there was no such thing as kitsch. During the centuries of human civilization that passed before the autonomy of the artist was installed, mass culture didn't exist. It needed the technologies of mass communication, mass production and mass distribution in order to come into existence. Mass culture definitely is an industry, in every sense of the word.

1. Boris Groys, 'Fundamentalismus als Mittelweg zwischen Hoch- und Massenkultur', in: Boris Groys, *Logik der Sammlung. Am Ende des musealen Zeitalters* (Munich/Vienna: Carl Hanser Verlag, 1997), 63.

Both the autonomous work of art and the culture industry were predicated upon social, economical and technological changes that followed the Industrial Revolution, the demise of the *ancien régime* and the emancipation of the middle classes. Walter Benjamin's intuition that modern reproduction technologies would forever end the realm of the contemplative, elitist work of art has proven unfounded. The relationship between the two forms is dialectical. Art and mass culture are each other's spinoff . . . each other's debris . . . each other's perversion . . . each other's disgrace . . . This is a mechanism that cuts both ways: art is a derivative of mass culture just as much as mass culture is a derivative of high art. Mass culture amounts to junk when measured against the standards of high art, and similarly high art turns into junk when judged with the standards of mass culture. Fredric Jameson proposes 'that we read high and mass culture as objectively related and dialectically interdependent phenomena, as twin and inseparable forms of the fission of aesthetic production under capitalism.'[2] They are like two continents drifting apart after having broken off from some legendary Gondwanaland.

2. Fredric Jameson, 'Reification and Utopia in Mass Culture' (1979), in: Fredric Jameson, *Signatures of the Visible* (New York/ London: Routledge, 1992), 14.

The twin sister of mass culture is autonomous art; or, more specifically, autonomous *modernist* art. Jameson: 'From a historical point of view the only form of "high culture" which can be said to constitute the dialectical opposite of mass culture is that high culture production contemporaneous with the latter, which is to say that artistic production generally designated as *modernism*.'[3] What does this mean for the situation in which we find ourselves today? Although we still admire and absorb the products of modernism in museums, libraries and concert halls, its ideology, its theoretical mainframe, is a thing of the past. The artistic and ideological collapse of modernism implies that mass culture – its dialectical counterpart – has also stopped being an identifiable entity. In many ways we have moved beyond the high/ low division, and entered the cold, postmodern universe of cultural differences. Meaning is everywhere. Culture is an endless array of differences. Producing differences has become the ultimate meaning of life. The more culture is produced, the higher the number of cultural producers that claim to be different, and the smaller the differences become.

3. Ibid., 15.

Culturally we live in a universe of *microdifferences*, as philosopher Boris Groys stated in 1996: 'The new . . . is being produced ever faster and in ever bigger quantities . . . because people increasingly understand what it means to be innovative. On top of that the techniques of today not only allow for the exact reproduction of originals, they also make it possible to automatically generate deviations from those originals . . . Wherever you look today, it is all differences that you see.'[4]

4. Boris Groys, 'Die Zukunft gehört der Tautologie' (1995) in: Groys, *Logik der* Sammlung, op. cit. (note 1), 87.

Here is an example. In 1996 German artist Thomas Struth made a photographic work that represents a cemetery in the centre of Tokyo. The work is titled after the location: *Aoyama Cemetery*. There is an interesting formal play between the rectangular shapes of the gravestones and funerary monuments, and the tall office and apartment buildings in the background. Now if you do a simple search on a website such as flickr.com, you'll find that many photographers, both amateur and professional, have taken pictures on the same location. And some of their photo's look remarkably similar to the one made by Struth. They are variations on the same motif. Perhaps a comparison will show that Struth is the better photographer, and that his photograph is the most interesting. But still this case demonstrates that even intelligent, serious artists need to come to terms with the cultural imperative to produce work that is 'different'; and that in this respect they are facing the same conditions as cultural producers working in any other niche.

High & Low

There is a complicating factor. What used to be high and low culture have equally become mere products in the hands of marketeers. In that respect they are interchangeable. Art museums and video game producers target audiences in ways that are more or less the same. The culture of marketing is a middlebrow culture – not high-brow nor low-brow but *middlebrow*. The M of *money* is also the M of *mediocrity*. The pervasive marketing of culture has further contributed to the blurring of boundaries between high and low. High and Low could be described as the treble and bass controls on a stereo amplifier: two buttons that cultural marketeers turn up and down, with a lot of flair and opportunism, in their never-ending quest for the commercial optimum – the best mix to match their sale strategies.

Recently *Junglebook* appeared as a series of supermarket promotion gadgets at Albert Heijn. Spend 10 euros and get 2 fluffy figurines for free. Soon we will see Bouvard and Pécuchet as mass-produced garden sculptures at our local garden centre. Where will this end? *Kafka the Musical*??

Yet how are we to criticize developments like these, if they result in more people getting acquainted with art and culture, albeit through a derivative spin-off? After all, that's perfectly in line with the educational ideology of museums and other cultural institutions. As a mode of self-legitimation, education is the bottom line for cultural institutions, when everything else has failed.

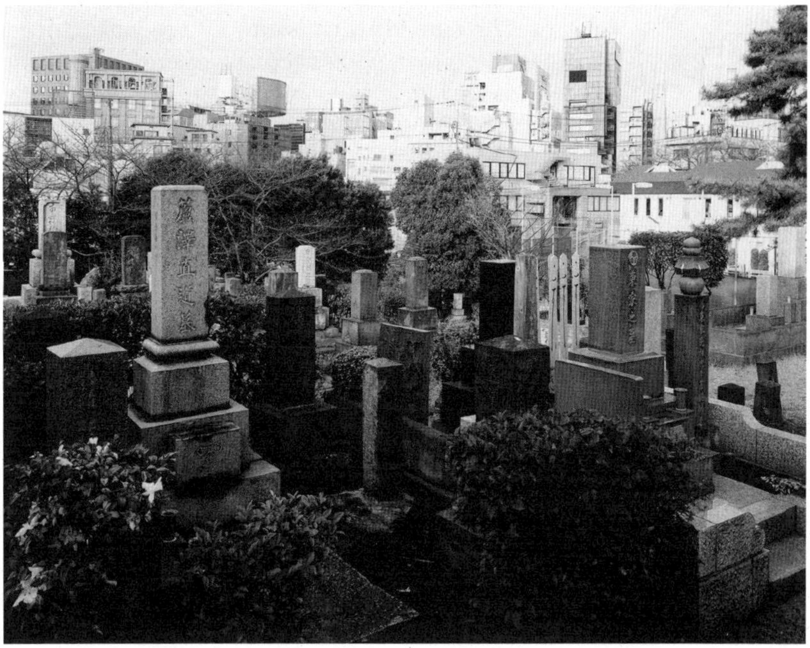

Thomas Struth, *Ayoma Cemetery 2*, Tokyo, 1996. © Thomas Struth.

The real problem of high and low is the fact that we lack terms to define it as a problem. We no longer have an intellectual or ideological foundation to base such a critique on. This explains why for the cultural consumer of today, the issue of high and low is not an issue at all. Consumers have a right to their own bad taste, and they are proud of it. They have other things to worry about. In the twentieth century the middle classes became aware of an urgent need for a cultural identity. As the higher and lower strata inevitably converge towards some gravitational centre, the middle classes discover that they lack a set of recognizable cultural signifiers or markers that are theirs and only theirs. This lack of a cultural identity is a major source of social anxiety. The anxiety is suspended – not resolved but suspended – by continuously absorbing and compounding bits of identity from other (older) classes and social layers: tokens and accessories, jammed together to form an uncertain heterogeneous ensemble. Tattoos used to be the trademark of sailors and prisoners; now even sales managers and real estate agents have them. The middle classes have become obsessed with lifestyle. In fact the obsession with lifestyle is the main cultural trait of the middle classes today.

Contemporary fashion design is just a formalized version of this anxiety-driven middle-class quest for a stable identity. Each 'look' in fashion is like a contrived montage of social and class signifiers:

The bohemian-bourgeois hippie-gypsy colonial look.
The military outfit meets Rasta coffeeshop hangout look.
The riding boots with carpenter's pants and nipple piercings look.
The ripped jeans with vintage geisha accessories look.
The closet-gay executive asshole meets old-money property-owner look.
The Mao-costume with pearl necklace look.
The late November fox-hunting seventies disco look.
The punky fluorescent secretary look.
The Louis Quatorze trampy homeless look.

If mass culture is the culture of the masses, the middle, the majority, who could pretend *not* to be permeated by it? Mass culture is not something you can step outside of. It's inside us. It's inside you, and inside me. The high/low tandem may have once been an objective division of cultural production, but now it's all in your head. High and low are two emotions, two distinct emotions, two forms of desire – two opposite forms of mental saturation . . . High and low are the cultural equivalent of *uppers* and *downers* in the drug department. And as everyone knows, the choice between uppers and downers is purely a matter of consumption, of consumer behaviour; the demand is strictly individual and may vary from moment to moment; the 'intake' has been stripped of moral qualifications.

If the Low is a *horizontal* state of mind, its opposite, High, is an emotional state related to the *vertical*. On the high end of the spectrum, there is the rush, a sensation of limitless energy, stimulation, euphoria. Your brain seems to expand, your sense of self dematerializes, you start to float, you no longer feel your own body. You are launched into a sublime void, a dematerialized universe. On the other end of the spectrum we find the low emotion, the cultural equivalent of a downer. It entails a slow move into 'dreamy nether regions' – the realm of relaxation, tranquillization and indulgence. This emotion is driven by the desire to give up all resistance and critical consciousness; to just follow the thick flow of bodily desire.

'Good Design'

Contemporary cultural production is determined by two general conditions. The first can be identified as *the regime of visibility*. This implies that nothing matters unless it has been clearly visualized. To be seen, to be noted, to stand out, to be different is the primary aim of any cultural or social act. Success equals visibility and visibility equals success.[5]

The second condition is *the dictate of professionalism*. Criteria of effective process management and good entrepreneurship increasingly dominate the cultural field. These general criteria of professionalism have become crucial for the recognition of quality in cultural production. Cultural producers are confronted with the imperative of effectiveness, competence, networking, efficient communication, audience targeting, rational budget management, total quality control, and so on and so on.

What does this imply for the realm of visual art? One implication is that, socially, culturally and economically, visual art is being pushed into the corner of *design*. It is not understood, and less and less accepted, why works of art could not have the same kind of direct public appeal and economic spin-off that the various sectors of applied art, such as fashion and industrial design, seem to have. Design stands out as a domain that bridges or transcends the dichotomy of art and mass culture. More efficiently than anything else, it brings together the realms of high and low. This explains why it has become an increasingly successful model of cultural production. Design makes the opposition between high and low culture seem obsolete. Everything becomes design in the sense that criteria of 'good design' are being applied to every single cultural domain.

Fundamentally, to use a phrase coined by Dutch design critic Hugues Boekraad, design is 'the quintessence of postmodern self-determination'. Boekraad says: 'The less we conduct our life in accordance with the precepts of tradition or inner conviction, the more it is influenced by professional languages and patterns of action and by categories of evaluation and observation. It is at that moment that designers make their appearance. The function of design – including the design of one's own life – has become so

5. Cf. Camiel van Winkel, *The Regime of Visibility* (Rotterdam: NAi Publishers, 2005).

dominant that it can serve as a metaphor for post-traditional life. In the absence of prescribed forms, life becomes a quest for new forms.'[6] So the paradox is that the professional tools and languages of design have become central to the lives of professionals and non-professionals alike.

6. Frederike Huygen and Hugues Boekraad, *Wim Crouwel: Mode en module* (Rotterdam: 010 Publishers, 1997), 189 and 192.

As regards the professionals, this image shows what they probably look like. It represents the Philips design department, as photographed for last week's issue of *NRC Focus* business magazine. The caption says: 'These individuals' task is to design products that make consumers happy and improve the quality of their lives.' I hope everyone hears the faint echo of Stendhal's *promesse de bonheur* in this job description.

In fact it is a very interesting group portrait. What you see here boils down to the corporate or 'lite' version of an avant-garde artist collective. The Philips product designers have been represented as a group of young, self-assured, metrosexual, ambitious and extremely focused team workers. They have surrounded themselves with all sorts of utensils for spontaneous artistic creation, ready to grab whenever a brilliant idea for a new Philips invention pops up. While pampered by the company, you can tell that on top of that these individuals are really the ideal employees of today, completely devoted to their work, utterly flexible, ready to prepare work presentations and answer e-mails in the weekend, as creativity knows no bounds.

My point is not that designers have become artists but, on the contrary, that designers provide the new role model for artists. Given the prominence of the criteria of 'good design', the notion of what a good work of art is has changed. A new consensus about what an artist is or does, what they can or should do, is being formed. This is partly the outcome of developments outside the domain of art, such as the successful rhetoric of the 'creative industry' and 'creative class', launched by Richard Florida.[7] But similar impulses have come from within the art milieu itself. Movements in contemporary art of the last ten to fifteen years have actually contributed to this gradual redefinition.

7. Richard Florida, *The Rise of the Creative Class: And How It's Transforming Work, Leisure, Community and Everyday Life* (New York: Basic Books, 2003).

So what exactly is the new consensus? Good art communicates with its 'users'; it is open and transparent. Good art is highly aware of its context and uses that awareness to responsibly create a 'place' for itself. More generally as well, it stems from a socially responsible attitude. Good art generates constructive communication between people. It avoids effects of alienation and estrangement. It does not impose any absolutes. It has a positive effect on a local community. It is interactive and brings out the best in people. It offers a unique experience. It generously accepts and stimulates an active response from individuals. Intended or not, these quality criteria move the work of art deeper and deeper into the rhetoric of contemporary design.

Of course, both among the general audience and in professional art circles you will still find the popular notion that art is

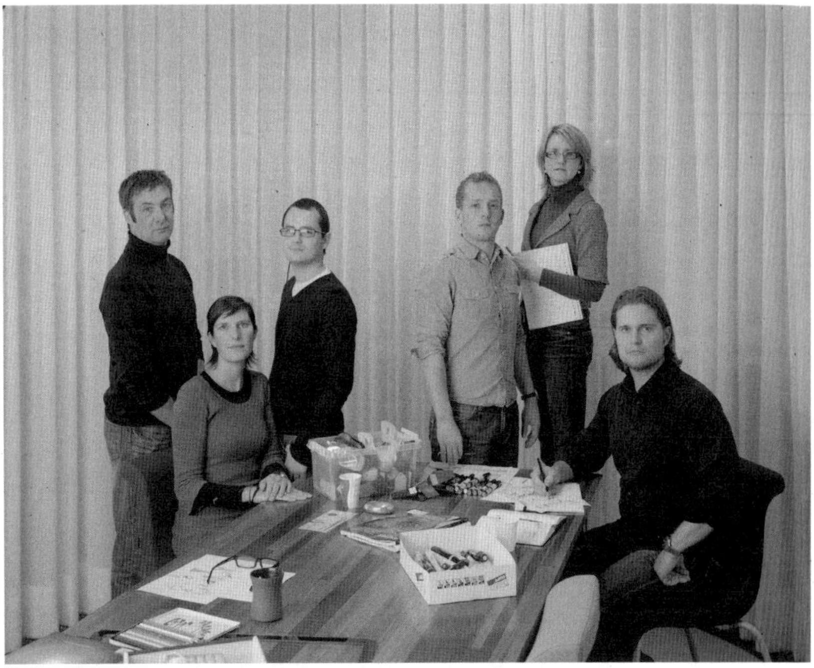

Henk Wildschut,
group photo Philips Design
Department, 2008.
© Henk Wildschut.

the domain of the unusual, the unexpected, the bizarre, the uncompromised, the domain where the mediocrity of everyday life can be overcome and transcended. But beneath or besides that notion one feels the presence of another kind of discourse, a discourse that increasingly gains strength, especially due to changes in the institutional and educational setting of art. According to this discourse, artists are educated, competent 'professionals' that aspire to learn and develop themselves all through their career. They have well-researched ideas *and* possess the ability to communicate and discuss those ideas. They feel responsible about the place and the effect of art in society. They keep themselves up-to-date with the latest developments in their profession. Of course they have a Master's degree and are thinking about doing a PhD . . .

Applied Concept Art

If all this appears to be a relatively recent trend, it also happens to be the culmination of an older process. Ever since it came into being as a distinct genre, around 1970, contemporary art has been the domain of a paradigm or ideology that is remarkably close to that of design. In fact you could say that what we call *contemporary art* is nothing but the result of the conditioning of visual art by the two forces that I have identified: the regime of visibility and the dictate of professionalism.

Contemporary art is a kind of 'applied concept art' – a hybrid of *form* and *concept*, applied to a specific *context*. These terms – form, concept and context – together make up the fundamental discursive triangle underlying the production and reception of art. The making of a contemporary work of art is a three-step process. First, an analysis of the context provides the artist with the specifications for the development of the concept. Next, the concept is executed and made to take form. And finally, the form is such that it can be productively applied to the original context. Just as in the case of the design professions, concept and execution are separate dimensions. The concept is primary; the execution may be subcontracted, handed over to assistants or skilled craftsmen, or done industrially, as long as the artist supervises the process, takes all important decisions, and determines the final outcome. In order to produce a work of art that is 'authentic' and 'authored', it is not necessary for the artist to do the execution, the material labour, him- or herself. This means that, at a fundamental level, works of art today are *designed* rather than just *made*. In contemporary art this has become so evident that we hardly think about it anymore. Conceptual art in the 1960s was already haunted by the spectre of design, as I have tried to show in my book *The Regime of Visibility*. Contemporary art is post-conceptual as a whole, in the double sense that it *comes after* and *is permeated by* conceptual art. The triangle form-concept-context essentially is a post-conceptual matrix that underlies the whole of contemporary art production.

Let's take a random work of art and see what the implications are for the measure of success in contemporary art: Damien Hirst, *The Physical Impossibility of Death in the Mind of Someone Living* (1992). Why is this such a successful work? You could almost say it is the quintessential model of success in contemporary art. I think anyone can tell you why it is successful. Here's why:

Its concept is simple.
It can be recognized from miles away.
Once you've seen it, you'll never forget it.
Whether you like it or not, it *works*.
It's great to take pictures of.
It has plenty of entertainment and spectacle value.
Anyone will feel addressed by it.
It's the trademark of its maker.
It's unpretentious *and* unbelievable.
It's unheard-of yet completely evident.
It suggests it is the universal symbol of . . . something.
And the media love it.

It can hardly be a coincidence that these characteristics perfectly match the list of criteria for the design of a successful logo, as provided by Gregory Thomas and Earl Powell in their book *How to Design Logos, Symbols & Icons*.[8] Thomas and Powell give ten criteria for the development of a successful logo. Let's go through them, while keeping Hirst's shark in mind.

8. Gregory Thomas and Earl A. Powell, *How to Design Logos, Symbols & Icons. 23 Internationally Renowned Studios Reveal how they Develop Trademarks for Print and New Media* (Cincinnati: North Light Books, 2000), 20.

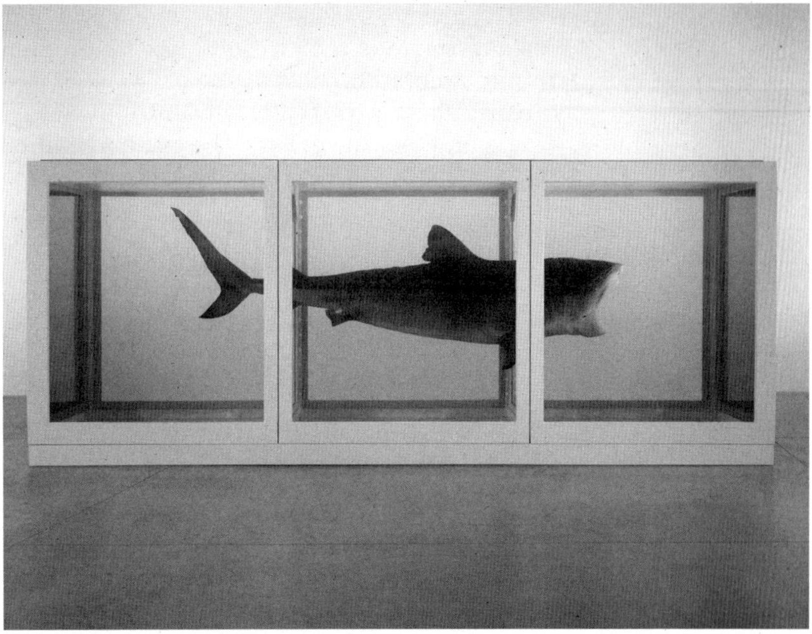

Damien Hirst, *The Physical Impossibility of Death in the Mind of Someone Living,* 1991, Metropolitan Museum of Art, New York. Photo: Prudence Cuming Associates. © Damien Hirst.

> *Visibility*: Will the logo stand out in its surroundings to provide quick and memorable identification?
> *Cross-media application*: How well can it be used in a variety of applications?
> *Distinctiveness*: Will it distinguish itself from its competition?
> *Simplicity and universality*: Is the concept easy to identify?
> *Retention*: Does the symbol give the viewer a sense of discovery and personal equity with the mark?
> *Effectiveness in colour and black and white*: Does it work in technologies that are unable to display the subtle nuances of some colour patterns?
> *Descriptiveness*: Does it reveal the nature of the company or product?
> *Timelessness*: Will it last?
> *Modularity*: Will the potential mark be adaptable to numerous applications?
> *Equity*: Does the mark respect the 'age, use and recognition' of its predecessors?

Even if Damien Hirst might fail that final test, the criterion of equity, he still gets a score of nine out of ten . . .

All this leaves us with the question whether there is a future for visual art as an autonomous discipline. Is there a way out of the current situation? Both art and the artistic profession will continue to develop – not in big quantum leaps, but slowly. These changes will always reflect the social demands and cultural aspirations of the period.

The artist-as-designer is a strong and highly contemporary format or model that will not lose its prominence any time soon. In fact it could be seen as the outcome of developments that already started in the early twentieth century and even has roots in the nineteenth century: the gradual collapse of the notion of a fine art métier, the growing obsolescence of the idea of the artist as craftsman, and the rise of the artist as 'professional without profession'. When seen in this light, the contemporary status of visual art as 'applied concept art' is the endpoint of a long process. At the moment I don't see any alternative for it, and the return to some kind of centralized craft or métier most certainly is not a solution. That road is definitely closed.

If the model of 'applied concept art' now starts to feel more restrictive and less productive than it has before, this says less about the model itself than about the way it is being implemented in the current socioeconomic order. I am referring to the increased pressure to consider the artistic occupation as a normal profession in compliance with general norms of professionalism and entrepreneurship. This restrictive application of the model is not inherent to the model itself.

There is one important thing to keep in mind: contemporary art will continue to have its own discourse, its own theories, its own frame of reference. Even when in form and appearance the differences between works of art and other cultural artefacts will have disappeared completely, there will always be the manic tendency towards self-reflection that characterizes the contemporary visual artist. Out of this self-reflection, possibilities may continue to arise to formulate alternatives to the dominant model – if only imaginary alternatives. More than ever the development of strong artistic discourse seems crucial.

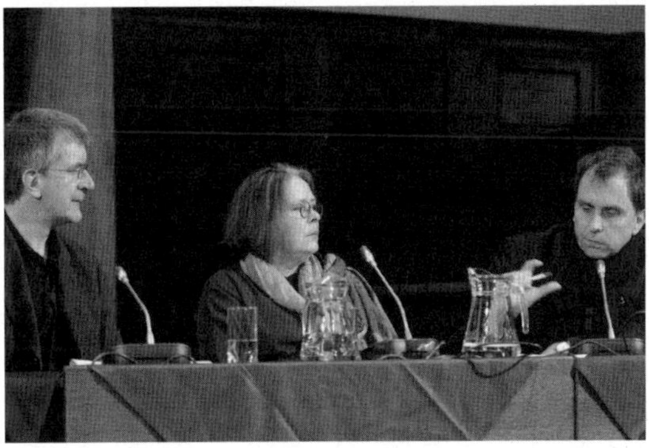

Rick Poynor, Frederike Huygen and Camiel van Winkel.

Discussion

The discussion was moderated by Frederike Huygen, design historian and critic specialized in Dutch Design.

Moderator: One thing we seem to agree on is that design is also part of consumerism, visibility, identities, marketing and commercial interest. Most designers we are talking about are trying to escape those areas of working. Camiel, in your lecture you mainly seem to associate design with a process, a strategy, with professionalism, almost as if you think that design is a managerial skill. But what kind of cultural values do you think design is about? Could you perhaps clarify your own position?

Camiel van Winkel: I am trying to get away from the discussion about cultural values, and from the high-low opposition. For me as a critic it is no longer productive to think in those terms. Rick Poynor wants to prove somehow that design is not inherently instrumental. I think it *is* instrumental, and there is nothing wrong with that. Design is part of an industrial production process, and most designers work for clients. Design is an applied art form. However, I don't want to attach old-fashioned value judgements to that. In my lecture I proposed a few mechanisms that could explain the success design has today, and I have tried to analyse how that influences the way we look at works of art.

Rick Poynor: There are designers who resist the notion of design as pure instrumentality. They look around for what seems to them a more workable model. Of course they look enviously in the direction of the artist. If you are trying to produce a kind of free autonomous work, where will it go, if not the gallery? The media which designers are adept at using present opportunities for all kinds of intervention and so does self-initiated work that makes use of an existing medium. So if a designer produces a book, well yes, this is a commodity, but it can have other purposes, other meanings, determined by the designer as a kind of author. I'm not suggesting that all design should aspire to do this, I'm simply saying that those possibilities exist and that they seem to be worthwhile as tools for reflection. This instrumental design we're talking about is the result of an abandonment of certain kinds of values. Is this not a worrying development? If art really cares about design so much, then at least we should address what design has been historically, what it thinks about itself and look at some examples of individuals who have tried to break with the norms. Camiel van Winkel's diagnosis in his lecture is spot-on. The question is: Can we do something about it, and is it desirable to do something about it? That's where we should start.

Camiel van Winkel: The problem I have with your approach is that you overestimate the effect of critical designers. I feel you have come here tonight with the intention to gain support for the idea of a critical-intellectual base in the design community. Just like you I'm happy that that base exists, but I think it is fairly marginal in relation to other things going on in society; on top of that it relies exclusively on an art context. To focus on this critical segment is a way of turning your back against the mainstream of design, which sits comfortably in the middle between the 'design thinking' adopted by corporations on the one hand, and the critical designers on the other. This is particularly unsatisfactory now that a lot of design thinking already has permeated society via the mainstream. Whether you like it or not, that's an interesting fact that we need to look at.

Rick Poynor: It's undeniably interesting and I also agree that critical design is a marginal activity at the moment. So I talk about it in the spirit of frantically trying to fan the flames, which I think we need to do, to create the possibility of development. This is at least a moment, a critical moment, when some designers seem prepared to name themselves, organize themselves, and commit themselves to thinking about the purpose of design and all of that seems to me culturally useful. Why give in to defeatism?

Moderator: Why is it so difficult to get across the importance that design can have as a social agent, let's say something integrated in the real world with an added value that is not necessarily the nice bag, or on the other extreme, the designer as an artist on the gallery wall?

Camiel van Winkel: I have the impression that the two of you, as intellectuals, feel slightly embarrassed by the enormous social success of design as a form of cultural production. Art museums increasingly show design objects rather than works of art, because they have trouble finding audiences and with design that seems to be easier to achieve. Design objects always look nice, they have a broad, general appeal, and they are not difficult to explain. Of course, designers love to show their work in museums because it gives them a higher status. Still there has always been this bad conscience in the design world, which I think goes back to the basic fact that designers are not artists. They come from the same modernist Bauhaus tradition, but they lack the autonomy that artists have. Especially when their commercial success increases, the embarrassment grows.

Rick Poynor: I don't think there's a contradiction. Design is all around us, we do inhabit it and the designer, as the creator, shaper and contributor to that world, is absolutely implicated. But being in the thick of things means we have to be honest and open in our communication about the nature of own complicity. We have to make that visible. Now, of course, that is an idealistic and utopian notion in itself and in practice, from project to project, day after day as a designer, fantastically hard to do.

Kaja Silverman - The Twilight of Posterity

NOW media

Laura U. Marks - Aniconism

Art & Theory

TIME

Media

Media in the field of the arts often generate a discourse of the 'new'. In the previous decades artistic interactions with film, TV and video were principally interpreted as an attempt to break with the ancient modernist desire for purity and medium specificity. New terms such as 'multimedia', 'mixed media' and 'intermedia' were created to describe these hybrid amalgams that offered the arts a bright future outside the white cube. The rupture with the past became even bigger in the 1990s, when the rise of the digital media inspired many to believe that nothing would ever be the same again. The 'new' media would lead the art world into a paradigmatic shift from the analogue to the digital, from the passive to the interactive, from producer to consumer, from the real to the virtual, from the visual to the synaesthetic.

In the new millennium the challenge for media art and its academic reflection, seems to be a distancing from, or even subversion of, this discourse of the 'new'. Probing questions that fuel such efforts are: Should we stop looking at the technological aspect of new media (art) and instead look at more structural characteristics? In what ways can we compare such characteristics to those of older, analogue forms of art? Should one practice 'media archaeology' and 'media art history' instead of a discourse of the new based on ruptures and paradigmatic changes?

In this line of thought, Kaja Silverman brings into play an installation by James Coleman in order to expose the historical embeddedness of contemporary media concepts, such as transitoriness and reproduction. Going as far back as Leonardo da Vinci's paintings and drawings, Silverman is able to rethink the relationships between contemporary new media art and the history of painting and drawing. Laura U. Marks makes in her contribution the argument that in order to understand the impact of the algorithmic and aniconic nature of contemporary media art we have to take a closer look at their correspondences with ancient Islamic art and thinking. In other words, Silverman and Marks show how in the twenty-first century the media have returned from the future in order to reconnect the new to the past.

Kaja Silverman (USA) is professor of rhetoric and film at the University of California, Berkeley. Silverman's research is essentially interdisciplinary, focussing on fields such as cinema, (time-based) visual arts, photography and literature. Her specialist topics include psychoanalysis, phenomenology and semiotics, with an ongoing commitment to feminism. Among Silverman's numerous publications are *The Subject of Semiotics* (1983), *Speaking About Godard* (1998), *World Spectators* (2000) and *Flesh of My Flesh* (2009).

Laura U. Marks (CAN) is professor of contemporary arts at Simon Fraser University, Canada. She specializes in new media art, experimental cinema, film theory and Arab and Islamic arts. Marks's publications include *The Skin of the Film: Intercultural Cinema, Embodiment and the Senses* (2000), *Touch: Sensuous Theory and Multisensory Media* (2000) and the forthcoming *Enfoldment and Infinity: An Islamic Genealogy of New Media Art*.

The Twilight of Posterity

Kaja Silverman

I

In June 2003, the Louvre mounted a major exhibition of Leonardo's work. It included many of the artist's drawings and manuscripts; sketches from the Verrocchio workshop, where Leonardo apprenticed; drawings from a number of his followers, the *Léonardesques*;[1] an 'intervention' by contemporary Irish artist James Coleman; and one of Leonardo's paintings, *Virgin and Child with Saint Anne*. Coleman's intervention had six components, dispersed throughout the exhibition space – a wall text, four small sets of black-and-white video editing monitors, and a large-screen digital projection of *The Last Supper*. The images on these five screens corresponded in complex ways both with the rest of the exhibition and with each other.

Inconspicuous, and lacking a room of their own, the four sets of editing monitors appeared to be 'informational' rather than aesthetic. Few visitors stopped to look at them. They displayed ghostly renditions of several works by Leonardo that did not appear elsewhere in the exhibition. The colour projection, on the other hand, was impossible to miss. In sumptuous colour, one image after another of Leonardo's painting *The Last Supper* filled an enormous screen. Sometimes this image was a 'shot' of the whole painting, taken via what appeared to be a stationary camera setup. At other times, the 'camera' focused on the left or right side of the painting, before slowly panning to the other side. On yet other occasions, it zeroed in on a detail of the painting, through sometimes so extreme a close-up that figuration gave way to pure abstraction. Each of these images occupied the screen for long enough to outgrow its status as a detail, and become a painting in its own right. But then another with an equal claim to be *The Last Supper* would fill the screen.

A text written by Coleman was printed on the wall at the beginning of the exhibition:

> Invité à concevoir un projet pour le musée du Louvre à l'occasion de l'exposition Léonard de Vinci, dessins et manuscrits,

1. This was a category created by the curators of the exhibition.

> James Coleman a restitué, à l'aide de documents, un certain nombre d'oeuvres de Léonard non présentes dans l'exposition. Les images qu'il a sélectionnées sont diffusées sur des écrans situés en différents points du parcours de l'exposition. La Cène du Réfectoire de Sainte Marie des Grâces à Milan dispose d'un espace à elle seule et est présentée par une projection numérique. Les oeuvres montrées constituent une sorte d'archivage ou de mémoire éphémère et leur réception est indissociable du contenu de l'exposition.

This text began conventionally enough, with the mention of the Louvre's invitation to Coleman to 'conceive a project . . . on the occasion of [its] exposition of Leonardo da Vinci, drawings and manuscripts'. His response to this invitation, however, took a surprising form, and one to which I will not be able to do justice in English. 'Il a restitué,' the wall text informed the viewer, 'a l'aide de documents, un certain nombre d'oeuvres de Léonard non présentes dans l'exposition.' The most obvious translation of this sentence would be: '[Coleman] restored a number of works by Leonardo which were not present in the exhibition.' However, this would be a misleading translation, because Coleman didn't restore any of the works he selected. There is also no one-to-one relationship between the French verb *restituer* and the English verb 'to restore'; the former could also be translated as 'to reconstitute', or 'to reproduce'. But neither of these verbs would be any more satisfactory, since the first would foreground the archival aspects of Coleman's project, but leave its aesthetic features unacknowledged and the second effect a reverse exclusion. For reasons that will become clear later, the only feature of any of these words which is adequate to the task at hand is the one they share with the original: the prefix 're'.

In his wall text, Coleman suggested that his digital images provided 'a kind of archive or ephemeral memorial' for Leonardo's work. 'Ephemeral memorial' is an oxymoron; it combines the notion of 'transitoriness' with that of a 'lasting testimony'. Coleman used the word 'ephemeral' in part because his intervention was site-specific, like Robert Smithson's *Spiral Jetty*. He also emphasized the ephemeral nature of his images because they constituted a process, rather than a product. The French word that I have translated as 'archive' is *archivage*, a neologism created to underscore the difference between his intervention, and a more conventional archive. Most archives work by lifting things out of time, and making them part of a synchronic system. Coleman's did the opposite; it provided the space within which a series of images could emerge, and then disappear. Finally, with the word 'ephemeral', Coleman served notice that he would not allow his intervention to be documented. When the exhibition closed, there was nothing to testify to its having-been-here – no photographic or video record of the sort that per-

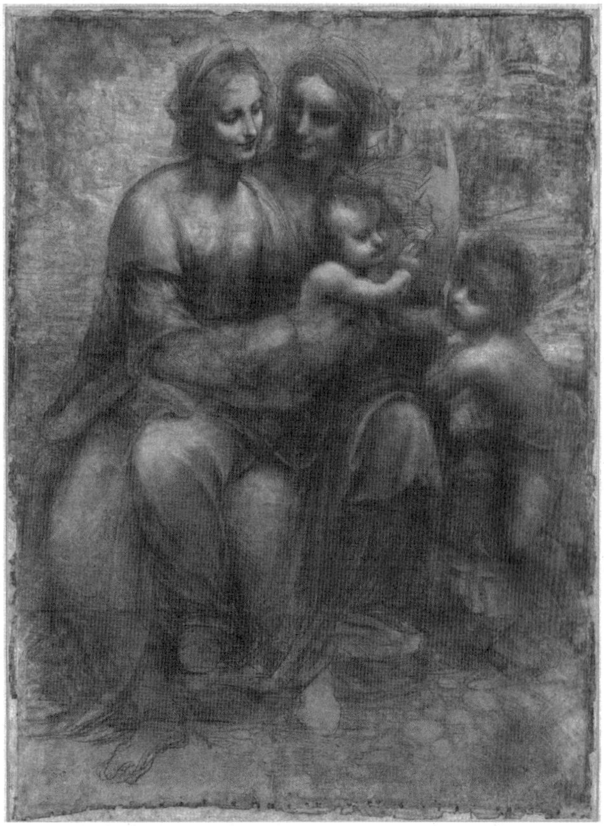

Leonardo da Vinci, *The Virgin and Child with Saint Anne and Saint John the Baptist*, 1499-1500. © National Gallery, London.

mitted us to visualize *Spiral Jetty* while it was still submerged in water.[2]

In the last sentence of Coleman's wall text, he did not say that his images were 'indissociable from the contents of the exhibition'; he said, rather, that their 'reception' was. The word 'reception' has a technological meaning; we use it when speaking about the transmission of audio, visual, or audio-visual information. In this context, it refers to the amount of information which is likely to arrive at a given destination; in some places radio or television reception is 'good', and in others 'bad'. Because Coleman used the word 'transmission' in the first sentence of his wall text, in connection with the editing monitors, 'reception' communicated this technological meaning when it emerged in the final sentence.

But 'reception' can also index what happens to a broadcast when it arrives at its destination. And whereas radio or television reception tends to be the same for everyone living on a particular block, an audio or audio-visual transmission will not be received by all of them in the same way. What such a broadcast represents to an individual viewer can also change dramatically over time. When the word 'reception' appeared in the last sentence of the wall text, it also conveyed this meaning, since it rubbed shoulders both with 'exhibition' and another word which cannot be

2. For a recent photographic documentation of *Spiral Jetty*, see Eve Meltzer, 'Now You See It: Robert Smithson's *Spiral Jetty*', *Frieze Magazine*, no. 72 (January 2003), 48-49. George Baker provides a brilliant discussion of Smithson's own filmic documentation of the work in 'The Cinema Model', in: Lynne Cooke and Karen Kelly (eds.), *Robert Smithson: The Spiral Jetty* (New York: Dia Art Foundation with the University of California Press, 2005), 79-113.

adequately translated into English: *memoire*. In addition to 'memorial', this last word can mean 'human memory' and 'hard-drive'. With it, Coleman challenged the notion that a computer is a storage system, which preserves what we put on it. He also reminded us that our memories are as provisional as the digital images of *The Last Supper*. Finally, he expressed his hope that the viewers of the Louvre exhibition would do for his images what he did for Leonardo's – provide them with an ephemeral memorial. It is in the spirit of this hope, and not as a documentation of Coleman's intervention, that I offer this analysis.

II

The meaning activated by Coleman through the verb *diffuser* has only been available for about a hundred years. The same is true of its English equivalent, 'to transmit'. During the nineteenth century, 'transmission' functioned primarily as a signifier for 'hereditary conveyance'. The values handed down from one generation to another throughout history have been heavily patriarchal, regardless of the agency of their transmission. Wealth and property have also passed from father to son, and even in cultures where women are allowed to inherit these things, men remain the only 'legal' recipients of another kind of legacy – that implied by the Name-of-the-Father.[3] Transmission is also a crucial component within the system of exchange upon which patriarchal cultures are based, a system within which men are the subjects, and women one of the things that circulate among them.[4]

Art has traditionally served as one of the most important vehicles for generational transmission. As Gregg Horowitz puts it: 'In all past art, we can locate an implicit conception of generations bound together through representational and affective practices. Succeeding generations were conceived as the bearers of a past in which the past imagined itself overcoming its finitude, and art was the sensuous vehicle of this transmission.'[5] Horowitz argues that since Kant, art has no longer been able to perform this function, but in making this claim he overlooks a crucial institution: the museum. Modernist art and aesthetics may, indeed, be 'born of a perception of the finitude of sensuous life', but this is not a perception available to most viewers, since museums treat contemporary paintings, drawings and sculptures in the same way they treat earlier ones: they preserve them for the future, and at the first sign of wear and tear they restore them. When a museum commissions a work of art, it is generally with the expectation that the artist will create something precious that can be added to its holdings, and transmitted – like the *Mona Lisa* – to posterity.

By characterizing this commission as an invitation to 'conceive' something, Coleman drew attention to the intimate connection between aesthetic transmission and paternal transmission. He himself, though, refused to step into the symbolic position of a 'father'. He also effaced himself as author, thereby removing

3. I take the notion of a paternal legacy from Jacques Lacan, who discusses it in 'Function and Field of Speech and Language in Psychoanalysis', in: Jacques Lacan, *Ecrits*, translated by Bruce Fink (New York: Norton, 2006), 197-268.
4. See Claude Lévi-Strauss, *Elementary Structures of Kinship*, translated by James Harle Bell and John Richard von Sturmer (Boston: Beacon, 1969); Luce Irigaray, *This Sex Which Is Not One*, translated by Catherine Porter (Ithaca: Cornell University Press, 1985), 170-197; and Gayle Rubin, 'Traffic in Women: Notes on the "Political Economy" of Sex', in: Rayna Raiter (ed.), *Toward an Anthropology of Women* (New York: Monthly Review Press, 1975), 157-210. I am emphasizing the phallic meaning of 'transmission', in spite of the fact that it is not part of the semantic field of *diffuser*, because this meaning was operative at so many other points in the exhibition.
5. Gregg M. Horowitz, *Sustaining Loss: Art and Mournful Life* (Stanford: Stanford University Press, 2001), 13.

one of the primary sources of aesthetic value; built an expiration date into his images; and prevented them from cohering into an independent work of art even during the brief tenure of their existence. Finally, he protected his images from a posthumous entification by making the human psyche the only possible agency of their memorialization.[6]

6. Douglas Crimp discusses a number of other contemporary artists who have a contestatory relationship to the museum in his important book, *On the Museum's Ruins* (Cambridge, MA: MIT Press, 1993).

7. Lacan, 'Function and Field', op. cit. (note 3), 230.

III

Although Coleman 'confused' the 'generations', as Lacan would say, the exhibition in which he participated seemed on a first viewing to 'knot and braid' the 'thread of lineage'.[7] As I have already mentioned, the Louvre displayed works by three different generations of artists, the first of whom transmitted a certain 'know-how' to the second, and the second of whom constituted a model for the third. The passage printed on the wall beside the door leading to Leonardo's early work also provided a classic instantiation of oedipal revolt; in it, the artist imputes to himself the capacity to create *ex nihilo*, thereby usurping not only his earthly father, but also God the Father. 'If the painter wishes to see beauties capable of inspiring love,' this passage reads, 'he has the ability [to create] them, and if he wishes to see monstrous things that frighten, or jests that cause laughter, or things that inspire piety, he is their lord and master. If he wishes to create landscapes, or deserts, or fresh and shady places in warm weather, he depicts them . . . If he wishes valleys, if he wishes to disclose great sweeps of land from the high peaks of mountains . . . he has the power to do so . . . all that exists in the universe through essence, real or imaginary, he has it first in his mind and then in his hands. And these are of such excellence that at a given moment they create a proportioned harmony taken in by the eye as the reality itself.'[8]

8. This is from an entry in the *Codex Urbanus* which has the heading 'How the painter is master of all sorts of people and of all things'. See Leonardo da Vinci, *Leonardo on Art and the Artist*, edited by André Chastel (New York: Dover, 2002), 51.

But in the first room of the exhibition, the yarn of lineage began to unravel. This room was divided into two parts: one devoted to drawings by Verrocchio and the artists in his atelier, and the other to a series of drapery studies. Although the Louvre identified Leonardo as the source of the drapery studies, and indicated that he produced them while he was Verrocchio's apprentice, their provenance remains unclear. Françoise Viatte suggests in 'The Early Drapery Studies' that many hands may have been involved in their original production; that other artists may have worked them over later; and that their apparent unity may be a retroactive construction, conferred upon them by a seventeenth-century collector. In an attempt to make theoretical sense of these attribution difficulties, Viatte says something that is highly germane to the present discussion: 'Perfection is anonymous . . . all we do is grant it its place without claiming to retrace its generation.'[9] And these are not the only ways in which the drapery studies refused to assume their pre-assigned place within the oedipal narrative. It is unclear whether they are free-standing works or preliminary

9. Françoise Viatte, 'The Early Drapery Studies,' *Léonard de Vinci: Dessin et manuscrits* (Paris: Musée du Louvre, 2003), 111-112. Francoise Viatte and Varena Forcione were the curators of the Louvre exhibition.

sketches for another work, and since the bodies that appear in them are headless and devoid of the usual markers of age, sexual difference, or socioeconomic status, we can say nothing whatsoever about the historical personages who served as their models.

But although the father of these drawings cannot be named, nor their models identified, the bodies in five of them are emphatically maternal. Three are seated, a position that was presumably chosen because it dramatically increases the number of folds in the fabric, but which also creates something which would not otherwise exist: a lap. The legs of two of the seated women are widely-spread, making their laps unusually capacious and inviting, and – at least to a contemporary eye – one appears to be pregnant. The second of these latter drawings breaks off just above the maternal figure's rounded belly, leaving nothing but dead space in the upper portion of the frame. Motherhood also made an appearance through Leonardo's early sketches of the Madonna and Child, and studies of a related subject, the Adoration of the Magi, and in almost every one of these drawings, the maternal figure is seated.

The image of a seated Virgin was of course a common one in medieval and Renaissance art. It is also ideally suited to the depiction of the Madonna as a physical support and aesthetic frame for the Christ Child. It therefore might not seem particularly surprising that the Florentine artist should privilege it. However, Leonardo refused to be bound by convention when working with this theme. In the *Virgin and Child with Saint Anne and John the Baptist*, he places the infant Jesus on his mother's lap, and Mary herself on her mother's lap. In the *Virgin and Child with Saint Anne*, the Madonna is again situated on St Anne's lap. Leonardo also makes her own lap unusually generous, and gives it pride of place. Rather than placing the Christ Child on his mother's lap, Leonardo locates him near the ground. Finally, instead of treating the Virgin Mary as a supporting player in a narrative which will soon transcend her, Leonardo connects her to her son in the same way he connects her to her mother: through a visual correspondence. She reaches out to hold the Christ Child, who repeats this gesture with a lamb.

And it is impossible to keep these two works out of the present discussion, since they are linked in several other important ways to the drapery studies. First, the torque of Mary's body in *Virgin and Child with Saint Anne and John the Baptist* echoes that of the figures in several of these studies. Second, the Virgin's lap is empty in *Virgin and Child with Saint Anne*, just as the laps in the drapery drawings are, and although the Louvre exhibition was devoted to Leonardo's drawings and manuscripts, the curators included this painting in it. And when we allow these works to communicate in this way, we realize how much they need each other. By placing Mary on St Anne's lap in *Virgin and Child with Saint Anne*, but having her reach out to a child who has either just climbed down from her own lap, or is about to return to it, Leonardo underscores the receptive aspects of motherhood. However, because there is still a tenuous connection between this tableau and the Christian narrative, it is possible to mistake this receptivity for that traditionally associated with the Virgin Mary. The drapery studies disable this reading. They liberate the mother from her role as the 'vessel' of God, allowing her to become the representative of a much more radical openness – one that is also instantiated by Leonardo himself.

IV

The room devoted to the *Léonardesques* provided the opportunity to think further about the issues raised in the first two. 'Room' might seem an odd word to use in this context, since the space in question was vast; it extended across the entire width of the exhibition. It was also divided into five smaller areas by walls. The symmetry of the room, though, overrode these divisions. Its two sides were architecturally identical, as were the smaller rooms onto which they opened. In both of these areas the names of Leonardo's imitators were also emblazoned on the floor. Finally, facing mirrors were attached to parallel walls at each end. The facing mirrors and the exaggerated symmetry of the room were obvious metaphors for the *Léonardesques*, who reprised the Florentine artist's style, themes, and even some of his works. Although imitation is often assumed to be the sincerest form of flattery, it is as fraught with potential violence as transmission. It is also informed by the same logic.

However, Leonardo did nothing to secure himself a posthumous existence. He did not have any children, and he chose his apprentices for their beauty, rather than their talent or eagerness to mimic him. Not surprisingly, given this, none of them became a disciple.[10] The Florentine artist also spent far more time on preliminary drawings than on the paintings to which they were supposed to lead, and he was notorious for leaving works half-finished. He even neglected to determine in advance whether the experimental technique he deployed when painting an important fresco would result in a lasting painting. In the *Codex Atlanticus*, Leonardo also advises artists not to imitate each other,[11] warning that 'the art of painting declines from age to age and is lost if painters have no other guide than what was done before them'.[12] Elsewhere, he inveighs against painters who reproduce themselves in their art. 'It is the greatest defect in painters to repeat the same movements and the same faces and draperies in a composition and to make most of the faces resemble their author.'[13]

Leonardo carried over the same principles into his paintings. He smudged the outlines of his figures, so that it was impossible to say where they ended and their surroundings began; used sketches he had produced in preparation for one painting as the basis for others; and generated two different versions of several

10. Kenneth Clark, *Leonardo da Vinci* (London: Penguin Books, 1959), 106-107, 171-172. It also seems safe to say that Leonardo would have been unperturbed if one of his apprentices had later outstripped him; he observes in one of his manuscripts that it is 'a poor pupil who does not surpass his master', Leonardo da Vinci, *Leonardo on Art and the Artist*, op. cit. (note 8), 86.
11. Ibid.
12. Ibid., 84.

13. Ibid., 193.

of his most famous paintings. He also pulled the rug out from underneath Albertian perspective by pointing out how different the same thing can look in the morning and at night, or when the weather is good, and when it is bad, and by suggesting that objects transmit light rays not in one direction, but rather in a dizzying number of different directions. The passage in which Leonardo advances the last of these propositions provides a startling contrast to the one used as the Louvre wall text. Far from being the 'lord' and 'master' of the universe, the painter is emphatically in the world. He can look in only one direction at a time, and see only one side of a phenomenal form – the side it turns towards him. He must also wait for a ray of light to carry this image to him.

Leonardo's ideal artist is neither an imitator nor a transmitter. He is, rather, a receiver. This is to some degree a given, because to perceive is to receive external images. 'If you look at the sun or another luminous body, and then close your eyes, you will see it again inside the eye for a long time,' Leonardo writes in the *Codex Atlanticus*, 'This is proof that the image entered it.'[14] However, the ideal artist also takes on the 'colours' of what he perceives – and because his psyche is as capacious as the maternal laps in the drapery studies, there is no limit to the number of things he can embrace in this way. 'The mind of the painter should liken itself to a mirror which always takes on the color of the thing it reflects and be filled by as many images as there are objects before it,' Leonardo writes in a famous passage in *Ashburnham 1*.[15]

14. Ibid., 90.

15. Ibid., 50.

V

Gravity is an important compositional principle in *Virgin and Child with Saint Anne*. Because the horizon is so high, only the upper third of the painting is devoted to the 'celestial', and even here the earth intrudes, through the tree on the right. The reiterative logic of the painting also unfolds from the upper left to the lower right, that is, via a falling motion. It could of course be argued that this downward movement is internal to Christianity itself, which recuperates it; Jesus descends to earth, but only to return to heaven, and make this ascent possible for mankind as well. But nothing in the painting speaks to the second half of this narrative. Both St Anne and the Madonna look down, rather than up, and the final term in the painting's unfolding is not even human. The infant Jesus and his two mothers also form a trinity, one which challenges both the primacy and the generative powers of God the Father.

Gravity figures even more prominently in *The Last Supper*. The title has an air of finality; it evokes the meal served to a prisoner before his execution. The painting itself is also under the sign of mortality. Because working with the fast-drying paint conventionally used in frescoes would have forced him to make quick, irrevocable decisions, Leonardo relied upon an experimental technique when painting *The Last Supper*: tempura on two layers of dry preparatory ground. The materials did not adhere properly to the wall, and the painting almost immediately began to decompose.[16] Over the years, there have been many attempts to halt this process, either by cleaning, restoring or repainting it, or by reproducing it in other, less perishable materials, like ceramic.[17] This preservation frenzy has continued unabated to the present. *The Last Supper* was recently restored yet again, and a high-tech laser system has now been installed to prevent it from disintegrating further. This system monitors the activity of the ground on which the Church of Santa Maria della Grazie stands, and immobilizes the mural wall at the first sign of a tremor.[18] But in spite of all of the efforts that have been made to arrest its decomposition, *The Last Supper* has continued to crumble.

The assumption on the part of the painting's restorers has always been that there is a 'true' version of *The Last Supper*, and that is the one that sprang to life when Leonardo applied his last dab of paint to the refectory wall. The Florentine artist also intended the painting to *last* – to survive the vicissitudes of time, like every other masterpiece. Each one of the changes it has subsequently undergone has therefore been both accidental and a corruption of its essence. The goal of the restorer should be to undo these corruptions, and recover as much of the original painting as possible. But although each new restoration initially seems to achieve this goal, it subsequently becomes yet another of the corruptions from which the painting must be liberated.

This might seem the moment to point out that *The Last Supper* is only a representation, and its restorations mere representations of this representation. However, the fresco doesn't function like a representation – not only because it corresponds with the space in which it is situated, but also because of its instability. Leo Steinberg observes that the energy of the painting 'expands into the space we ourselves occupy', and that 'perspective . . . seems to reverse itself'.[19] Both he and Arasse also comment on the compositional agitation caused by all of the pointing fingers, and the 'temporal sfumato' created through multiple durations, and the co-presence of different moments in the Christian narrative.[20]

Coleman corresponded with this aspect of Leonardo's work by constantly changing the images in his large-screen projection, and by using computation to absolutize the concepts of absence and presence.[21] When the Louvre exhibition ended, most of Leonardo's work was removed from the walls of the museum, but it did not vanish. It was absent there, but present elsewhere – in a private collection, another museum, or a vault in the Louvre. However, when the Louvre stopped showing the digital *Last Supper*, it ceased to exist – and this was also true of each image as soon as it left the screen. If we had cut open the computer at any point during the exhibition, we would have been unable to locate anything it permitted us to see, because when a digital image disappears, it

16. Pietro C. Marani, *Leonardo da Vinci: the Complete Paintings* (New York: Harry N. Abrams, Inc., 2000), 228; Marani, 'Leonardo's *Last Supper*', in: ibid., 22.
17. Richard Turner, *Inventing Leonardo* (Berkeley: University of California Press, 1992), 89-93; Marani, 'Leonardo's *Last Supper*', op. cit. (note 16), 1-57.
18. This information derives from Coleman, who a visited the room behind the fresco when shooting the photographs for his digital *Last Supper*.

19. Leo Steinberg, *Leonardo's Incessant Last Supper* (New York: Zone Books, 2001), 150.

20. Ibid., 19-29; Daniel Arasse, *Leonardo da Vinci* (William S. Konecky Associates, 1998), 362-383. In *Leonardo on Art and the Artist*, Chastel also suggests that *The Last Supper* registers and makes visible 'the imperceptible movement of the organs and the play of emotions', Chastel, op. cit. (note 8), 124.
21. Coleman alerted us to this dimension of his 'intervention' in his wall text. He 'presented' some works that were not 'present' in the exhibition through a 'numerical projection'.

decays into the 'dust' of numerical data. This data could of course be used to create a computationally identical image, but this image would still be *new*.

The ever-changing numbers at the bottom of each image in the large-screen projection indicated how close the computer was to completing the next image. This process was live; it happened in real time, before our very eyes. But the escalating numbers also helped us to see that until this image-in-the-making was visible, it would not exist – that its life would begin only when it appeared, and last only as long as it stayed there. Since Coleman laid his digital *Last Supper* to rest when the Leonardo exhibition ended, he seems to have concluded this *fort/da* game with a resounding 'gone'. It will not be long, though, before an analogous work emerges. We will never come to the end of *The Last Supper*.

Revised from: Kaja Silverman, *Flesh of my Flesh*, Copyright © 2009 by the Board of Trustees of the Leland Stanford Jr. University. All rights reserved. Used with the permission of Stanford University Press, www.sup.org.

Aniconism

An Islamic Idea Blooms Anew in Contemporary Media Art

Laura U. Marks

Imagine you are gazing up at *Hemisphere* (2006-2007), an artwork by Ulf Langheinrich: a suspended dome, plunged in darkness to which the eyes slowly adjust, begins to twinkle and shimmer with patterns beamed from five projectors poised around the dome's edge. Simple algorithms determine how the beams interact, giving rise to shifting meshes of polygons and five-pointed stars that, in the darkness, seem to arise on the viewer's own eyes. The experience is hypnotic and overwhelming. It is also collective, for you are aware of other viewers ensconced in the beanbag chairs Langheinrich provides, each lost in his or her perceptual space.

Now imagine you are under the fourteenth-century dome of the Friday Mosque at Yazd, Iran. Its brick decoration of concentric zigzags and star shapes performs a spinning firmament of astonishing geometric complexity. From a whirling rosette of 16 petals in the centre radiates a series of concentric zigzags — as though God had thrown a rock into the water, creating ripples. And from the edge of the ripples a seemingly infinite line arises; the eye is stymied whether to follow the line's path or to admire the shapes it produces, which gleam softly like blond stars in a blue sky. Mind-bogglingly, the designer of the dome has produced a concentric pattern of stars whose number of points increases from four, to five, to six, to seven: 16 seven-pointed stars twinkle at the edge of the dome.

Two domes, one analogous, one digital; one 700 years old, the other from our time: both invite the people gazing up to lose themselves in their shifting patterns, giving rise perhaps to dizziness, perhaps to exaltation, but certainly to a release, however temporary, from subjectivity. In both cases an abstract and algorithmic pattern passes through the beholder's embodiment and lifts her consciousness out of herself. Here are profound parallels in the experience of algorithmic, non-imagistic art in two historically and geographically distinct practices – the formative

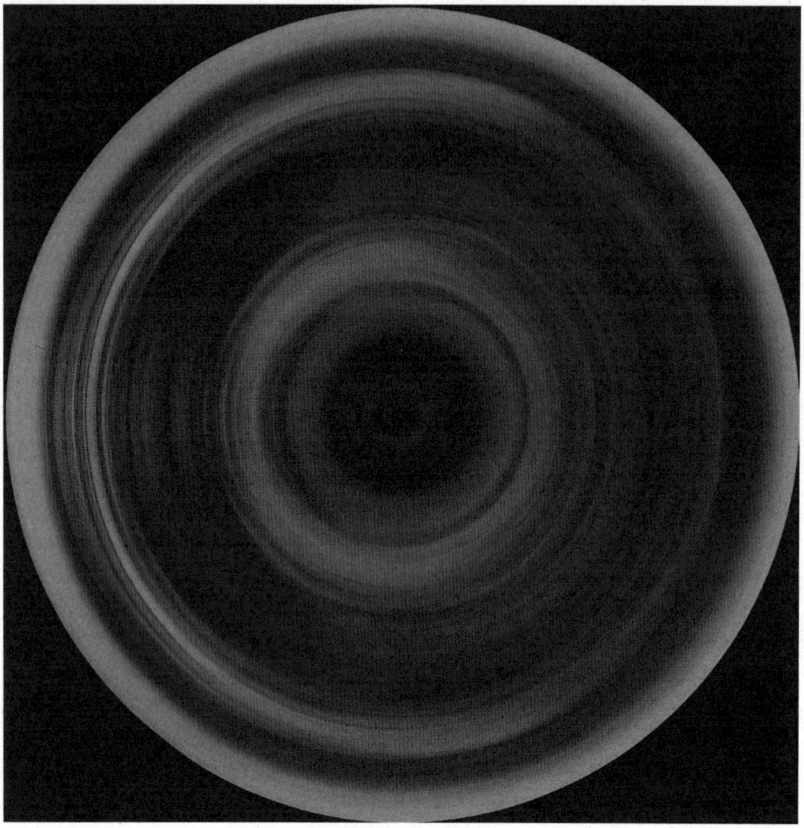

Ulf Langheinrich, *Hemisphere*, installation 2006. © Ulf Langheinrich.

centuries of Islamic art, spanning continents, and recent decades of abstract, algorithmic and digital art. Even as a 'medium' both works show an interesting correspondence, although it may seem strange to deploy this term for an ornamental-looking work of art like the Yazd dome. But classical Islamic art emphasizes its role as a medium, one whose reception is subjective and individual for each person – for believers, a medium from the divine to the human, but also a medium of contemplation that can soothe and diffuse the sense of self. Kaja Silverman has long suggested that the most creative acts of perception are those that undo subjectivity in some way, rather than buttress the illusion of the perceiver's mastery and corporeal solidity.[1] The images we are looking at here also cajole the viewer to loosen up her subjectivity, to experience perception in the body and in time, and to feel herself dissolve in a larger (for believers, a Divine) whole.

Another parallel between Islamic art and contemporary media culture can be found in the fact that what we perceive visually and audibly is often the end result of processes of information. The underlying code is the real subject. All around us computer screens, LED screens, mobile phones and other hand-held devices, the television screen subdivided into flows of information, signage and advertising, commercial radio, and the audio alerts that fill

1. See for example Kaja Silverman, 'Fassbinder and Lacan: A Reconsideration of Gaze, Look, and Image', in: Kaja Silverman, *Male Subjectivity at the Margins* (New York: Routledge, 1992), 125-126; and Kaja Silverman, *The Threshold of the Visible World* (New York: Routledge, 1996).

the urban soundscape all demand cognitive attention not as sensuous material to be experienced, but as information to be processed. The visible and audible skin of these media is permeable, permitting passage of the underlying layer of information. Gilles Deleuze predicted this shift from visual to information culture in his brief discussion of electronic and 'numerical' images: 'The screen itself, even if it keeps a vertical position by convention, no longer seems to refer to the human posture, like a window or a painting, but rather constitutes a table of information, an opaque surface on which are inscribed "data", information replacing nature, and the brain-city, the third eye, replacing the eyes of nature.'[2]

2. Gilles Deleuze, *Cinema 2: The Time-Image*, translated by Hugh Tomlinson and Robert Galeta (Minneapolis: University of Minnesota Press, 1989), 265.

The new images provide a window not out to the perceptual world but in to abstract worlds of information. In this, new media art, and the arts of the information age in general, are *aniconic*. So is most Islamic art, the strongest parallel to the visual media of our age, in that it gives text precedence over image. Both seem to follow Hegel's dictum that art make the invisible visible; what is particular to them is that the invisible is filtered through the Word in Islam, or through information in new media.

Islamic art is often considered simply decorative. Only recently has it become clear that Islamic art has a structural aesthetics. Its elements, which include aniconism, performativity, emphasis on reception, the importance of abstract line and haptic space, and even a quality of autopoeisis or nonorganic life, reoccur in twentieth-century and contemporary art, including new media art. Western culture is not so distant from Islamic culture, but it took modernism, and then code-based, algorithmic culture, to make this apparent.

A Positive Definition of Aniconism

I have chosen to focus on a much-discussed aspect of Islamic art, namely its aniconism, because it provides such a strong parallel to new media art. However, it's important to note from the outset that Islam's rejection of image-making has been exaggerated. The Qur'an does not prohibit representational images. Some of the *hadith* (a collection of sayings attributed to Muhammad) criticize mimetic representation as a prideful attempt to imitate God.[3] However, much Islamic art embraces mimetic images, notably in Shi'i Islam.

3. Oleg Grabar, *The Formation of Islamic Art*, revised edition (New Haven: Yale University Press, 1987), 78-83.

For aniconic art – Byzantine Christian and Jewish, as well as Islamic – the avoidance of images indicates that the divine, being infinite, cannot be represented. The image compels the worshipper to gaze into its absence, beyond it, towards the unknowable face of God. This is the beautiful challenge that Islam sets its artists, craftspeople and worshippers.

Contemporary artists also rise to the aniconic challenge when they deal with the fact that a phenomenon is impossible to represent. A single striking example is Trevor Paglen's project *The Black World*, an ongoing multimedia documentation of clandestine US military installations. The object of Paglen's investigation is assiduously carried out 'below the radar' of public scrutiny, because its purposes, such as the extraordinary rendition of prisoners, are illegal. To make that world of secret Information available, Paglen had to come up with all kinds of devices. He attends gatherings of top-secret pilots (who turn out to be quite chatty) and deciphers their cryptic badges. He camps in the desert outside the vast restricted areas where black-world bases are located, and photographs them through a high-powered telescope.[4] The images Paglen comes up with are mere traces, for, as Deleuze wrote, power is the ability to hide things in the image.[5] Yet these images are in a position to unfold information, and thus connect it back to the world.

4. See www.paglen.com/pages/projects/nowhere.

5. To paraphrase Deleuze, *Cinema 2*, op. cit. (note 2), 45.

In both Islamic art and computer media, the invisible unfolds to perception, through a filter of information. In Islamic neo-Platonism the universe emanates from and reflects God, in a descending series of levels from the unrepresentable God, to the representable names of God, and finally to the material. The Islamic neo-Platonist universe is a cascade of unfoldings, from the divine to the earthly. Digital media are also structured so that each level unfolds from the previous one: from the deepest level of the machine code, which interfaces with hardware, to the higher-level program code, and finally to the graphical user interface, which conceals most of the work carried out on the lower levels.

Abstract Line and Haptic Space

In Islamic art aniconism gave rise to two characteristic forms: abstract line and haptic space. Deleuze and Guattari called the abstract line (a term borrowed from Wilhelm Worringer) a line that is not tamed into a contour. The companion form, haptic space (a term adapted from Alois Riegl), is a space that invites not distant contemplation but intimate involvement, the eyes moving over the surface as though touching it.[6] Both of these allow form to unfold in the visible without generating a figural image. When line and shape are freed from depiction, lines become abstract; sculptural form dissolves into haptic space; and meaning is deferred to the subjective discovery of the viewer.

6. Gilles Deleuze and Félix Guattari, '1440: The Smooth and the Striated', in: Gilles Deleuze and Félix Guattari, *A Thousand Plateaus: Capitalism and Schizophrenia*, translated by Brian Massumi (Minneapolis: Minnesota University Press, 1987), 492-493.

Abstract line and haptic space are the liberated versions of drawing and colour, whose priority artists fiercely debated in the Renaissance. But they were not really free to be themselves until Western art loosened its attachment to figuration. However, the lively abstract line and the porous haptic space Deleuze and Guattari describe were already thriving in Islamic art as early as the eighth century. Early Islamic art's tendencies towards abstraction, flow and infinite growth culminate in what art historians call the 'bevelled style'. This new style arose during the flurry of building construction that took place in Umayyad Iraq in the ninth century: an abstract form, somewhere between plant and geometry, that is both linear and sculptural. Deep carving makes

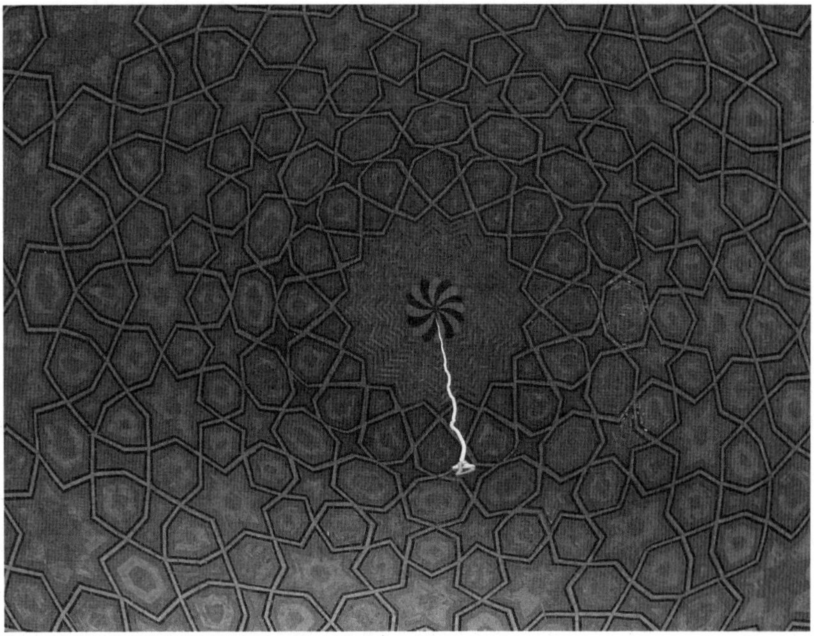

Interior of the Dome of the Friday Mosque at Yazd, Iran, 1324-1328. Photo: Laura U. Marks.

this style look, frontally, like sculpture, yet from the side, like linear ornament. Looking at it from different angles one sees a shimmering surface; fluid lines; fleshy curves; and the occasional biomorphic surprise, like the toothy rabbits that greeted my eyes when I first laid them on the bevelled-style panels from the ninth-century Balquwara Palace, now in Berlin. Both abstract line and haptic space originate in this flowing ornament, which seems constantly to shift between figure and ground, space and void.

This style became all the rage, and spread quickly across the Muslim world in the ninth and tenth centuries. When we see interlocking tiles, arabesque ornament, and geometric patterns in which figure and ground shift back and forth,[7] we are witnessing the descent of haptic space and abstract line. And when space has multiple access points, it is the eye that draws abstract lines. Deleuze wrote of digital images: 'The new images . . . are the object of a perpetual reorganization, in which a new image can arise from any point whatever of the preceding image.'[8] This precisely describes the bevelled style of Islamic art, and the many kinds of overall pattern that developed from it, in that it can be approached from any point.

It's interesting that Deleuze and Guattari value in abstract line and haptic space the resistance to figuration. In the late nineteenth century Alois Riegl had ultimately condemned this resistance. Riegl described the breakdown of figure-ground distinction and the resulting 'shimmering of light and shade'[9] approvingly in the case of late Roman and early Christian art. He noted that the 'tactile disintegration' of works that repress figuration 'is not just a sign of subjectivity or spirituality, it actually provides an

7. Richard Ettinghausen, 'Originality and Conformity in Islamic Art', in: A. Banani and S. Vryonis (eds.), *Individualism and Conformity in Classical Islam* (Wiesbaden: Harrassowitz, 1977), 92-93.

8. Deleuze, *Cinema 2*, op. cit. (note 2), 265.

9. Alois Riegl, *Historical Grammar of the Visual Arts* (1897-1899); quoted in: Margaret Iversen, *Alois Riegl: Art History and Theory* (Cambridge, MA: MIT Press, 1993), 42; Iversen's translation.

occasion for the exercise of our imaginative faculties'.[10] Yet he was harshly critical of Islamic art to which the same description could apply. This is because he believed that Christian art had a spiritual (or 'conceptual') purpose, while he had already dismissed Islamic art as only functional or decorative. His prejudice is echoed by those who dismiss ornament as meaningless.

10. Alois Riegl, *Late Roman Art Industry*, quoted in ibid., 43.

On the other hand, Riegl found the most lively expressions of *Kunstwollen*, or art's tendency to grow and change, to arise in the decorative arts, relatively free, as they are, from concerns with figural representation. The 'low' forms I examine here, 'ornamental' Islamic art and 'nerdy' computer art, are prime loci for their cultures' expression of the will of art. Contemporary critics often shun computer-based art for much the same reason that Riegl found ornament to be meaningless: it may be novel as a visualization of algorithmic activity, but it seems frivolous from a humanist perspective. Yet I argue that abstract line and haptic space, and their new-media manifestations, are meaningful precisely because they require a subjective approach. One can begin looking at any point and allow the eye to be guided by the forms, in a subtle shift of agency from the beholder to the beheld. In these art forms – and in the best of new media art – the body is no longer the object or vision, but the medium of perception.

Artificial Life

Qualities of nonorganic life and self-organization are other provocative commonalities between new media art and much Islamic art.[11] Contemporary philosophy and science are expanding the concept of life to include both macro-organisms, such as ecosystems, and micro-organisms, as well as non-carbon-based matter. Life is not exclusive to biological beings; it is 'a property of the organization of matter', in the words of artificial-life pioneer Christopher Langton.[12] Artificial life is 'emergent', meaning that it gives rise to forms or activities that cannot be predicted from its component parts.[13] It is produced by genetic algorithms, an example of which is the cellular automaton, an array of cells programmed to change according to simple rules governing life, propagation and death.[14]

Islamic artworks in many media exemplify the generative processes that contemporary algorithmic art carries out in time. Early Islamic artists, rather than imitate biological life, produced artificial life: a set of abstract art forms that were generative, self-organizing, dynamic systems. They did not try to imitate a body or a consciousness but to actually build something small, some cells or some sorting mechanisms, like the *muqarnas* dome built of small repeatable cells. Islamic patterns are cellular automata in stone, stucco and paint. Carpets and the beautiful painted frontispieces to Qur'ans and illustrated books are other examples.

The earliest cellular automaton in our age was devised by mathematician John Conway's *Game of Life* (1970). The program

11. See Deleuze and Guattari, '1440', op. cit. (note 6), 497-499; Niklas Luhmann, *Art As a Social System*, translated by Eva M. Knodt (Chicago: University of Chicago Press, 2000); Manuel DeLanda, 'Non-Organic Life', in: Jonathan Crary and Sanford Kwinter (eds.), *Zone 6: Incorporations* (New York: Zone Books, 1992); Mitchell Whitelaw, *Metacreation: Art and Artificial Life* (Cambridge, MA; MIT Press, 2004).
12. Christopher Langton, 'Artificial Life', in: Christopher Langton (ed.), *Artificial Life*, Santa Fe Institute in the Studies of Complexity, vol. 6 (Reading, MA: Addison-Wesley, 1989), 5; quoted in Whitelaw, *Metacreation*, op. cit. (note 11), 7.
13. Whitelaw, *Metacreation*, op. cit. (note 11), 209.
14. Ibid., 9.

could run for a very long time, producing complex ecosystems. The *Game of Life* is not art; but some artists produce beautiful and sophisticated images with genetic algorithms. Mauro Annunziato uses genetic algorithms to create vectors that have self-organizing, emergent 'behaviours'. In the effort to live as long as possible, the vectors in Annunziato's digital print *Migration* (2000) dart across space, seek uninhabited spaces in which to grow, produce offspring and curl in on themselves. Like the bevelled style and the arabesque, Annunziato's picture suggests an infinity of directions for the eye to follow and produces a shimmering surface that confounds the difference between figure and ground, space and void.

Erwin Driessens and Maria Verstappen have made some genetic artworks that are notably carpet-like in appearance and activity.[15] Their *Ima Traveller* (1996) generates a colourful visual field that seems to expand infinitely in any direction the user looks, including infinitely into depth. Zooming along the surface of *Ima Traveller* is like gazing into the vast, colourful field of a carpet. It unfolds a haptic space before your eyes in real time, just as a carpet reveals yet more fascinating details to the attentive beholder. This work, like much of Driessens and Verstappen's oeuvre, reflects their interest in how self-organizing processes give rise to something new and absolutely particular, in the true sense of virtuality.

15. http://www.xs4all.nl/~notnot/ima/traveller_a.mpg; http://www.xs4all.nl/~notnot/E-volverLUMC/evo-a.avi.

The self-organizing abstract lines and haptic spaces of new media also occur in social space. Vast user-produced online networks like Facebook and Second Life use algorithmic organizing principles to set up a basic grid. That grid is subdivided again and again by the actions of users, giving rise to seemingly infinite series of ever more detailed events of great variety and particularity. However, their infinity is often of the 'lame' nature, an infinite amount of more or less the same thing, as I will discuss shortly.

Fana'

What happens when people gaze into these infinitely multiplying spaces? The mystically tending scholar Seyyed Hossein Nasr suggests that: 'There is an aspect of nothingness or void which lies in the very nature of the whole created order and which is a direct consequence of the fact that, in an absolute sense, only God is real . . . The arabesque enables the void to enter into the very heart of matter.'[16] For Islamic mysticism, the non-existent side of every existent thing stimulates *fana'*, the mystical obliteration of the difference between things and God. Sufism, central in the thought of the thirteenth-century Andalusian philospher Ibn al-'Arabi, reasons that if God is One and changeless then the separateness and changefulness of the world must ultimately be an illusion.[17] This impossible concept causes a painful dialectic between One and Many, in a universe expanding and contracting like a pumping heart, 'whose most characteristic movement,' Ibn al-'Arabi

16. Seyyed Hossein Nasr, 'The Significance of the Void in Islamic Art', in: *Islamic Art and Spirituality* (Albany: State University of New York Press, 1987), 185-186.

17. Oliver Leaman, *An Introduction to Classical Islamic Philosophy* (Cambridge: Cambridge University Press, second edition, 2002), 194-195.

writes, 'is one of pulsation: towards God and away from Him.'[18] This mystical view embraces dissolution of the Many back into the One, and the individual path of dissolution or *fana'*.[19]

A similar dissolution of the individual in the universe occurs in the thought of Deleuze. I must be clear that Deleuze's philosophical goal is not *fana'*; it is creativity, the capacity for new perceptions, affects and thoughts. However, something rather like *fana'* takes place in the destruction, which Deleuze and Guattari emphasized again and again, of the usual limitations of the individual. The psychic organization that both allows us to survive and prevents us from really being alive must be destroyed.[20] The conventional expressions that permit us to communicate but prevent us from saying or making anything new must be trampled to smithereens.[21] The human 'dividual' that might result after these processes of destruction will be crazy, as crazy as the goofy and grinning Sufi dervishes painted by Riza-yl 'Abbasi. Those dervishes are mad with God-realization, the mystical certitude that there is no difference between themselves and God. Deleuze and Guattari's schizo is not thinking about God, a concept the philosophers find has been used to discipline and destroy creativity. Rather to become schizo is to think about the universe, to be madly free from any pre-determined attachment to any part of it, to be in a position to discover it from any point whatsoever.

Subjective contemplation is one of the ways one can begin to approach the Whole, or even to get a glimpse of the Open, in Deleuze's philosophy as it is informed by Henri Bergson. Deleuze chose cinema as the medium that best approximated the 'zone of indetermination' capable of seeing more than interested human perception could. Some of the same processes are at work in

18. Quoted in Tarif Khalidi, *Classical Arab Islam: The Culture and Heritage of the Golden Age* (Princeton: Darwin Press, 1985), 75.

19. Indeed he was called *ibn Aflatun*, son of Plato. Michael Barry, *Figurative Art in Medieval Islam and the Riddle of Bihzâd of Herat* (Paris: Flammarion, 2004), 168.

20. See for example Gilles Deleuze and Félix Guattari, '1914: One or Several Wolves?', in: Deleuze and Félix Guattari, *A Thousand Plateaus*, op. cit. (note 6), 26-38.

21. See for example Gilles Deleuze, 'The Painting Before Painting' and 'The Diagram', in: Gilles Deleuze, *Francis Bacon: The Logic of Sensation*, transated by Daniel W. Smith (Minneapolis: University of Minnesota, 2002), 71-90.

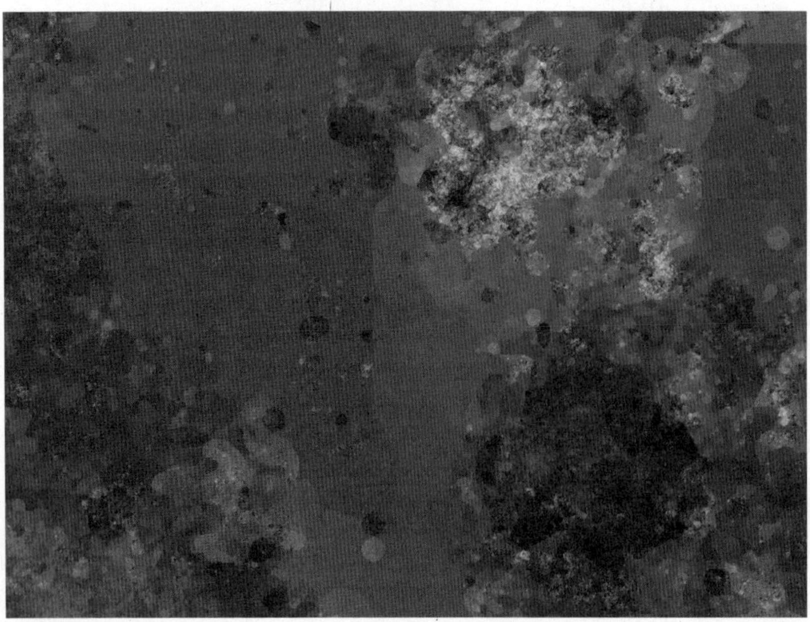

Driessens and Verstappen, *Ima Traveller*, 1996. Courtesy of VOUS ETES ICI Amsterdam.

Islamic art, an art that is both subjective and impersonal. Ultimately it brings contemplators back into the ideological fold of the religion, but its 'zone of indeterminacy' is large (given its relatively non-representational nature), allowing her more space and time to become disinterested and to enlarge her inner capacity for feeling and thought.

Lame Infinity

In our time, the creative thought process of discovering the infinitely Open is rare. However, it is often simulated. This simulation is what I call *lame infinity*, a lame term for a dispiriting phenomenon. The Infinite of Islam, like of other religions, is a qualitative infinity: one can never know the number of stars in the universe, but God does; and so it inspires awe, humility and gratitude toward the One who comprehends the universe. The infinity of information technology, by contrast, is a quantitative infinity. Computers' capacity for calculations inspires a sort of awe; web pages number in the billions; there is more out there (and in there, in the mysterious universe of existing code) than we can possibly imagine. But it is all the same kind of thing: endless iterations of a few possibilities, usually generated for profit-driven ends.

The lameness of digital infinity is also the reason that Deleuzians cringe when computer-generated spaces are referred to as 'virtual' worlds. For Deleuze and Guattari's concept of virtuality is that which does not yet exist, but has the potential to exist: the Deleuzian virtual is the truly infinite ground against which the fewest actual entities emerge. By contrast, computer-generated 'virtual worlds' are as actual as can be, for they are the product of programs written to produce these worlds. Even though the software is responding to specific input of users, the resulting new elements are new only quantitatively. So-called 'virtual worlds' provide at best a lame virtuality. Looking out the window is a better way to come into contact with the virtual, because when you look out the window, something may come into being for your perception for the first time ever.[22] Yet our computer-animated world does possess, in an immanent rather than transcendent way, the quality of infinity that religious believers revere in God. This is because computer media enfold the world that produced them, in its infinite materiality. The best new-media works open to an immanent Infinite that is more profound than the algorithms that produce them.

22. Steve Reinke suggests a criterion for art in his video *Afternoon (March 22, 1999)*: Is it more interesting than looking out the window?

A beautiful work in which the digital world opens onto immanence is *OneTrees* (2004), a project by Natalie Jeremijenko. For this project a thousand California Black Walnut trees were cloned from a single tree and planted around the San Francisco Bay Area in places where kindly hosts would monitor them. Since the trees are all identical, the difference in how they thrive would effectively measure the differences in their environments. Meanwhile, a thousand trees were planted in 'digital' terrain and programmed to respond to the concentration of carbon dioxide at the site of their corresponding botanical trees. Combining both carbon- and silicon-based life forms, *OneTrees* mirrored physical trees in digital analogues in a way that permitted a critical look at both environments, one too susceptible to chance and pollution, one too pure. Instead of converging on unity, as in religious thought, the artwork shows that the physical and social world is *more* infinite than the Information world that it reflects.

It might seem that the strongest parallel between Islamic art and the computer-made art of our time is the algorithmic nature of their construction. But the beauty of an algorithm is not in its visual manifestation alone. In Islamic art, it is the algorithm's ability to indicate God's creative power: the transcendent Infinite. In our time, algorithmic artworks are most powerful when they point to the social, material and historical connections among us: this is the immanent Infinite. What replaces divine aesthetics are something like relational aesthetics, which we hope will not be lamely compliant but will, in their resistance to incorporation, open up new virtual worlds.[23] In the best examples of contemporary media art, their algorithmic basis is the means to a social, political or material end.

23. Claire Bishop, 'Antagonism and Relational Aesthetics', *October*, no. 110 (Fall 2004), 51-79.

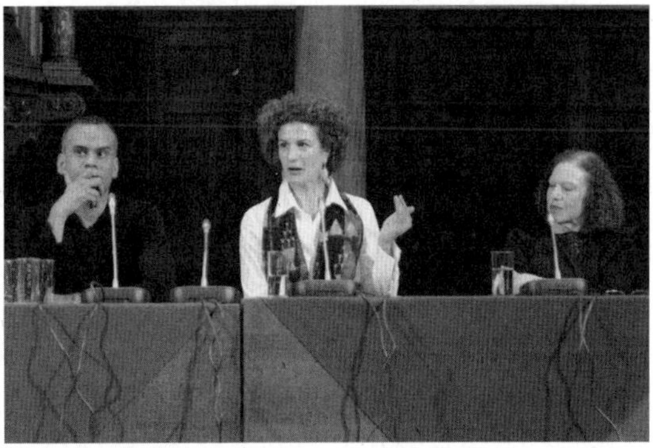

Sudeep Dasgupta, Laura U. Marks and Kaja Silverman.

Discussion

The discussion was moderated by Sudeep Dasgupta, assistant professor at the Department of Media and Culture of the University of Amsterdam.

Moderator: In both your arguments media art seems to function as a portal to an absent history of non-computer-generated art. Or, to use a Freudian term, make explicit that which is 'latent'. What is the purpose of such an argument? How does it help us to rethink 'media' or 'new media art'?

Kaja Silverman: Laura and I both challenge the 'newness' of new media art by linking computation to much earlier representational practices. I see Coleman's digital *Last Supper* as another stage in the metamorphosis of Leonardo's *Last Supper*, a metamorphosis that began almost as soon as Leonardo applied the last dab of paint to the refectory wall, and that will never end. I have also come to think of digitalization as a process rather than a product – the giving over of things to their 'becomingness'. This concept is already present in the work of a number of earlier figures, including Ovid, Leonardo, Bergson, Proust and Deleuze. For all of these writers and artists, forms are constantly decomposing and being reconstituted, and this process not only links every being to every other, but is also the means whereby individual beings perdure.

Laura Marks: But how can we rethink the medium? I am sure that some people are spooked out to have religion be brought into the context of contemporary new media art. What I tried to do is to posit the deity of Islamic art and other kinds of religious art and then say: rather than such an infinite deity, we can think of the art of our age as trying to make contact with or constitute an 'imminent infinity'. Deleuze uses this term for everything that is both actual and virtual. Art can be a medium to this, just as Islamic art is a medium to the divine. So the new media art of our day is a medium in two ways: both a subjective medium of contemplation and a medium of connection between us and between people, things and history.

Kaja Silverman: Wouldn't it be interesting, both in the case of your talk and mine, to think of an aesthetic medium the way we think of a psychic medium: as something that 'channels' the past, thereby reviving it? Benjamin describes film and photography in these terms in 'The Work of Art in the Age of its Technological Reproducibility'. He writes that when Abel Gance proclaimed that 'all legends, all mythologies, and all myths, all the founders of religion, indeed, all religions' were awaiting 'their celluloid resurrection,' he was 'inviting the reader . . . to witness a comprehensive liquidation.' Film and photography may now be on the other side of this equation: dead forms, awaiting their digital resurrection.

Laura Marks: That really is a beautiful addition. There's a lot of continuity between your idea that as mediums continue as they die they also continue to live and Riegl's idea of *Kunstwollen* which you could translate as the will of art or, art's desire to grow. When a work of art travels from one culture to another, it is transformed and new things are drawn from it. And that happened in the transmission of Islamic aesthetics to the West.

Audience: What about historical models? I sense both the model of continuity and rupture in your arguments. For example, Laura, is there a continuation between Islamic algorithms and those of the new media art works or is it a history filled with gaps?

Laura Marks: Indeed it works both ways: There has been a great deal of loss of the knowledge that was developed by scientists, artists and philosophers in the Muslim world that did not reach the West. But I also think that there is a lot of historical continuity, in that there is actually an abstract line of Islamic aesthetics that creeps its way into the West, starting during the Renaissance and continuing in Holland in the seventeenth century. Think for instance of genre paintings with one of those Persian or Turkish carpets on the table. Even as early as the seventeenth century, in a solidly figurative genre, there was this moment of abstraction with those carpets and the ideas of the people who wove those carpets, the ideas about abstraction, in some cases algorithmic ideas.

Audience: You seem to suggest, though, that we are leaving a paradigm dominated by visual culture and entering an aniconic one?

Laura Marks: In so many ways we are in an information age where the images we see are the product of processes of information. Of course this is not entirely true, because there continue to be things that we can perceive with our own naked senses. But so many of the things we perceive are mediated through a filter of information and really what we are seeing is not an image, but an image window to some software. So in that way our perceptual culture is really the by-product of an information culture. This is why I think it's really good to look out of the window.

NOW

Romanticism

Jos de Mul - Radical Romanticism

Jörg Heiser - Romantic Conceptualism and the Trouble with the Sublime

IS THE

Art & Theory

TIME

Romanticism

Some say that Romanticism, which emerged in the eighteenth century, has remained with us to this very day. But even these believers in the persistence of romantic thought must acknowledge that interest in Romanticism fluctuates considerably over time and is more in evidence in some periods than in others. After a rather cynical period in art and art theory, we are now seeing renewed interest in what is known as one of the most idealistic, if not outright dreamy, of art-historical movements. Countless illustrations could be given of Romanticism's contemporary relevance, and scholarly studies of the phenomenon have become equally innumerable. One useful place to start examining present-day thinking is Rüdiger Safranski's book *Romantik. Eine deutsche Affäre* (Romanticism: A German Affair), which has become a standard point of reference in the international debate about the current status of Romanticism. Jos de Mul and Jörg Heiser both refer to Safranski, emphatically contrasting their aesthetic view of Romanticism with Safranski's tendency to freight its legacy with political significance.

Basing his argument on his recently reprinted book *Romantic Desire in (Post)modern Art & Philosophy* (1990), Jos de Mul describes how the romantic desire for unity is linked to a tragic sense of the ultimate impossibility of that desire ever being fulfilled; the enthusiasm and persuasive power of Romanticism are accompanied by irony, which tempers overwrought desires. In his view, this makes the romantic experience, with its all too familiar qualities of enthusiasm and inspiration, a precursor of postmodern scepticism and irony, or indeed of any form of doubt about the 'controllability of happiness'.

Similarly, Jörg Heiser uses romantic thought to arrive at a deeper understanding of contemporary art, but it is not the irony of Romanticism that he focuses on, but its opposite, the sublime. Having developed the idea of Romantic Conceptualism, he uses it to penetrate to the core of the conceptual art of the final quarter of the twentieth century. As Heiser sees it, conceptual art is generally described in rational and therefore un-romantic terms. The purpose of his investigation is to uncover the highest ideals of this understated art form, which hark back to the romantic concept of the sublime. Heiser presents a new and broader context for the work of several well-known conceptual artists, such as Bas Jan Ader, whose romantically tinged art is easier to understand and appreciate now, in the early years of the twenty-first century, than it was when it was first created.

Jos de Mul (NL) studied philosophy, art history and law at the universities of Utrecht and Amsterdam. Since 1993 he is full professor of philosophy of Man and Culture at the Faculty of Philosophy, Erasmus University Rotterdam. Among his book publications are: *Romantic Desire in (Post)Modern Art and Philosophy* (1999), *Cyberspace Odyssey* (2002) and *The Tragedy of Finitude: Dilthey's Hermeneutics of Life* (2004).

Jörg Heiser (DE) is a Berlin-based art critic and co-editor of *frieze* art magazine. He contributes regularly to several German newspapers and international art magazines and journals. Heiser curated the exhibition *Romantic Conceptualism* (Kunsthalle Nuremberg and BAWAG foundation Vienna, 2007) and co-edited the accompanying catalogue. He recently published the book *All of a Sudden: Things that Matter in Contemporary Art* (2008), and is guest professor at the Kunstuniversität Linz, Austria.

Radical Romanticism

Art in the Age of the Technological Sublime

Jos de Mul

In many, the word 'romantic' effortlessly evokes the cliché image of romantic lovers in moonlit forests and on tropical beaches. A cliché image that might be called sentimental or even pathetic, yet one that is, at a superficial glance, rather innocent. However, Rüdiger Safranski leads us to believe that Romanticism is significantly less innocent than this cliché image seems to suggest. In his book *Romantik: Eine deutsche Affäre*, Safranski presents this movement, which emerged around 1800, with a generous touch of German self-hatred, as an explosive mixture of art, religion and politics, that brought European culture to the rim of a bottomless abyss.[1] While the romantic desire for a better, congenial world of poets such as Novalis, Hölderlin and Schlegel can still be easily cast aside as rather innocent *Schwärmerei,* things went seriously awry, says Safranski, when later romanticists such as Marx, Wagner and Nietzsche primed themselves to truly realize this desire. From there, according to Safranski, it is only a small step towards Joseph Goebbels' *stählerne Romantik* (stealed Romanticism).[2] The catastrophe that sprang from National Socialism appears to have brusquely awoken the Germans from their romantic glow. According to Safranski, the counterculture of the 1960s, so critical of the existing social structure, which ended in the terrorist violence of the Rote Armee Fraktion, teaches us that romantic desire is a lasting threat to democratic culture that finds its roots in Enlightenment.

Romanticism, viewed as a form of counter-Enlightenment, indulging in irrationalism and nationalism, and ending in an orgy of violence. It is a popular narrative. Twenty years ago Alain Finkielkraut told a similar story in his *La défaite de la pensée*.[3] In the following I will defend an opposing interpretation. The calamities that Safranski mentions and that have tormented Europe over the last two centuries, to my mind should be ascribed to a

1. Rüdiger Safranski, *Romantik: Eine deutsche Affäre* (Munich: Hanser, 2007).

2. Quoted in Jeffrey Herf, 'Der nationalsozialistische Technikdiskurs: Die deutschen Eigenschaften des reaktionären Modernismus', in: W. Emmerich (ed.), *Der Technikdiskurs in der Hitler-Stalin-Ära* (Stuttgart/ Weimar: Metzler, 1995), 87.

3. Alain Finkielkraut, *La défaite de la pensée* (Paris: Gallimard, 1987).

lack of Romanticism rather than to a surplus thereof. In an age and a country [which country?] in which opinion-makers gladly refer back to the heritage of 'Radical Enlightenment' it is, therefore, worthwhile to shed light once more on the heritage of Radical Romanticism.[4]

4. Jonathan Irvine Israel, *Radical Enlightenment: Philosophy and the Making of Modernity, 1650-1750* (Oxford/New York: Oxford University Press, 2001).

Radical Romanticism

Contrary to what Safranski and Finkielkraut claim, the young romanticists did not take a hostile stance towards the ideals of Enlightenment at all. Most of them were fervent supporters of the French Revolution, which had its roots in these ideals. However, the bloody Jacobin terror that resulted from this revolution made it clear to the young romanticists that an enlightened mind is no guarantee for a better world. According to the romanticists, who in this respect followed Friedrich Schiller's analysis in his influential collection of letters entitled *Über die ästhetische Erziehung des Menschen* (On the Aesthetic Education of Man, 1795), the fiasco was caused by the one-sided intellectualism of Enlightenment thought, which had not managed to balance the 'sensual passions' of man with his high rational ideals.[5]

5. Friedrich Schiller, *Über die ästhetische Erziehung des Menschen* (Stuttgart, 1981).

The 'disenchantment' of the world, instigated by the Enlightenment, also led to a crude utilitarianism. We live in an age, the romantic philosopher Schelling notes in 1800 ironically, 'in which the improvement of the *mangelwurzel* counts as the highest achievement of the human mind'.[6] The remedy that the romanticists propose, following Kant and Schiller, is to aestheticize the world and life, to make them into a grand piece of art, so as to increase the sensibility for moral ideals.

6. F.W.J. Schelling, *System des transzendentalen Idealismus* (Hamburg: Felix Meiner Verlag, 1957), 291.

In a secular, post-religious culture only art can give us the inspiration and communal spirit that was previously offered by religion. Novalis notes around 1798: 'By endowing the commonplace with a higher meaning, the ordinary with mysterious aspect, the known with the dignity of the unknown, the finite with the appearance of the infinite, I romanticize it. This procedure is reversed for the higher, the mystical, the infinite . . . It gets a common expression. The humble self is identified with a better self through this operation.'[7]

7. Novalis, *Schriften: die Werke Friedrich von Hardenbergs*, edited by P. Kluckhohn and R.H. Samuel, 4 volumes (Stuttgart: Kohlhammer, 1977), vol. II, 545.

In his book, Safranski calls Romanticism a continuation of religion through aesthetic means. There is truth in that claim, but the continuation is marked by a noteworthy difference. Europe's major religious wars and the fiasco of the French Revolution made the romanticists aware of the fact that striving for the Absolute – in religion, politics and love – can easily turn into bloody violence, when it comes with the conviction that these things can and *must* actually be realized, if necessary through force. For the romanticists, the desire for the Absolute is accompanied by a tragic realization of the unattainability of that goal. Romantic desire is, to use one of Hölderlin's poetic phrases, *heilignüchtern* (solemn-soberly).

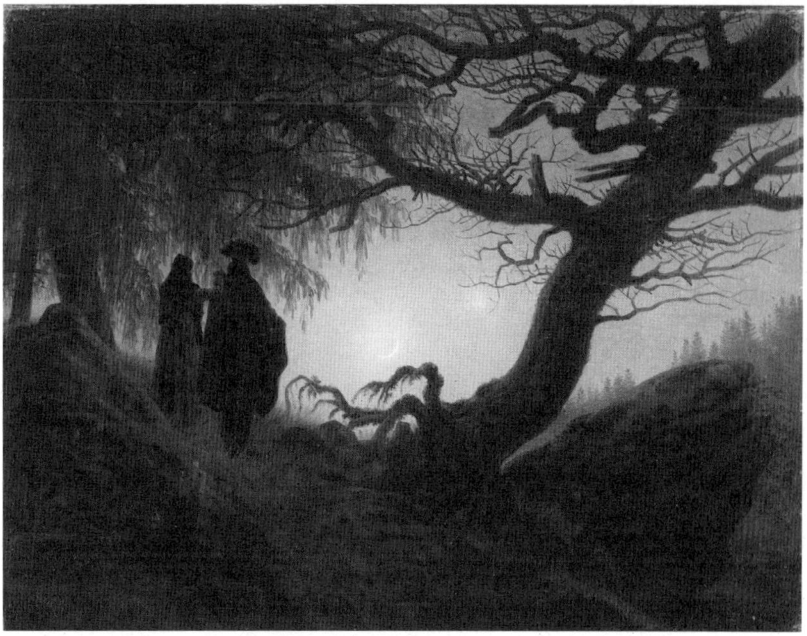

Caspar David Friedrich, *Mann und Frau in Betrachtung des Mondes* or *Mann und Frau den Mond betrachtend*, around 1818-24. Courtesy of bpk / Nationalgalerie, Staatliche Museen zu Berlin.

This is also the reason why Friedrich Schlegel defines romantic desire as 'an eternal oscillation between enthusiasm and irony'.[8] Without enthusiasm – which stems from the Greek *enthousiasmos* (ἐνθουσιασμός) and means 'a divine possession' – an individual or a society will lapse into cynicism and nihilism. But without ironic distancing, high ideals all too easily lead to terror. When the romanticists look upon the ideal and call it forth with irony, they do so to prevent this taunting ideal from calcifying, and to stop themselves from falling for the dangerous illusion of the manipulability of human happiness. Romantic irony, therefore, is much more than a mere stylistic trope. Rather, it has an ontological meaning, which expresses the radical limitedness of our capabilities to realize our unlimited desires. At the same time, the ironical stance expresses the transcendent character of romantic desire. Irony takes us beyond existing beliefs and truths. Thus it embodies the fundamental openness towards new experiences.

8. F. Schlegel, *Seine prosaischen Jugendschriften*, edited by J. Minor (Vienna: Konigen, 1882), vol. II, 361; cf. Jos de Mul, *Romantic Desire in (Post)modern Art and Philosophy* (Albany, NY: State University of New York Press, 1999), 9-14.

With its emphasis on the necessity to find new forms of inspiration in a post-religious culture, without falling into the traps of dogmatism or fanaticism, Radical Romanticism remains an inspirational model for European culture. This is all the more so, because the romanticists' call quickly drowned in the unbounded enthusiasm of modernity. Viewed from a romanticist perspective, political, scientific and artistic modernity is characterized by a dangerous lack of irony. It is precisely on this point that the reconstruction of European history, as presented by Finkielkraut and Safranski, goes amiss.

We cannot deny that the secular ideals of Marx and communism have been inspired, among other things, by the revolutionary *élan* of early Romanticism. However, what Marx and his revolutionary heirs lacked entirely was the sense of irony that so deeply characterized Romanticism in equal measure. This is why it is remarkable that Safranski, without much ado, presents Marx as a romanticist in his book.[9] The romantic position, however, was expressed much more distinctly by Marx's friend Heinrich Heine, who sympathized with Marx's communist ideals in many respects, but at the same time also warned of the dangers of an excess of enthusiasm in razor-sharp irony. As he expressed this famously in his play *Almansor* (1821): 'Where they have burned books, they will end in burning human beings.'

9. Safranski, *Romantik*, op. cit. (note 1), 248.

Wagner, who dreamed of radically renewing German culture by transforming it into a *Gesamtkunstwerk*, can be called a semi-romanticist for exactly the same reason as Marx. Particularly his thoroughly anti-Semitic nationalism and his return to Christianity, openly preached in *Parsifal*, (a temptation, by the way, for which several early romanticists fell in old age), testify to the fact that he radically lacked a sense of ironic distance.

Nietzsche is a more complex figure. As a young man he was an idolatrous fan of Wagner's operas, but he soon developed a wicked-ironic aversion towards their weighty mythology. '*Maybe there is a future for laughter*,' Nietzsche wrote,[10] after he had sobered from the Wagnerian glow, but European history has since given little cause for cheerfulness. National Socialism, in any case, has shown very little ironic self-deprecation, and the results of National Socialism are there to show for it.

10. Friedrich Nietzsche, *Sämtliche Werke: Kritische Studienausgabe*, 15 volumes (Berlin: De Gruyter, 1980), vol. III, 370.

And although Safranski rightly points out that the counterculture of the 1960s has known terrorist excesses, these excesses emerged precisely when the ludic irony was silenced and a fanatical enthusiasm became dominant. Even in its secular guises, every belief in the Absolute that is not held in check by irony will let nothing stand in its way.

While modernity is characterized by an excess of enthusiasm, an unconditional belief in the possibility of realizing the Absolute – in religion, politics and love – the postmodern response consists of radically deriding the Absolute. What sets Romanticism apart from both modernity and postmodernity is that it doesn't entrench itself in either one of the two poles, but rather tries to maintain the oscillation between enthusiasm and irony. The result is an ambiguous attitude towards the Absolute, which itself appears as an utmost ambiguous matter. This becomes especially clear in the romantic conception of the sublime. In tracing the development from the natural to the technological sublime, which characterizes (post)modern culture, the current-day relevance of the romantic ambiguity will be become clear as well.

From the Natural to the Technological Sublime

When we call a landscape or a piece of art 'sublime', we express the fact that it has particular beauty or excellence. Note, that the 'sublime' is not only an aesthetic characterization; a moral action of high standing or an unparalleled goal in a soccer game may also be called 'sublime'. The sublime is something that exceeds the ordinary. This aspect of its meaning is expressed graphically in the German and Dutch synonyms for the sublime: the 'exalted' (*das Erhabene*). In the latter term we also hear echo's of the religious connotation that the phrase often contains. The sublime confronts us with that which exceeds our understanding.

The notion of the sublime has a long history. It stems from the Latin *sublimis*, which – when used literally – means 'high up in the air', and more figuratively means 'lofty' or 'grand'. One of the oldest essays on the sublime dates back to the beginning of our calendar. It is a manuscript in Greek entitled *Πεϱὶ ὕψους* (On the sublime). For a long time it was ascribed to Longinus, probably incorrectly so. The author does not give a definition of 'the sublime' and some classicists even doubt whether 'the sublime' is even the correct translation of the Greek word *hypsous*. Using a number of quotes from classical literature, the author discusses fortunate and less fortunate examples of the sublime. For one, it must discuss grand and important subjects and be associated with powerful emotions. For pseudo-Longinus the sublime landscape even touches upon the divine. Nature 'has implanted in our souls an unconquerable passion for all that is great and for all that is more divine than ourselves'.[11]

11. Longinus, 'On the Sublime', in: T.S. Dorsch (ed.), *Classical Literary Criticism* (Baltimore: Penguin Books, 1965), 146.

Longinus's essay was hardly noticed by contemporaries, and in the centuries that followed we only rarely find references to this text. The essay was published in print for the first time as late as 1554 in Basel. But only after the French translation by Boileau (1674) and the English translation by Smith (1739) did the text begin its victory march through European cultural history. From the period of baroque onwards, which culminates in Romanticism, the sublime grows to become *the* central aesthetic concept. At the time, the sublime was often associated with the experience of nature. In the eighteenth century we find it predominantly in descriptions of nature by a number of British authors, who portray the impressions they collected on their Grand Tours through Europe in the Alps – a common phenomenon for young people from prosperous families in those days. These authors use the term to put the often fear-inducing immensity of the mountain landscape into words.

The sublime refers to the wild, unbounded grandeur of nature, which is thus contrasted starkly with the more harmonious experience of beauty. In *A Philosophical Inquiry into the Origin of Our Ideas of the Sublime and Beautiful* of 1756, Edmund Burke defines the sublime as a 'delightful terror'.[12] That the forces of nature can nevertheless lead the viewer into ecstasy is connected with the fact that the viewer watches these forces from a safe distance.

12. Edmund Burke, *A Philosophical Enquiry into the Origin of Our Ideas of the Sublime and Beautiful: And Other Pre-Revolutionary Writings*, Penguin Classics (London/New York: Penguin Books, 1998), 101-102.

However, in German Romanticism the sublime loses its innocent character. Especially the work of Immanuel Kant has been of critical importance in this respect. In the *Kritik der Urteilskraft* (1790) Kant, following Burke, makes an explicit distinction between the beautiful (*das Schöne*) and the sublime (*das Erhabene*). Beautiful are those things that give us a pleasant feeling. They fill us with desire, because they seem to confirm our hope that we are living in a harmonious and efficient world. A beautiful sunrise gives us the impression that life is not that bad, really. The sublime, on the other hand, is connected with experiences that upset our hopes for harmony. It is evoked by things that surpass our understanding and our imagination, by their unbounded, excessive, or chaotic character.[13]

13. Immanuel Kant, *Kritik der Urteilskraft*, volume 10: *Theorie-Werkausgabe* (Frankfurt, 1968), B74 ff.

Kant makes a further distinction between the mathematical and the dynamic sublime. The first, the mathematical sublime, is evoked by that which is immeasurable and colossal, and pertains to the idea of infinitude. When we view the immensity of a mountain landscape or look up at the vast night sky, we are overcome by a realization of our smallness and finitude. Kant associates the second, the dynamic sublime, with the superior force of nature. The examples he uses include volcanic eruptions, earthquakes and turbulent oceans. Here, too, we experience our smallness and finitude, but in these cases this understanding is complemented by the realization that these forces of nature can destroy us with their devastating power. The dynamic sublime evokes both awe and fear, it induces a 'negative lust'. Attraction and repulsion melt into one ambiguous experience in these cases.

Since the sublime remains primarily an aesthetic category in Kant's work, he maintains the idea that the experience of the sublime is characterized by keeping a safe distance. When looking at a painting of a turbulent storm at sea, one can allow oneself to contemplate the superior force of nature, while resting comfortably assured that one is safely in a museum and not at sea! Friedrich Schiller, in contrast, takes things one step further and 'liberates' the sublime from the safe cocoon of the aesthetic experience in a series of essays – deeply impressed as he was by the political terror that had sprang from the French Revolution under the Jacobin rule.

In order to accomplish this liberation Schiller rephrases Kant's distinction between the mathematical sublime and the dynamic sublime in his 1793 text *Vom Erhabenen* (On the sublime). Schiller argues that the mathematical sublime ought to be labelled the theoretical sublime. The immeasurable magnitude of the high mountains and the night sky evoke in us a purely *reflexive* observation of infinitude. When nature shows itself as a destructive force, on the other hand, we *experience* the practical sublime, which affects us directly in our instinct for self-preservation. On top of that, according to Schiller, we need to make yet another distinction. When we view life-threatening forces from a safe distance – for instance by watching a storm at sea from a safe place on land – we may possibly experience the grandeur of the storm, but not its sublime character. An experience can only be truly sublime when our lives are actually endangered by the superior forces of nature. And even that is not enough. Human beings have an understandable urge to shield themselves both physically and morally from the superior force of nature. Whoever protects his country by building dykes, attempts to gain 'physical certainty' against the violence of a westerly gale; whoever believes that his soul will live on in heaven after death, protects himself by means of 'moral certainty'. Whoever truly manages to conquer his fear of the sea or of death shows his grandness, but loses the experience of the sublime, according to Schiller. Truly sublime is he who collapses in a glorious battle against the superior powers of nature or military violence. 'One can show oneself great in times of good fortune, but merely noble [sublime only] in times of bad fortune' (*Groß kann man sich im Glück, erhaben nur im Unglück zeigen*).[14]

In Schiller's work the sublime is transformed from an ambiguous aesthetic category into a no less ambiguous category of life. History doesn't stop, however. During the nineteenth and twentieth century, the ambiguous experience of the sublime is gradually transferred from nature to technology.

Our current time is viewed as the age of secularization. God is retreating from nature and nature is gradually 'disenchanted' in the process. Nature no longer implants in us, as was the case with Longinus, 'an unconquerable passion for all that is great and for all that is more divine than ourselves', but principally invites technical control. Divine rule has become the work of man. The power of divine nature has been transferred to the power of human technology. In a sense the sublime now returns to what it was in Longinus's work: a form of human *techne̊*. However, these days it no longer falls into the category of the alpha technologies, such as rhetoric, but rather we find ourselves on the brink of the age of beta technologies. Modern man is less and less willing to be overpowered by nature; he vigorously takes command of nature instead.

As David Nye has documented in great detail in his book *American Technological Sublime*, the Americans initially embraced the technological sublime with as much enthusiasm as with which they had previously embraced the natural sublime.[15] The admiration of the natural sublime, as we may experience it in the Grand Canyon, was replaced by that of the sublime of the factory, the sublime of aviation, the sublime of auto-mobility, and the sublime of war machinery.

Nevertheless, it would be quite premature to think that we have banished the dark side of the sublime from history. With the transfer of power from divine nature to human technology, the ambiguous experience of the sublime, also, has nested in the latter. In our modern world it is no longer the superior force of nature that calls forth the experience of the sublime, but rather the superior force of technology. In the era of technology it is

14. Friedrich Schiller, 'Vom Erhabenen', in: *Sämtliche Werke* (Munich: Hanser, 1962), 502.

15. David E. Nye, *American Technological Sublime* (Cambridge, MA: MIT Press, 1994).

technology itself that gains a confounding character in its battle with nature. On the one hand, technology is an expression of the grandeur of the human intellect, but at the same time, we experience it progressively as a force that controls and threatens us. Technologies such as nuclear power and genetic manipulation, to mention just two paradigmatic examples, have a double-faced head: they gather both our hopes for the prosperity that human technology may bring, and our fears for its uncontrollable, destructive potential. This is why it is often said, in relation to such sublime technologies, that we 'shouldn't play God'.

Modern man, however, has been denied the choice to *not* be technological. The biotope in which we used to live in the modern age has been transformed entirely into a techno-tope. We have created a technological world without which we can no longer survive. The idea that we could return to nature is an unworldly illusion. As noted, we do not only have to regret that. Enthusiasm for technologies' accomplishments is certainly justified. Modern technology has given the average European and American a level of comfort in life that mediaeval royalty could only dream of. However, as the sublimity of war machinery has taught us, that which applies to the sublime in general also applies to the technological sublime: without ironic distancing the means can be far more brutal than the troubles they are supposed to mend. It is too easy to attribute all the horrors of the Nazi regime to irrationalism. It's far too easy to blame irrationalism for the factory-like organization of the concentration camps. It was motivated by an enthusiastic faith in the technical manipulability of society as well. In a similar vein, the American belief in nuclear bombs and the destruction of Hiroshima and Nagasagi displayed a one-sided enthusiasm for the technological sublime. And more recently, the American attempts to bring 'democracy' to Vietnam and Iraq exhibited a politico-technological enthusiasm that borders on recklessness. Likewise, many of the ecological problems we are encountering today stem from an excess of technological enthusiasm.[16]

16. Cf. Jos de Mul, 'Prometheus Unbound: The Rebirth of Tragedy out of the Spirit of Technology', in: A. Cools, et al., *The Locus of Tragedy* (Leiden: Brill, 2009).

According to David Nye, this is the reason why, throughout the twentieth century, the enthusiasm for the technological sublime has turned into a fear. Especially atomic energy and genetic research evoke fears in us regarding the fact that we may be creating forces that will eventually destroy us. Since Mary Shelley's *Frankenstein* this has been a recurrent response to the technological sublime.

Living the Sublime: Beyond the Opposition of Enthusiasm and Irony

By no means do I want to argue that irony is a solution to every problem. From the perspective of Radical Romanticism the ironic *rejection* of technology would be no less naïve than the uncritical embracement of technology. Indeed, when the fiascos that spring from modern enthusiasm entail that we entrench ourselves in a surplus of irony, we will have no progress whatsoever. This is what the history of postmodernism shows. Postmodernism has accompanied modernism from the start in the guise of a critical shadow. As a result of the atrocities of modern European history the voice of postmodernism has grown louder as time has passed. Undoubtedly, we should take the critique that the postmoderns have put forth against the modern enthusiasm to heart. But where irony gets the upper hand and enthusiasm is extinguished, only cynicism and nihilism remain. And these are no less lethal to cultures. Exit postmodernism.

What we can learn from Radical Romanticism today is the fact that we have to maintain the precarious balance between enthusiasm and irony, as if we were walking on a tightrope. With respect to the technological sublime, too, we need to go beyond the unproductive opposition of enthusiasm and irony, of optimism and pessimism. In our current age of high technology we can no longer expect – as for example Nietzsche still did under the spell of Romanticism – that art will save us. Nevertheless, this does not imply that art has lost its part to play. In these times art may help us feel at home with the technological sublime.

The romantic oscillation, eternally going back and forth between enthusiasm and irony, might also be just the right attitude in the multicultural societies that have emerged in Europe. In such societies, one form of enthusiasm easily provokes a radically opposite form of enthusiasm. That explains why Enlightenment fundamentalism often resembles the Muslim fundamentalism it attempts to combat to a sinister degree. If history can teach us anything, it is that these forms of radicalism are a guarantee for raving fires that spread far and wide. Ironic distancing is a wonderful extinguisher, particularly when it takes aim at our own enthusiasm. But we must not forget that with an excess of irony we may also miss our goal. Whoever ridicules the other entirely is past any form of dialogue. And for whoever can only ridicule himself, even the monologue becomes devoid of expression. If, as Nietzsche suggests hopefully in *The Gay Science*, laughter has a future, than let laughter be spent together, on matters that are truly holy to us all. There is quite a bit of romanticizing left to do.

Romantic Conceptualism and the Trouble with the Sublime

Jörg Heiser

What do I mean when I say Romanticism? In brief, not a synonym for the kitsch of love and desire, but an abbreviation for the cultural techniques of emotion and for ideas of the fragmentary and the open. My argument is that an actualized idea of Romanticism is important to the understanding of conceptual art, and that it has not just been a minor aspect within the realm of conceptualism, but a central – though often ignored – strand of it. In short, what I have termed 'Romantic Conceptualism'[1] is an abbreviation for artistic practices that bring up the question of whether the conceptual can be productively invested with what appears to be its antithesis: Romanticism.

Andy Warhol's *Kiss* (1963). The screen lights up and without further ado – no titles, no violins, no cuts, no camera pan, no voice off – we see a black-and-white close up of a kiss. Real kissing, aroused looks for endless minutes before the screen whitens, flickers and falters, as if Warhol had simply let the film in his camera run out (which is what he did). The screen remains white for a brief moment, and then the next uninterrupted close-ups include male on male kisses, or an African-American man and a white woman (in 1963, the year the film was made, this was an extremely daring statement).

Warhol's *Kiss* seems in many respects to obey in 1963 what were subsequently to become the shared methodological axioms

1. See also Jörg Heiser, 'Emotional Rescue', *frieze*, no. 71 (November 2002), 70-75, and the catalogue, edited by Ellen Seifermann and Jörg Heiser, accompanying the exhibition *Romantischer Konzeptualismus/Romantic Conceptualism*, Kunsthalle Nürnberg and BAWAG Foundation Vienna, 2007 (Bielefeld: publisher, 2007)

of conceptual art: the direct and simplest possible execution of an idea; serial repetition; actions dictated by instructions ('embrace and kiss for the duration of a reel of 16mm film'); documentation of the results. But at the same time, a voluptuous bliss and lack of regulation overwhelms the rigidity of the conceptual execution.

It is no coincidence that Sol LeWitt's 'Paragraphs on Conceptual Art' from 1967 includes the following: 'It is the objective of the artist who is concerned with Conceptual art to make his work mentally interesting to the spectator, and therefore usually he would want it to become emotionally dry . . . The expectation of an emotional kick, to which one conditioned to Expressionist art is accustomed . . . would deter the viewer from perceiving this art.'[2] At the time, in 1967, it may have appeared fundamentally necessary to set conceptual art strictly apart from that which had long become a cliché of artistic expression: the emotional pathos of expressionism.

But why should a viewer not be able to find a work 'mentally interesting' *and* be touched by it emotionally? Why would an 'emotional kick' inevitably deter the viewer from perceiving the conceptual? Might not the exact opposite be the case: that charging a concept with an emotional investment – or examining the 'conceptual' aspects of emotions themselves – is what actually could make the work 'mentally interesting'?

Two years later, in 1969, LeWitt published his 'Sentences on Conceptual Art', in the first issue of *Art-Language*. In a context where Marxism, linguistics and analytical philosophy were gospel, he turned against a purely rationalistic understanding of conceptual art. In the first of 35 sentences, he proclaimed: 'Conceptual artists are mystics rather than rationalists', 'they leap to conclusions that logic cannot reach.'[3]

Mystic, but emotionally dry – to let this elegant dogma implode took more than irony. What it took for example were several works by Dutch artist Bas Jan Ader. Such as *I'm too sad to tell you*, a short film from 1971. The piece is about the unspeakable: the artist crying, in a static close-up, no cuts, no sound. Instead of looking hysterically theatrical, he seems racked by a more profound grief. With *I'm too sad to tell you*, Ader tells me that he *can't* tell me, while he goes on to *show*. This absence of explanation produces a strong paradox: it is as if I am being shown a basic human behavioural trait, crying, using common facial expressions (head back, then forward again, mouth half open as if in pain), almost in the scientific style of educational, anthropological films. But at the same time, Ader's crying moves me. The antipode to Warhol's *Kiss*, eight years later: together, the two works form a conceptual melodrama . . . which means it's a melodrama devoid of any narrative motivation.

The colour photograph *Farewell to Faraway Friends* (1974) is the most direct reference in Ader's oeuvre to historical Romanticism. The lone artist on the sea shore, silhouetted by a beautiful

2. Sol LeWitt, 'Paragraphs on Conceptual Art', *Artforum*, 5:10 (Summer 1967), 79-84; reprinted in Alexander Alberro and Blake Stimson (eds.), *Conceptual Art: A Critical Anthology* (Cambridge, MA and London: publisher, 1999), 12-16, here 12.

3. Sol Lewitt, 'Sentences on Conceptual Art', *Art-Language*, no. 1, vol. 1 (May 1969), 11-13, reprinted in Catherine Moseley (ed.), *Conception. Conceptual Documents 1968-1972* (Norwich: publisher, 2001), 82-83, here 82.

sunset, with his back to the viewer. Of course, this recalls Caspar David Friedrich's sea scenes. But also, perhaps more strongly, the tradition of kitschy postcards that developed out of these portrayals of landscape. It is as if Ader is mourning the very history of this motif, as if his *Farewell to Faraway Friends* is addressed to those Romantic artists of the early- to mid-nineteenth century whose discovery of nature as a mirroring of psyche and emotion now seemed worn and battered, if not obsolete.

In 1800, Friedrich Schlegel defined art as 'an intentionally determined utterance, or clearly thought delimitation . . . an outline and principle of treatment'.[4] William Wordsworth knew and admired the writings of Schlegel; the very same year, he remarked that good poetry, and art in general, was characterized by 'the spontaneous overflow of powerful feelings'.[5] But crucially, Schlegel had also written that it is 'equally deadly for the mind to have a system and to have none. It consequently will have to decide to connect both states.'[6] Schlegel had expressed an important aspect of Romanticism, favouring the fragmentary and the open over the systematic and the conclusive: allowing the mind to adjust to a contradictory reality instead of doing the opposite and fitting reality to its own parameters.

So what about the supposed conflict between emotion and reason? And between Romanticism and conceptualism? Should one act simply as if this conflict didn't exist? Is it the case that emotions always had a place in the conceptual method? While it was also the case that a dominant discourse on conceptual art did not consider this dimension? And was this the case because conceptual art was vehemently combated from the outset, which made emotions seem far too *unreliable* to support an authoritative position?

Feelings are Facts (2006), the title of a volume of memoirs by artist, choreographer and filmmaker Yvonne Rainer, is an implicit reference to the rhetoric of 'just the facts' upheld by minimalists like Donald Judd, who denied feeling this status in a bid to set minimalism apart from the expressionistic.[7] Similarly, conceptual artists gave their works intense theoretical buttressing, especially Joseph Kosuth and Art & Language, not least in an attempt to exclude from the conceptual-artistic production anything that cannot be *controlled* – also ruling it out in the philosophical-inductive sense. For a long time, this was the common denominator of minimal and conceptual art; it was not marginal, but dominant, its influence also felt in fields such as structuralist film and art criticism. An eloquent illustration of this is provided by Carolee Schneemann's famous work *Interior Scroll* (1975). As shown in the photograph documenting the performance, the artist pulls a long strip of paper out of her vagina and reads what is written on it: an account *as* poem – of her encounter with a structuralist filmmaker. She is charming, he tells her, but her films, with all their self-indulgent emotionality, are truly unwatchable. He, on the other hand, has chosen a clear process with a logic of its own

4. Ernst Behler (ed.), *Kritische Friedrich-Schlegel-Ausgabe*, Vol II (Munich: publisher, 1967), 290, quoted from Herbert Mainusch, *Romantische Ästhetik* (Bad Homburg, Berlin and Zurich: publisher, 1969), 11.
5. Nowell C. Smith (ed.), *Wordsworth's Literary Criticism* (London: publisher, 1905), quoted from Mainusch, *Romantische Ästhetik*, op. cit. (note 4).
6. Behler, *Kritische Friedrich-Schlegel-Ausgabe*, op. cit. (note 4), 13.

7. See Yvonne Rainer, *Feelings Are Facts. A Life* (Cambridge, MA and London: publisher, 2006), 391.

– he has rid himself of all these self-important artistic affectations – 'emotion, intuition, inspiration' – and she should do the same. She decides in favour of a clear process of presentation that establishes its own system, but which will always remain 'contaminated' with all of what the man quoted thinks he has neatly rid himself of. Romantic Conceptualism shares this mistrust of an attitude that considers itself above the entanglements of subjectivity and emotion. However, instead of opposing it with the demonstrative presence of the artist's own body like Schneemann, it prefers to sensualize the supposedly 'clear process with its own logic' itself.

The paradox of this opening up of conceptualist practices lies precisely in the fact that the notion of Romantic Conceptualism only makes sense if, for all this openness, its limits are clearly drawn. It is therefore important to state that it is *not* about creating a label for anything in the orbit of conceptualism that is in any way poetic or otherwise 'atmospherically emotional' (and which, for this very reason, can all too easily be branded as de-politicized). For Joseph Kosuth, the idea itself is the art, for Sol LeWitt, its realization[8] – but Romantic Conceptualism is not the poetic version of this linguistic idea. It's not about wallowing in imaginative visual and experiential worlds. Rather it's about releasing the emotive potential of ideas while bypassing the iconographic, multi-sensual or narrative machinery usually brought to bear in such cases: no titles, no violins, no cuts, no camera pan, no storyteller voice, no monumental elements. If at all 'poetic', then Romantic Conceptualism, rather than a flowery elaboration, is a haiku.

8. See also Alexander Alberro, 'Reconsidering Conceptual Art, 1966-1977', in: Alberro and Stimson, op. cit. (note 2), 87.

Another possible misconception would be to think that Romantic Conceptualism is about injecting conceptual art with *narration* and the artist's *soul*. No, it confounds the false alternative between subjectivist, narcissist inwardness on the one hand and, on the other, desubjectivized and cool discursive transmission that supposedly is selfless and engaged and thus emancipates the viewer. This false alternative is an ideological staple of the discourse on conceptual art – eloquently put, for example, by Rosalind Krauss in her text 'Sense and Sensibility: Reflection on Post 1960s Sculpture' of 1973. She distinguishes between artists like Robert Barry, Douglas Huebler and On Kawara, in whose work the idea 'is understood as a prior mental event which we cannot see but for which the work now serves as testimony that it occurred'[9] and artists like Sol LeWitt or Mel Bochner. Here, the work only takes its meaning from interaction with the viewer. This distinction is questionable, first, since it is based on the assumption that the artist's intention controls the reception of the work – or, in other words, that this intention corresponds directly to the actual impact of the works, preventing the viewer from interacting. Secondly, it's not even clear that an artist such as Barry was not intending the work to take its meaning from interaction with the viewer. When in his *Psychic Series* in 1969, Robert Barry

9. Rosalind Krauss, 'Sense and Sensibility: Reflection on Post 1960s Sculpture', *Artforum*, no. 3, vol. 12 (November 1973), 46.

notes the following sentence: 'Everything in the unconscious perceived by the senses but not noted by the conscious mind during trips to Baltimore, during the summer of 1967', then of course one can say that the emphasis here is on the impossibility to communicate a private mental space that is not fully accessible even to the artist; but the point is that he still communicates this very refusal to communicate. He forcefully prompts discussion of its meaning as an artwork by not tying it up in definitions. No narration, no soul here (the unconscious is only indexed in regard to its inaccessibility to the conscious mind of the artist).

In principle, there is little to be said against moving away from the esoteric understanding of the gifted artistic soul that is to be interpreted. Early Romanticism did not necessarily see it this way in the first place: Friedrich Schlegel's text 'On Incomprehensibility', for example, puts forth the idea that ironic modes of writing continue to release new meanings for hundreds of years after the writer has died.[10] In some way this is more advanced than a late-modernist understanding of the artistic work as a normative set of rules dictating which modes of perception and production are allowed to form its basis.

10. Friedrich Schlegel, 'On Incomprehensibility', in: J.M. Bernstein (ed.), *Classic and Romantic German Aesthetics* (Cambridge: Cambridge University Press, 2003), 297-307.

The irony is that things precisely start to get interesting when one looks through the supposedly merely subjective confessional quality of a work to see the conceptual idea on which it is based. Bas Jan Ader's *I'm too sad to tell you* remains the most compelling example of this: of course I could speculate whether Ader just wanted to narcissistically present himself as a suffering soul, a man in pain. Almost in the same breath, I could claim that this is all just a clever parody of that very myth. But I can only make either of these statements at the price of completely ignoring the fact that the title *I'm too sad to tell you* binds me as the 'you' into a scenario where the 'I', like that of an actor, can be anyone's – the work is, after all, not called *Bas Jan Ader is too sad to tell you*, or *The artist is too sad to tell you*.

But despite of this openness – doesn't the emphasis on emotional or even unconscious levels mean to deprive conceptual practice of its critical potential, making it erratic, arbitrary? Well, Felix Gonzalez-Torres made the point quite clear. In a 1991 interview, he stated that: 'There is no private space anymore. Our intimate desires, fantasies, and dreams are ruled and interpreted by the public sphere.'[11] And: 'We are always shifting back and forth between the personal and the public. One day I want to make something from what I read in the paper and the next day I want to make a work about a memory I have of eating a delicious meal with my boyfriend in Italy.'[12] What is decisive here is that the conceptual method allows intimate material to be treated publicly *without* subjecting oneself to the regulation, for example, resulting from a detailed biographical account of suffering generating pity (which can easily turn into homophobic stigmatization). In the concrete case of Felix Gonzalez-Torres, this means

11. 'Felix Gonzalez-Torres: All the Time in the World', interview with Robert Nickas in: Julie Ault (ed.), *Felix Gonzalez-Torres* (city: publisher, year), 39.
12. Ibid., 45.

that instead of telling in his works the full story of his partner who died of AIDS, he uses allusions and simple serial techniques to refer to it, but without really relinquishing this personal space. This interplay between allusion and abstraction is a model of how 'private' subjectivity can be dealt with in public without submitting to the confessional mode. In 1991, on 24 billboards in Manhattan, Gonzalez-Torres published a black-and-white photograph of an empty bed of which the pillows still held the imprints of two heads (*Untitled*, 1991). The piece was a personal expression of mourning for the artist's own partner, who had died the same year, but at the same time it was also a fitting comment on the AIDS crisis and a coded subversion of the divide between individual health problem and social interest.

This is, incidentally, a succinct way to approach the distinction that runs through Hannah Arendt's entire philosophy and which presents us with, to put it in very broad terms, the psychological confession of the self as being a fundamental hindrance to the political emancipation of sovereign humans able to develop feelings of social interconnectedness (one can see how Richard Sennett, with his notion of the 'tyranny of intimacy' developed in his *The Fall of Public Man* of 1974, is a direct heir to Arendt in this).

Hannah Arendt's deep-seated scepticism of Romanticism – understood as a movement hailing the importance of the psychic self – is laid out already in her first major work, the biography of Rahel Varnhagen. Varnhagen was a key figure of early Romanticism, a German-Jewish writer hosting a salon in Berlin around 1800 that became the meeting place for eminent figures such as the Schlegel brothers, Schelling, Schleiermacher, Alexander and Wilhelm von Humboldt, and Ludwig Tieck, to name but a few. Written in Germany from 1929 to 1933 and completed in exile in France in 1938, it wasn't until 1958 that the book was published (*Rahel Varnhagen: The Life of a Jewess*).

Her point is that Romanticism offered Varnhagen a deceptive way out of the pressures of negating her own Jewish identity. Romanticism, according to Arendt, severs reflection from fact, and love from the object of love, while offering up the intimate as public, in the form of indiscrete speculation and gossip. Reason and emotion become free-floating, an all-pervasive fantasy – in short, Romanticism is portrayed not only as escapist, but as a seduction to Jewish self-neglect.[13] One can understand Arendt's frustration with Varnhagen's continuing repudiation of her Jewish background.

In a short period between the 1790s and 1806, Jewish salons like that of Varnhagen, for the metropolitan intelligentsia, offered a kind of utopian retreat from the strict social orders and conventions. Arendt readily describes it this way, but holds this *against* these salons, saying they were merely *Lückenbüßer* (stopgaps) between 'a perishing and a not yet stabilized form of conviviality'.[14] It seems that to denounce early Romanticism for

13. Hannah Arendt, *Rahel Varnhagen. Lebensgeschichte einer deutschen Jüdin aus der Romantik* (Munich: Piper, 1981 [2008]), 65.

14. Ibid., 71 (my translation).

this historic development towards a resurgence of patriotism and anti-Semitism in Prussia of the 1810s, and for Varnhagen's increasing neglect of her Jewish heritage, is to throw out the baby with the bathwater. Wasn't her salon an actual and very real, consistent counter-example to the nationalist-chauvinist backlash of the *Tischgesellschaft*, not only in regard to the emancipation of Jewish intellectuals but also female intellectuals (a point that Arendt curiously and consistently ignores)? One can't help but think that the Romanticism that Arendt despises in Varnhagen is the Romanticism of her own time, the amplified and overblown Wagnerian sublime that became a tool of Nazism.

Which leads directly to the crucial question only implied or alluded to so far – how does Romantic Conceptualism actually deal with the Romanticist sublime? Doesn't it – just like a good part of historic Romanticism – present us with an artist conveying to us the experience of the sublime, whether it's actually spelled out or not? And what would the problem be with that?

First of all, just to clarify, what notion of the sublime are we talking about? The Romantics favoured different variations of Edmund Burke's and Immanuel Kant's notion of the sublime, but in any case they located the experience of the sublime neither merely in physiological perception nor in reason, but in the 'soul', today we might say: the affects. According to Jean-François Lyotard, modernist avant-gardes are dealing with the 'the incommensurability of reality to concept which is implied in the Kantian philosophy of the sublime'.[15] His conclusion is that it's the job of art to insist that there is always an unrepresentable surplus that the work cannot and shall not console, or offer relief for, for example by way of a merely pleasant form.

15. Jean-François Lyotard, 'Answering the Question: What Is Postmodernism?', in: Jean-François Lyotard, *The Postmodern Condition: A Report on Knowledge*, translated by Geoff Bennington and Brian Massumi (Minneapolis: University of Minnesota Press, 1984), 79.

However, there is a problem with Lyotard's concept: a work of art that *negates* perceptive relief through sensual representation or spelled-out narration of the sublime still remains in the paradigm. It implies the biblical command to not make images of the sublime – which in itself is sublime. This is the attitude we can detect in artists from Malevich through Ad Reinhardt to Joseph Kosuth. This can be described as the strategy of borrowing or internalizing the power of the sublime precisely by stating – and at that point the artist becomes a priest – that we can and shall not approach it.

Of course the coolness, the matter-of-factness of minimal and conceptual art were meant to negate the actual presence of the sublime as it was still projected in Mark Rothko's or Barnett Newman's paintings, for example. As Sol Le Witt writes in the aforementioned 'Paragraphs on Conceptual Art': 'When a viewer is dwarfed by the large size of a piece this domination emphasizes the physical and emotive power of the form at the expense of losing the idea of the piece.'[16] Yet ironically the internalization or impersonation of authority and power connected with sublimity is still palpable in minimal and conceptual art.

16. LeWitt, 'Paragraphs on Conceptual Art', op. cit. (note 2), 14.

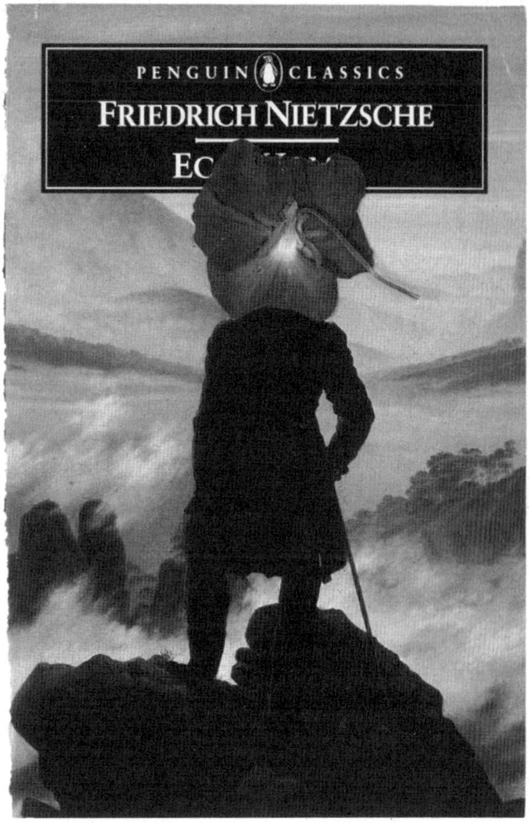

Frances Stark, *Ecce Homo Series: 6,* 2000. Courtesy of the artist and Galerie Daniel Buchholz, Cologne.

I understand Romantic Conceptualism as a critique of this strategy of a 'cool repression of the sublime'; but it doesn't wallow in the sublime either. While it may involve the artist's own, actual experience of the sublime, it refuses to translate that experience into a representation of magnitude. It does so for the sake of allowing the viewer to more actively *imagine* partaking in it, rather than just to *identify* with the artist representing it. This is arguably why, for example, Robert Barry, in his *Inert Gas Series* (1969), does not represent the act of releasing the gas, whether on the beach or in the desert, in grand landscape photos, as he could have done, but in descriptive texts accompanied by a small photo print, or an actual slide.

Or take Frances Stark's homage to Nietzsche in the guise of parody. The protagonist of Caspar David Friedrich's famous painting *Wanderer above the Sea of Fog* (1818), printed on the cover of a Penguin edition of Nietzsche's *Ecce Homo* (1888), suddenly has a pansy for a head – the real blossom resting neatly on the shoulders, turned towards the landscape, not us – which not only dwarfs the male body in proportion, but also covers most of the ambitiously pompous title of the book. With a simple, one-step juxtaposition, Friedrich's sublime is played off against Nietzsche's scrutiny, the figure against the ego; most crucially, the very concept of the sublime as being masculine – which from Burke and Kant on has always been implied – comically collides with the supposedly feminine beautiful and pretty.

In any case, speaking of Nietzsche: maybe his not necessarily flattering in-depth analysis of Wagner and his audience in his *Thoughts out of Season* is paradigmatic for the problem with the sublime: 'We therefore leave it to those who doubt Wagner's power of discerning the proper time for action, to be concerned and anxious as to whether what is now taking place in Bayreuth is really opportune and necessary. To us who are more confident, it is clear that he believes as strongly in the greatness of his feat as in the greatness of feeling in those who are to witness it.'[17] This is not, as in the case of Stark, homage in the guise of parody, but parody in the guise of homage, or more precisely and pathologically: intended homage that, as if unconsciously, can't help but smack of bitter ridicule. What Nietzsche from this point on, and increasingly so later in his life, seems to have taken issue with is not the experience of the sublime in the work of art, but the way it is impersonated by the artist vis-à-vis his audience. What we feel suspicious about in pathos and heroism is not the sublime, but its internalization and knowing impersonation. It's like internalizing authority, submitting to it, but selling this defeat off as a victory.

17. Friedrich Nietzsche, *The Complete Works of Friedrich Nietzsche*, edited by Oscar Levy, translated by Anthony M. Ludovici, Volume One: *Thoughts out of Season*, part one, 'Wagner in Bayreuth' (New York: The MacMillan Company, 1911), 102.

This is also why Romantic Conceptualism is anti-theatrical: it shares the interest in evoking the sublime, but dismisses the self-indulgent show-offiness that comes into play once it *is* actually evoked. Precisely for the sake of saving the imaginative space that Romanticism opens up, Romantic Conceptualists circumvented its tendencies of self-obsession, of locating essence in the artist's soul. The idea of the open artwork demands this; if meaning is to be established through interaction with the viewer, then some sort of humbleness on the part of the artist comes into play. Maybe this is also why Romantic Conceptualism sometimes comes across as the shy sibling of physical comedy. Both undermine magnitude, whether it's the magnitude of Wagnerian sublimity or Kantian moral superiority. The hero is always a failing one, but not necessarily tragically so.

Again, one last time, a work by Bas Jan Ader: In Ader's silent film *Broken fall (organic), Amsterdamse Bos, Holland*, 1971, we see the artist hanging from the branch of a tree until his strength fails him and he falls into the narrow ditch beneath. The artist has knowingly put himself at risk, but apart from maybe a bruised ankle, Ader escapes unharmed – it's hard to create the right tension between the sublime and abstraction, between horror and comedy, and between Romanticism and conceptualization.

Endlessness, boundlessness, today resides on the Internet. Arendt's assumption that Romanticism, essentially, is a hindrance to proper interconnectedness, is going through odd new twists in cyberspace. If Felix Gonzalez-Torres was still alive, a contemporary version of the aforementioned quote would probably be:

'There is no private space anymore. We readily make our intimate desires, fantasies, and dreams available for being ruled and interpreted by the public sphere – because we fear we would otherwise not be able to love and be loved, would otherwise be excluded.' Gonzalez-Torres' work already provided an example of how to navigate this virtual space of connection, confession and commodification: refusing to succumb to the confessional mode, while proactively playing with coded allusions and abstractions.

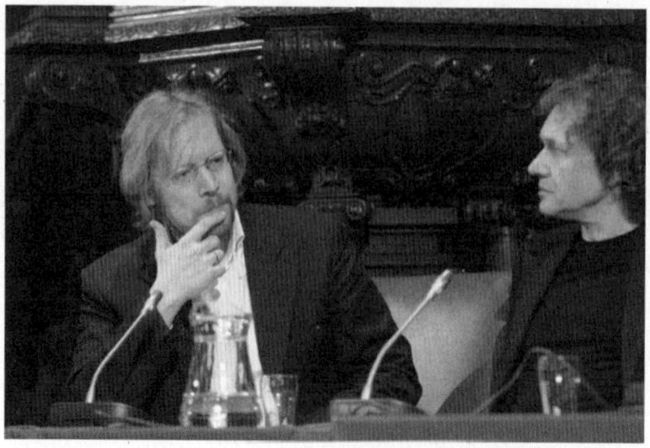

Jörg Heiser and Jos de Mul.

Discussion

The discussion was moderated by Thomas Lange, Professor at the Institut für Bildende Kunst und Kunstwissenschaft, University of Hildesheim, Germany.

Moderator: In his lecture Jos de Mul spoke about the delicate balance between enthusiasm and irony, the struggle between two completely different concepts that are brought together in the historical concept of romanticism. In my mind this is one of the most difficult things to understand. People like Schlegel or Runge understood that there is an approach to the world that cannot take the whole, but splits up into an emotional and a rational side. Both sides have their own discourse. When you lean to one side, and neglect the other, you get chaos, destruction, death. Jos de Mul argues that this should be tackled by taking it as an advantage, by being aware of these things as a modern condition in our world. Take for example what Runge notes on a famous debate he had with his art teacher. When Runge showed his *Four Times* drawings to his teacher for the first time, the teacher took them home and spent several days looking at them. When he came back to Runge he was very upset. He said: 'I tried to read them, but I couldn't understand what you intended to say.' Runge replied that this was the wrong way to go about it. He should just let go and see what the drawings do to him, while reading them. Let the pre-formed ideas about things go and come into the dialogue with this piece of art, or with these lines. It was in fact a progress of lines . . . It was about things . . .

Jörg Heiser: I think it is important to point out that this shouldn't be confused with the widely held idea that art shouldn't be explained. This story on Runge is not about negating the idea that the viewer should enter some kind of discourse about the work, or that the artist is not allowed to talk about it. I'm talking about the work in itself, and the way it uses 'narrative' elements or neglects them. With this whole thing about enthusiasm and irony there is one point where I start to question it. In the 1960s, 150 years later, we had a situation where first of all irony had become a kind of ritual in many ways, on all levels of society. And within the art context there is, starting with Duchamp and not Liszt, the whole idea of certain parodies that are very silent and very to-the-point. I think that one has to be aware that this idea is not isolated. Talking about Bas Jan Ader. There is humour in his work and there is slapstick in it. But I don't see irony in it. Irony, as a way of cautioning enthusiasm, would be a problem I think. It seems to be a kind of tempering down. For many of these artists physical comedy has replaced the function of irony in terms of dealing with the question of how to keep the void in this kind of sublime horror in check.

Jos de Mul: I find this analysis very interesting. However, I am somewhat sceptical about it. Romantic art was very ambitious from the very start. On the one hand – and this is the enthusiastic dimension – it really wanted to change society and life. On the other hand, the romantic artists also from the very start realized that this ambition could never be fully realized. The Absolute in love, art, politics is more a relative ideal than a realizable state of affairs. For that reason the romantic artists and philosophers intentionally ironized the ideal in order to prevent themselves from falling into the trap of dogmatism. This romantic attitude was continued in the twentieth century by the historical avant-gardes like Dada, surrealism and futurism. After the Second World War this changed profoundly. Especially when the centre of the art world moved from Paris to New York, art became institutionalized and commercial. All the avant-gardes end up in museums, which is sad in a certain sense. I think that this took away the revolutionary spirit of art. Hearing your story made me think of Slavoj Žižek, who speaks about a fear of reality. That's why we want to have beer without alcohol, cigarettes without nicotine and politics without politics. Everything has become innocent. In the same way you could say that the neo-avant-garde artist wants to have the sublime without the destructive part in it. Perhaps slapstick is a good phrase to refer to that, because slapstick is a way to make a serious experience seem innocent. Bas Jan Ader in this sense expresses in his work the sublime without sublimity.

Thomas Lange: Was irony, at least during historical romanticism, not a way to communicate horror, the unknown, or sheer fear through mirroring it, like in the Medusa effect: you can't look directly into Medusa's eyes, but you can look at her image in a polished shield. Could art have a function like that?

Jos de Mul: There was a lot of disappointment in the ambitions of traditional romantic art after the Second World War, because it had become an institution. It lost a lot of its vitality and became a discourse for specialists. I think that's one of the reasons for the new appearance of romanticism. There is something at stake there, which is not innocent. It has to do with life, with serious things. In the 1970s and '80s, and the moment of postmodernism, this irony became a kind of all-consuming attitude. But since the 1990s a whole series of movements are aimed at going beyond irony. These movements are heavily influenced and inspired by the romantic attitude.

Audience: I have a question for Jos de Mul. If I may summarize your lecture, you basically advocate the oscillation in romantic thinking between irony as a form of distance and as an engaging model. How can that be put into practice and translated into a political or artistic attitude?

Jos de Mul: I don't think it should be a kind of manic depressive oscillation between those two states. It is better to compare this to the tragic experience in politics. Absolute principles are splendid for the gods, but they are oversized for human beings. In politics it's often very good to have your principles and try to realize them, but you also have to realize that too much of a good thing can easily turn into its opposite.

Acknowledgments

The lecture series and publication *Now Is the Time: Art and Theory in the 21st Century* are the result of a unique partnership between several Dutch cultural and educational institutions: Stedelijk Museum Amsterdam, University of Amsterdam, W139, Stedelijk Museum Bureau Amsterdam and Metropolis M.

To all the speakers, the moderators and those posing critical questions during the debates, the organizers – Jelle Bouwhuis, Ingrid Commandeur, Gijs Frieling, Domeniek Ruyters, Margriet Schavemaker and Christel Vesters – would like to express their gratitude for their contributions to the project. They would also like to thank everyone who attended the lecture series at Amsterdam's Oude Lutherse Kerk in the fall and winter of 2008-2009, for turning *Now Is the Time: Art & Theory in the 21st Century,* – like its preceding project *Right About Now: Art and Theory since the 1990s* – into a great success.

This project could not have been carried out without the generous financial support of the Netherlands Foundation for Visual Arts, Design and Architecture, the Mondriaan Foundation, the Prins Bernhard Cultuur Fonds, and our own institutions, especially three affiliated with the University of Amsterdam: the Amsterdam School for Cultural Analysis, the Institute of Culture and History, and the department of Art, Culture, and Religious Studies.

We are also grateful to all the volunteers and staff members at the participating organizations who lent their support to the project. Finally, we would like to extend our special thanks to a number of individuals: the project manager, Christel Vesters, for her unflagging commitment; the project interns Femke Gerritsma, Catharina Koerts and particularly Hendrik Folkerts; the designers of the fantastic brochure and book, Janna and Hilde Meeus; the photographer, Cassander Eeftinck Schattenkerk; the copy editor Solange de Boer, and Barbera van Kooij at NAi Publishers. Our very special thanks goes to Jowon van der Peet and Geer van der Klugt; without their support over the past two years, this project could never have taken place.

Credits

Editors: Jelle Bouwhuis, Ingrid Commandeur, Gijs Frieling, Domeniek Ruyters, Margriet Schavemaker, Christel Vesters

Coordinating Editor: Christel Vesters

Contributors: Terry Eagleton, Boris Groys, Hou Hanru, Jörg Heiser, Laura U. Marks, W.J.T. Mitchell, Jos de Mul, Robert S. Nelson, Ruth Noack, Rick Poynor, Kaja Silverman, Sean Snyder, Julian Stallabrass, Camiel van Winkel

Translations Dutch-English: David McKay, Open Book Translation

Copy editor: D'Laine Camp

Intern: Hendrik Folkerts

Illustration editors: Hendrik Folkerts, Christel Vesters

Production: Solange de Boer, Christel Vesters

Graphic design: Janna and Hilde Meeus

Photography: Cassander Eeftinck Schattenkerk

Lithography and printing: Drukkerij Die Keure, Brugge

Paper: Reviva Offset

Publishers: Now Is the Time / NAi Publishers, Rotterdam

This publication results from the series of lectures with the same name held between October 2008 and January 2009. The lecture series was organized by Stedelijk Museum Amsterdam, University of Amsterdam (UvA), W139, Stedelijk Museum Bureau Amsterdam (SMBA) and Metropolis M.

Stedelijk Museum

University of Amsterdam

W139

SMBA

METROPOLIS M

This publication was made possible thanks to the generous support from the Netherlands Foundation for Visual Arts, Design and Architecture (Fonds BKVB); the Mondriaan Foundation and the Prins Bernhard Cultuurfonds.

F The Netherlands Foundation for Visual Arts, Design and Architecture BKVB

Mondriaan Stichting (Mondriaan Foundation)

Prins Bernhard Cultuurfonds

For works of visual artists affiliated with a CISAC-organization the copyrights have been settled with Pictoright in Amsterdam.
© 2009, c/o Pictoright Amsterdam

Although every effort was made to find the copyright holders for the illustrations used, it has not been possible to trace them all. Interested parties are requested to contact NAi Publishers, Mauritsweg 23, 3012 JR Rotterdam, the Netherlands, info@naipublishers.nl

© 2009, Now Is the Time, the authors and NAi Publishers, Rotterdam. All rights reserved. No part of this publication may be reproduced, stored in a retrieval system, or transmitted in any form or by any means, electronic, mechanical, photocopying, recording or otherwise, without the prior written permission of the publisher.

NAi Publishers is an internationally orientated publisher specialized in developing, producing and distributing books on architecture, visual arts and related disciplines.
www.naipublishers.nl

Available in North, South and Central America through D.A.P./ Distributed Art Publishers Inc, 155 Sixth Avenue 2nd Floor, New York, NY 10013-1507, tel +1 212 627 1999, fax +1 212 627 9484, dap@dapinc.com
Available in the United Kingdom and Ireland through Art Data, 12 Bell Industrial Estate, 50 Cunnington Street, London W4 5 HB, tel +44 208 747 1061, fax +44 208 742 2319, orders@artdata.co.uk

ISBN 978-90-5662-721-8

NOW IS THE TIME - Art & Theory in the 21st Century - NAi Publishers, Rotterdam

Terry Eagleton - Boris Groys - Hou Hanru - Jörg Heiser - Laura U. Marks -
W.J.T. Mitchell - Jos de Mul - Robert S. Nelson - Ruth Noack - Rick Poynor -
Kaja Silverman - Sean Snyder - Julian Stallabrass - Camiel van Winkel

Editors: Jelle Bouwhuis - Ingrid Commandeur - Gijs Frieling -
Domeniek Ruyters - Margriet Schavemaker - Christel Vesters